Teaching for Moral Imagination

Teaching for Moral Imagination

An Interdisciplinary Exploration

Pamela Bolotin Joseph

University of Washington Bothell

INFORMATION AGE PUBLISHING, INC.

Charlotte, NC • www.infoagepub.com

Library of Congress Cataloging-in-Publication Data

A CIP record for this book is available from the Library of Congress
http://www.loc.gov

ISBN: 979-8-88730-607-0 (Paperback)
979-8-88730-608-7 (Hardcover)
979-8-88730-609-4 (E-Book)

Printed in the United States of America

Contents

Preface ix

Acknowledgments xiii

Introduction xv

1 **Morality, Ethics, and the Moral Imagination** 1
- Morality 3
  - *Ideal and Real Values* 3
  - *Customary and Reflective Morality* 4
  - *Moral Competencies* 5
- Ethics 10
  - *Definitions of Ethics* 10
  - *Ethics and Morality* 11
- Moral Imagination 12
  - *Components of Moral Imagination* 13
  - *Importance of Moral Imagination* 16
- References 17

2 **Human Nature and Morality** 23
- Assumptions About Human Nature and Morality 24
- Moral Predispositions 25
- Dependency and Attachment 29
- Ongoing Human Needs and Moral Capacity 33

Transcendent Human Needs: Moral Agency and Identity 35
Survival Needs and Moral Dysfunction 36
References 40

3 Becoming Moral: Emotions and Reasoning 45
Moral Emotions 46
The Ethic of Care 50
Moral Reasoning 52
Rational Morality and the Ethic of Justice 57
Integrating Heads and Hearts 60
References 62

4 Becoming Moral: Culture and Socialization 69
Culture and Morality 70
Influence of Culture on Values 71
Childrearing: Cultural Moral Learning 73
Moral Socialization 75
Key Socialization Theories 76
Childrearing: Moral Socialization 77
Moral Socialization: Peers and Media 82
References 85

5 Moral Socialization and School Culture 91
Moral Socialization and Schooling 92
Moral Socialization and Discipline 95
Culture and Schooling 102
References 107

6 Moral Schools and Classrooms 115
Ethical School Cultures 117
Climate 117
Ethos 119
Moral Classroom and School Practices 120
Caring Community 120
Democratic Community 123
Service Learning 125
Just Community 128
Restorative Justice 131
References 133

7 Moral Education Curricula: From Tradition to Transformation......141
Traditional Values and Virtues 142
Cultural Heritage 144
Character Education 148
Ethical Reasoning 154
Moral Conversation 154
Philosophy With Children 155
Ethical Inquiry Across the Curriculum 157
Transformative Moral Education 160
Moral Education for Transformation 161
Transformative Curricula and Pedagogies 162
References 166

8 Ethical Teachers and the Moral Imagination 179
Teaching as a Moral Profession 180
Virtuous Teachers 180
Professional Codes of Ethics 182
Moral Dispositions 183
Teachers and the Moral Imagination 184
Moral Emotions: Caring and Moral Calling 185
Moral Perception: Presence and Identity 188
Ethical Reasoning: Ethical Knowledge and Obligations 190
Critical Reflection: Ethical Dilemmas and Introspection 192
Visioning: Moral Agency, Transformative Pedagogy, and Activist Identity 194
References 199

About the Author 207
Index 209

Preface

Background

Since becoming a teacher, I have been fascinated with the moral dimensions of education. As a social studies and language arts teacher in high school and middle school, I became aware of conflicting values that surfaced in my classroom—my moral beliefs as well as those of my students, all influenced by our parents, communities, and cultures. My first published writing dealt with teachers' value conflicts: how not being aware of the inherent moral dilemmas could contribute to a teachers' anxiety and how consciously dealing with such conundrums could enhance efficacy. Correspondingly, in my doctoral studies and early writing as a teacher educator, I focused on the study of moral development and how educators must view the teaching of values as a complex expression of rationality, emotions, and culture. I also grappled with difficult inquiries: Why do human beings devote their energies to cruelty and destruction? How do schools engage in practices and create environments that thwart moral development?

Over the years, I have written about various facets of the moral dimensions of education. I have investigated how teachers conceptualize their ethical decisions and dilemmas as well as their perceptions of themselves as moral educators. I also have studied my practice as a teacher educator and my students' reflections in courses specifically focused on moral development and education. Moreover, the content of moral education has held a keen interest for me and I have written critiques of practices based on

Teaching for Moral Imagination, pages ix–xii

simplistic, culturally insensitive, and unfounded assumptions about moral development. As I have studied various approaches to moral education, from the conventional to the transformative, I have expanded my view of moral education to write about the moral imagination and teachers' obligation to challenge an ecology of violence in human discourse, action, and in relationship to the Earth.

A major focus of my professional work has been to bring the moral dimensions of education into the academic curriculum for beginning and experienced teachers in graduate programs and undergraduate students in educational studies and other majors who wanted to know more about ethics, parenting, and schooling. I have organized these classes around major themes and guiding questions:

- Moral philosophy: How do we make sense of morality, ethics, and moral imagination?
- Moral development: What must educators understand about human needs and moral capacity as well as how children and adolescents learn values and the influence of families, peers, and culture?
- Classrooms and schools as moral communities: How can educational settings become moral milieus that emphasize ethics, justice, and caring?
- Moral education: What are key orientations—both traditional and transformational—for fostering moral development in classrooms and schools?
- Teachers' ethics and moral agency: How do educators understand the ethical dimensions of their work and their responsibilities as moral educators?

Teaching courses about moral dimensions has been a work in progress—as there never is enough time to fully explore the rich field of moral development and education and there are numerous choices of content, learning activities, and outcomes. For this reason, I also have encouraged students to identify areas of interest to them and to use course knowledge as a springboard for myriad further investigations, among which have been cross-cultural moral education, the moral development of bullies and morally disengaged adolescents as well as moral dimensions of coaching, moral education across the academic curriculum, and adults' moral distress when faced with dilemmas. Such independent and collaborative studies have given my courses added depth and breadth and I have learned a great deal from students' studies; certainly, my expanded horizons are represented in this book.

I have especially come to know that teachers savor the chance to think deeply about their roles as moral educators and to be informed about a wide range of moral education approaches, including how they can encourage their students (of all ages) to ponder ethical questions when studying the academic content. I also recognize that when having the opportunity to reflect upon their ethical responsibilities in the classroom, teachers often profoundly consider their moral obligations. So too, students who are not educators find the subject matter fascinating and describe how such classes challenged their initial assumptions about morality and childrearing.

Overall, as a result of my experiences as a teacher educator and scholar, I contend that teachers need to gain expertise about the moral dimensions of education and to explore the concept of the moral imagination. The cultivation of such knowledge is important, not only to enhance teachers' understanding of teaching as a moral profession—a standpoint that should be infused throughout teacher preparation and professional development—but because it is crucial to help educators become aware of their moral identities and to realize their full potential as moral agents. For these reasons, I have written this book.

Focus

Teaching for Moral Imagination: An Interdisciplinary Exploration examines the multifaceted nature of morality and ethics, moral development, and moral education so to provide educators with a clear yet complex understanding of theories, issues, practices, and curricular content. This text is intended to be an accessible work of academic significance that inspires educators' deliberation about personal and societal values as well as approaches for fostering children's and adolescents' moral development, cultivating ethical classrooms and schools, and creating transformative moral education curricula. This book is organized by interrelated components:

- Moral philosophy, ethics, and moral imagination
- Human nature and morality
- Moral emotions and reasoning
- Culture, morality, and moral socialization
- Moral socialization in classrooms and schools
- Classrooms and schools as moral communities
- Moral education curricula
- Ethical teachers and the moral imagination

I hope that *Teaching for Moral Imagination* will be a pertinent text for educational studies courses that specifically focus on the moral dimensions of education as well as more comprehensive classes about teaching, teachers, and classroom culture. Such classes are offered in undergraduate and graduate teacher preparation programs, professional studies for experienced teachers, educational studies courses in the liberal arts, and doctoral seminars for students becoming teacher educators and educational leaders. This book also is intended as a source for teachers' professional development in schools and for reading groups. Finally, in our contemporary societies emphasizing extreme individualism, competition, conformity, and prejudice as well as unexamined beliefs leading to violence in words and actions, it is crucial to consider how schools can encourage ethical reasoning, compassion, and transformative alternatives for moral education.

Acknowledgments

I cherish the memory of Northwestern University faculty Lee Anderson, Christopher Boehm, John Lee, Joe Park, and Lindley Stiles who many years ago insisted that conceptual inquiry is a crucial form of educational research and encouraged me to investigate moral philosophy and development, culture, and moral education. I am indebted to contemporary researchers investigating the moral dimensions of teaching who continue to revitalize this area of scholarship. As well, I have been inspired by scholars of peace education who have extended my understanding of ethics and moral imagination. As always, I am grateful to Sara Efrat Efron and Edward Mikel, dear friends and colleagues, for their contributions to my thinking and writing and to my husband Mark Windschitl for his support and for his example as a writer and researcher. I also very much appreciate the University of Washington librarians who consistently and promptly supported my scholarship throughout this project. Finally, I especially wish to thank all the teachers whose writing enhanced mine through their reflections on ethics, moral dilemmas, and agency.

Teaching for Moral Imagination, page xiii

Introduction

Purposes

From the past to the current day, a typical notion of a moral educator is that of a teacher—a virtuous role model who bestows rewards or imposes punishments to maintain students' socially acceptable behavior—who stands before students in an orderly classroom replete with lists of sanctioned values and traits decorating the walls. Less usual is the idea of an educator who has a vital role to play in fostering students' moral development by widening ethical perspectives, encouraging critical reflection on values, stimulating new perspectives about how to be moral human beings, and creating just and caring classroom and school communities. Yet, if we care deeply about children and adolescents—as well as the people these students will become and the world that will be left for them—it is not enough to exemplify and reinforce rudimentary morality. Instead, teachers need to go beyond given roles to realize their potentials as moral agents who transform classrooms and schools into places that nurture students' moral growth and imagination—their ethical reasoning, sensitivity, and empathy.

Teaching for Moral Imagination: An Interdisciplinary Exploration examines the multifaceted nature of morality and moral development, moral dimensions of teaching, and moral imagination. Drawing from conceptual and empirical scholarship from the fields of philosophy, psychology, anthropology, sociology, curriculum studies, and educational research, this text considers how children and adolescents become ethical human beings. It also

Teaching for Moral Imagination, pages xv–xix

delineates how classrooms and schools can contribute to students' moral development by cultivating caring communities and through curricular content that stimulates ethical perspectives. Moreover, it critically analyzes conventional moral education orientations and disciplinary practices, calling for moral educators to broaden their ethical responsibilities by challenging acceptance of violence in human interactions and toward the Earth

This book brings to light a number of ethical, developmental, and pedagogical issues to encourage critical and holistic thinking about moral education and teachers' roles as moral agents—to illustrate their many choices for practices, curricula, and ultimate aims. Appreciation of complexity helps educators to challenge often unexamined ideas about moral development and education and everyday conceptions of what is morality and a moral classroom. Lastly, through the framework of the moral imagination, it explores facets of the wide-ranging literature on the moral dimensions of teaching and includes the voices of teachers to reveal their ethical purposes, concerns, and dilemmas.

In particular, the field of curriculum studies—especially the concept of curriculum inquiry—has deeply influenced the writing of this text—both in regards to the questions it poses and its organization. Curriculum inquiry itself is an ethical activity because it allows us to scrutinize fundamental values of teaching and schooling. As such, to engage in curriculum inquiry about the moral dimensions of teaching leads to questions such as: What do we mean by "moral"? What does it mean to be a moral person and an ethical teacher? What values should be represented in guiding children toward moral growth? As well, an essential curriculum inquiry heuristic—the curricular commonplaces (Connelly & Clandinin, 1988; Schwab, 1973)—has shaped this book's structure. Accordingly, after investigating the philosophical concepts of morality, ethics, and moral imagination in the first chapter, the following chapters illuminate the curricular commonplaces of moral education by exploring *learners, the milieu, curricular content,* and *teachers.* Through this lens we apprehend theories of moral development to better understand learners' capacities for moral growth as well as what experiences that lead to the suppression of their moral impulses, classroom and school environments that foster or hinder moral development, curricular content that enhances or stifles young people's moral growth, and teachers' perceptions of their moral identities, ethical dilemmas, and possibilities for practice.

Most importantly, *Teaching for Moral Imagination* is written with the perspective that educators need to care not only about the character traits of their students but also about young people's agency in creating the world that will be left for future generations. Besides having the aim of providing an interdisciplinary knowledge base, this book was written to inspire concern about violence in discourse and action—as reflected in the modern worldview that emphasizes intense competition rather than cooperation, exploitation of peoples and all living forms, and environmental degradation. Instead of viewing the goals of nonviolence and environmental healing as outside of the mainstream, peace and ecojustice education are included within the repertoire of moral education approaches. In this sense, a purpose of this book is to cultivate teachers' moral imagination as well as their own moral presence and agency for challenging violence in discourse, human interactions, and in relationship to all life forms and the Earth.

Chapter Descriptions

Chapter 1, "Morality, Ethics, and Moral Imagination," introduces elements of moral philosophy to allow readers to contemplate their baseline knowledge, perceive commonplace assumptions, and develop more complex understanding of the concepts of morality, ethics, and moral imagination as well as moral concern, responsibility, and character. *Teaching for Moral Imagination* begins with this chapter because of the rationale that when we ponder the meanings of these ideas, we are better able to name, clarify, and expand our aspirations and practices as moral educators.

Chapter 2, "Human Nature and Morality," focuses on significant yet confounding quandaries about human nature and what influences children and adults to become moral beings. It explores evolutionary theories of moral capacity and the particular circumstances of human life that become catalysts for moral development. This chapter emphasizes theories of human needs and how satisfaction of needs contributes to moral functioning and even to altruism, concluding with an investigation of how moral dysfunction can result when human needs are not fulfilled. As well as considering why individuals have difficulty reasoning and acting morally, this chapter discusses violence and aggression stemming from individual and group narcissism.

Chapter 3, "Becoming Moral: Emotions and Moral Reasoning," familiarizes readers with prominent psychological theories of moral development. The first thread attends to the affective realm involving the development of empathy, shame, and guilt as well as other intrinsic factors such as moral identity for which moral action may depend. The second thread emphasizes the cognitive realm and the concepts of rationality, reasoning, and reflection. This chapter concludes with the perspective that educators need to informed by an integrated theory that takes into consideration both emotion and reasoning.

Chapter 4, "Becoming Moral: Culture and Socialization," extends the discussion of moral development to include values transmission through culture and socialization. It attends to how children learn their culture's moral standards, how families teach moral values and behaviors, and how peers and media influence children's moral development. This area of scholarship informs us that children learn about moral values from various sources, including through families' explicit moral teaching and reactions to children's missteps or wrongdoing—especially those digressions that flaunt deeply held cultural beliefs. Caregivers correct moral misbehaviors in diverse ways; some encourage empathy and reflection and some merely model power and aggression. Eventually, peers, media, and teachers convey a myriad of moral messages to children and adolescents.

Chapter 5, "Moral Socialization and School Culture," posits that schooling also has a role in moral socialization. Schools overtly promote cultural and societal values deemed right and proper—exposing students to notions of morality throughout their daily experiences. As well, there are cultural patterns of beliefs and behaviors that may be implicit, deeply ingrained, and unquestioned. This chapter considers how moral socialization takes place in classrooms and schools, the role of discipline in moral socialization, and how we might think about classrooms and schools as moral universes.

Chapter 6, "Moral Schools and Classrooms," highlights the development of democratic practices that promote perspective taking and deliberation and how schools can become fair and caring environments. It explains how educators create and sustain moral classrooms and schools, beginning with discussion of the various factors that foster ethical environments. It also explains how teachers develop caring and inclusive classroom cultures and use classroom management strategies that promote students' moral growth. In particular, it emphasizes the importance of intentional moral classroom and school practices and explores scholarship on the caring community, democratic community, service learning, just community, and restorative justice.

Chapter 7, "Moral Education Curricula: From Tradition to Transformation" elucidates and critiques numerous ways to deliberatively teach moral education in addition to or embedded in academic curricula. It explores transmission of cultural values and virtues through an international perspective, moral conversations for the development of reasoning about ethical issues including in specific subject areas, and transformative moral education for countering violence and injustice and for imagining a peaceful world. There are various moral education curricula described in this chapter: cultural heritage, character education, philosophy with children, ethical inquiry across the curriculum, critical pedagogy, human rights education, ecojustice education, peace studies, conflict resolution education, global education, and environmental education.

Chapter 8, "Ethical Teachers and the Moral Imagination," reveals ways in which teaching is viewed as a moral profession and how teachers themselves perceive their moral identities and dilemmas. This chapter draws from the fields of educational history, sociology, and teacher education to explore community and professional requirements for teachers to maintain high ethical standards. It also depicts teachers' perceptions stemming from qualitative educational research featuring interviews and reflective journals; these perceptions are analyzed through the framework of the moral imagination encompassing emotions, reasoning, reflection, and visioning.

References

Connelly, F. M., & Clandinin, D. J. (1988). *Teachers as curriculum planners: Narratives of experience.* Teachers College Press.

Schwab, J. J. (1973). The practical 3: Translation into curriculum. *School Review, 79,* 501–522.

1

Morality, Ethics, and the Moral Imagination

> *Within the flickering inconsequential acts of separate selves swells a sense of the whole which claims and dignifies them. In its presence we put off morality and live in the universal. The life of the community in which we live and have our being is the fit symbol of this relationship.*
>
> —John Dewey, 1922, *Human Nature and Conduct*, pp. 331–332

In everyday life, the word *moral* is commonly used to refer to choices we make, dilemmas we experience, and principles by which we live. But seldom do we stop to inquire how a moral decision might differ from another kind of a decision or how a moral dilemma is different from other types of conundrums that we experience. Nor do we typically take the time to find out if moral means to one person the same as what it means to another. For that reason, when teaching a course on the moral dimensions of education, I begin by asking students these questions:

Teaching for Moral Imagination, pages 1–21

- How do I define morality?
- How do I define ethics?

As they individually write their answers, share definitions in small groups, and debrief as a class, students often grasp essential differences between morality and ethics but also notice how difficult it is to pin down answers and that these familiar terms are not easy to discuss with confidence. In fact, students mention, during class or later in their written reflections, that this introductory session leaves them with far more questions than answers and that they experience disequilibrium—a state of feeling unsettled. Throughout this course, students continue to grapple with definitions and expand their knowledge base about morality, ethics, moral development, and moral education. Eventually, the course focuses on another pertinent question:

- What is the meaning and significance of moral imagination?

Still, it is not my intention to leave them with certainty; rather, I want my students to discern the complexity of these matters and the many options for them when they strive to become moral educators.

This work of analyzing the meaning of morality, ethics, and moral imagination has taken on certain urgency in the context in which we live—within "a pervasive ideology of individualism that supports the competitive adversarial way of life" (Noddings, 1989, p. 189) and "amidst an ecology of violence in human interactions, discourse, and relationships with the natural world" (Joseph & Mikel, 2014, p. 317). Increasingly I have introduced into such courses opportunities to consider personal viewpoints and for teachers to help their pupils to think more creatively, more empathically, and, above all, to transcend conventional reasoning—to develop "citizens who are capable of thinking for themselves, arguing with tradition, and understanding with sympathy the conditions of lives different from their own" (Nussbaum, 2002, p. 301). This rationale calls for both educators and the students whom they teach to look beyond their immediate situations and to become free of habitual thinking processes (Kim, 2009).

The process of understanding the moral realm begins by exploring the nature of morality, ethics, and moral imagination. To engage in curriculum inquiry about the moral dimensions of education, we need to consider the meaning of these complex ideas and interrogate commonplace beliefs before learning how to create and sustain moral classrooms and schools.

Morality

At first glance, morality refers to an individual's judgments about what is right and wrong or what is good and evil (Hinman, 2012; Ray, 1996; Solomon, 1992). Morality also means "a prescriptive understanding of how individuals ought to behave toward each other" (Smetana, 1999, p. 312). As such, morality refers to a person's standards of behavior or beliefs concerning "what is and is not acceptable for them to do" (Hobson, 2004). Moreover, morality becomes a guide for making and acting on choices.

However, as scholars from the fields of philosophy, anthropology, and psychology seek to explain the meaning of morality, we learn that it is not an uncomplicated concept—not only because of the various definitions given but because of the thorny issue of inconsistency; although people may recognize what is right or wrong, they do not always make moral decisions and act on them. Because of discrepancies between beliefs and actions, recognizing morality is not as simple as recognizing explicitly stated moral values. Unfortunately, too often research on morality relies on "artificial replication of situations, and experimental or survey settings to investigate moral judgement" rather than studying morality in its "real-life complexity" (Walker, 2020, p. 2).

Ideal and Real Values

The disparity between moral beliefs and actions can be understood in part because of the gap between *ideal* and *real values.* Scholars perceive that there are principles that are ideal or "govern human interaction in an ideal situation" (Barrow, 2006, p. 8). Anthropologist Christopher Boehm noted that in "in every culture there is an ideal moral code" that consists of

> a series of behavior propositions about how things ought morally to be. The ideal values that are represented in our Bill of Rights and in the Ten Commandments are good examples because realistically we know we cannot hope to fully live up to all of them. (Boehm, 1977, p. 30)

Although these ideal values influence moral beliefs, within cultures there also are "real" values that are part of individuals' moral code and may exert a more potent influence upon people's moral functioning.

> While we may have difficulty in even beginning to live up to an ideal more code, we are saved from this strain by the existence of a second (also universal) kind of moral code consisting of real values. Real values contrast

> with ideal values in that they are not involved in lip service to the idea of a perfect moral life based upon higher principles that an average individual may scarcely hope to fulfill.... In a way, real values may be seen as rules for breaking rules. (Boehm, 1977, p. 30)

In a sense the real values are guidelines for following the ideal values, such as telling inconsequential lies in certain circumstances, for example, so not to hurt someone's feelings, but for the most part being honest and trustworthy.

There are various reasons why there are differences between ideal and real values. People realize that they cannot hope to live consistently according to the high standards of ideal values, the ideal values have not kept up with "the realities of a changing culture" so the ideal values function more as memories, or the ideal values "probably never have been in agreement with the goals of the real culture" and these values may have been more "honored in the breach" rather than in actuality (Linton, 1945, p. 53). Once more, people in a culture may cherish idealistic explanations of their values or their society's values, preferring to not expose the more realistic moral code influencing behavior.

Customary and Reflective Morality

A number of scholars inform us that there are two categories of morality: *customary* and *reflective*. Philosopher John Dewey (1908/1932) contrasted moral codes handed down from family and culture that are unquestionably accepted with examined moral values that are chosen deliberately. He explained that "the intellectual distinction between customary and reflective morality is clearly marked. The former places the standard and rules of conduct in ancestral habit; the latter appeals to conscience, reason, or to some principle which includes thought" (p. 3). These starkly different interpretations of morality raise the question of if we can even characterize customary beliefs as morality if people do not consciously weigh principles and develop personal moral philosophies.

Customary morality has been described as a set of beliefs and values that are usually "taken for granted and followed unconsciously" with "most moral decisions follow[ing] in a routine way the commonsense recipes that have been learnt to the present" (Musgrave, 1978, p. 33). Correspondingly, such morality is labeled as "habitual"—morality "based on repetition"—as people rely on "ingrained habits of interpreting moral situations" (Colby, et al., 2003, p. 106). This characterization of morality "connotes conformity to the rules of 'right' conduct" (Park & Barron, 1977, p. 3). In addition, morality may stem from "precepts set forth by authority"—by the state or religion (Reardon, 2015, p. 52) and that function of a "moral system" "is to keep individual behavior harmonized" to function within society and "conform to society's norms of behavior" (Boehm, 1977, p. 25; Mullerat, 2013, p. 179). Certainly, this view of morality suggests that morality is not necessarily "conscious, rational, reflective, and deliberate" (Colby, et al., 2003, p. 105) and that people intuitively develop or accept moral beliefs.

In contrast, reflective morality is not automatic or unconscious; rather it "involves careful evaluation and justification" (Colby, et al., 2003, p. 105). Reflective morality begins when "the right course of action is not obvious or when one's initial moral response is challenged and there is time to reflect" (p. 105). Descriptions of reflective morality suggest that an individual's moral system must be chosen through a deliberative process and that reflection is a crucial element in living a moral life (Kekes, 2006, p. 4) as "morality is entirely bound up with how our best reflective experience tells us we should meet and treat each other" (p. 99).

Reflective morality leads to the development of moral theory, beginning when individuals ask, "Why should I act thus and not otherwise? Why is this right and that wrong? What right has anyone to frown upon this way of acting and impose that other way?" (Dewey, 1908/1932, p. 5). In the bigger picture, a danger of customary acceptance of values is that society's morality can deteriorate when principles become so settled as to be second nature so that people act without thinking. When people no longer adapt principles to new circumstances, they lose their ability to make moral decisions (Hare, 1966, pp. 219, 220). The power of reflective thinking is to enable people to thoughtfully adopt an ethical code and adapt more rules to changing situations if examination of morality reveals deficiencies.

Reflective morality also promotes questioning of religious beliefs. Yet, this version of morality does not call for rejection of all faith traditions. Through thoughtful study and consideration of a religion's ethical tenets, individuals may become devout because they wish to live in accordance to religious embodied values and teachings. Conversely, they may distance themselves from certain religious beliefs or practices if they discern the potential for harm rather than moral behavior.

Moral Competencies

There are myriad ways to define what it means to be moral and it is not possible here to do justice to the many traditions and theories that describe how we should live as righteous people and bring about societal good. However, to understand what should be teachers' moral aspirations and aims of moral education, three concepts are critical: *moral concern, moral responsibility*, and *character.*

Moral Concern

An essential quality of morality is moral concern. This capability allows for "recognition" of others beyond immediate family members and realization of their "moral standing" and "obligation to protect, invest, or defend" their "wellbeing" (Neldner et al., 2022, p. 2). Scholars conclude that moral concern characterized as an ethic of care is "deeply embedded in classical enduring traditions" of religion and philosophy in the East and the West and that this "core moral sentiment... consists of an empathetic and sympathetic concern for the well-being of others and active engagement in facilitating and sustaining worthy and fulfilling life to fellow humans" (Aloni, 2020, p. 99).

Others write that "care is, first and foremost, a relationship... not achieved by simply following a set of guidelines or principles" (Epley, 2015, p. 882). Similarly, "the Confucian moral ideal quite strongly resembles the moral ideal of care ethics" in which relationships carry moral value in a manner distinct from ethical systems that "hold principles or personal virtues as the moral ideal" (p. 888). The ethic of care is a moral endeavor, the "activity of caring" (Cockburn, 2005; p. 73). This perspective views human beings as "embedded in community" and having the capacity to "care about others and about their hurts and concerns" (Kegley, 2011, p. 122). As well, this conceptualization exists through the sub-Saharan African conception of morality: "our deepest moral obligation is to become more fully human and to achieve this requires one to enter more deeply into community with others" (LeGrange, 2012, p. 331).

Care, as "an ethical act" (Niedermeyer, 2017, p. 187) also can be understood "as a social process and as a daily human activity" (Sevenhuijsen, 2000, p. 12). The ethic of care is founded upon the inherent interdependence existing between individuals as "people live in connection with one another" and "lives are interwoven" (Gilligan, 1998, p. 342): it includes "caring for the self, for the inner circle, for strangers and distant others, for animals, plants, and the Earth, for the human-made world, and for the world of ideas" (Noddings, 1992). Moral concern makes the difference between understanding a moral principle and being motivated to act on such knowledge. Thus, caring awakens "a sense that 'I must' do something" (Noddings 2002, p. 13).

Moral Responsibility

A corresponding competency to moral concern is moral responsibility, conceptualized as our moral obligations to each other, to other life beings, and to the planet. It begins with people affirming the principle of *beneficence*—"to do only good and to not to do any harm" (Frankena, 1973, p. 45). Thus, "we have moral obligations to help, just as we have moral obligations not to harm"; This obligation calls for scrutiny into what we "do and omit to do" with the "priority of reducing or preventing suffering" (Singer, 2009, p. 66) and prompts us to question if our inaction can be harmful and therefore unethical. Striving for beneficence means that a individuals take "into account the interests of all those affected by [their] decision[s]," choosing "the course of action that has the best consequences, on balance, for all affected" (Singer, 2000, p. 16).

In contemporary times, various philosophers write about moral responsibility as honoring the connection between self and others, the interdependence of humankind, and the relationship between humans and the natural world. One way to express human interconnectedness is through the concept of *cosmopolitanism* that focuses on human's obligations to each other and "taking an interest in the practices and beliefs that lend them significance" (Appiah, 2006, p. xv). This means that we care not just about helping others but about knowing and cultivating relationships with them—including people from different cultures and outlooks—informed by "a sense of moral responsibility and an aspiration to move beyond what is required" (Merry & De Ruyter, 2011, p. 4). In this vein, morality comprises awareness that we must go beyond thinking only about humans' connections to each other to recognize that "humans are a part of a world of ever-evolving interdependence" and that "ecosystems and all living beings possess intrinsic value." This way of thinking encompasses "vital attitudes of care, respect, and appreciation for world of nature—even empathy and love for more than human life" (Joseph & Mikel, 2014, pp. 324).

Ultimately, morality involves "the idea of something bigger than the individual" (Singer, 2000, p. 14). For instance, philosopher Kurt Baier (1958) explained that "we should be moral because being moral is following rules designed to overrule self-interest whenever it is in the interest of everyone alike...." (pp. 314–315). Particularly eloquent is Dewey's (1922) description of what it means to override self-interest (as quoted above). Dewey affirmed that morality itself may be inconsequential when we do not take into consideration "the life of the community" and "living in the universal" (pp. 331–332). He calls on human beings to not be content with being good as individuals, to not be satisfied with being obedient or for merely refusing to harm to others. Such moral stances are limited and ephemeral; they do not bring about a more lasting contribution to humanity, to others outside of one's lesser sphere.

But although moral responsibility involves weighing self-interest with the needs of others, this is not moral masochism for the self, as part of the human race, should also be respected. Even though it may never be possible "ever to be fully responsible" "or never responsible enough" (Ronell, 2009, p. 41), the moral imperative is to not become disconnected, separate, and uncaring. Framing the question of how are we to be morally responsible in another way, moral philosopher Peter Singer (2009) asks, "How are we to live?"

> We make our life most meaningful when we connect ourselves with some really important causes or issues and we contribute to them. So we feel that because we live, something has gotten a little better than it would otherwise; we have contributed in however small a way to making the world a better place. (p. 86)

The above reply provides a description of how we can be morally responsible by minimizing self-interest and yet create lives of consequence and integrity.

This answer also is a germane description of the moral calling and sense of obligation experienced by those who become teachers. Undoubtedly, most teachers deeply understand that they make the world a better place and have lives of meaning. Likewise, teachers can inspire and guide students toward understanding their own moral obligations and realizing lives of connection and meaning—thereby cultivating moral responsibility also becomes an aspiration for moral education. Beyond helping students to achieve socially acceptable behavior and a level of kindness toward others, we might also hope for them to build their moral capacities so to attain critical awareness, the desire to confront violence and injustice, and imagining of just and moral possibilities for society.

Character

Another concept linked fundamentally to morality is character—a designated, although often unexamined—aim of moral education. In commonplace political and educational discourse, character refers to virtuous traits exemplifying "a person's attitudes, actions, and conduct" (Taylor, 2006, p. 279). However, moral philosophers and psychologists disparage equating character with a list of good qualities, pointing out that such traits may not be "stable and enduring," but also are "capable of change over time and across situations" (Cohen & Morse, 2014, p. 45). Others write about character traits as "a folk conception" (Harman, 2009, p. 241) or insist that although individuals may affirm and even at times demonstrate their honesty, compassion, or courage, "character is not a collection of virtues or personality traits" (Nucci, 2019, p. 76). Instead, scholars highlight the complex nature of character as an influence on moral functioning and delineate constituents of character that encompass moral principles arrived at through reflection, moral identity, habit, and action. In sum, character includes "those capacities and characteristics that motivate and enable the individuals to act as moral agents" (p. 74).

An important component of character refers to moral choices and judgments "centering on issues of fairness, welfare, and rights distinct from judgments about consensually determined conventions" (Nucci, 2019, p. 75). As such, character has a cognitive basis—understanding and choosing moral principles based on "objectivity and truth" as guides to judgment and adherence to "deeply rooted moral commitments" (Narvaez & Lapsley, 2009, p. 242). According to philosopher R. S. Peters (1962), application of reason to morality creates "autonomous" moral individuals who do not merely invent and live by their own standards; rather, they

> follow rules in a rational discriminating manner and who also have character. To do this, individuals must subscribe to some higher order principles which will enable them both to apply rules intelligently in the light of relevant differences in circumstances and in empirical knowledge about the consequences of their application. (p. 46)

Thus, to have character is to live habitually by examined moral principles. Moral people "become to a large extent responsible for the formation of their habits and their own way of life," in which case, habit becomes chosen action, "a matter of logic and understanding, not merely a matter of repetitiousness of behavior" (Hamm, 1975, p. 428). As well, reflection should begin by acknowledging moral principles "that are capable of rational proof"—some principles that "allow for different rules for different conditions" and some that are "fundamental and changeless" (Singer, 2002, p. 13).

Furthermore, "an autonomous choice is only possible against the backdrop of shared standards and criteria which belong to our human heritage" (Cuypers, 2009, p. 196). Various philosophers affirm that "you cannot undertake practical rational deliberation at all without some kind of idea of what is good" (Baggini, 2016, p. 154). In this way, established moral principles are "resources" for reflection about individuals' beliefs and actions (Besser, 2020, 288). But, as Dewey and Tufts (1932) advised, a moral principle is "not a command to act" but "a tool for analyzing a special situation, the right or wrong being determined by the situation in its entirety, and not by the rule as such" (p. 309).

Another important connection between cognition and character is the concept of moral identity as "a mental image of what it means to be a moral person" (Hardy & Carlo, 2011, p. 213), a "cognitive representation of the moral self that reflects the degree to which moral traits are central to one's self-concept" (Narvaez & Lapsley, 2009, p. 247). "Once more, "the cognitive motivation for moral action springs from this sense of fidelity to oneself-in-action" and "toward self-consistency" (p. 242). Character also signifies that people develop an "authentic inner-compass" informing them on "what is truly important" and what they "really value and need" (Assor et al., 2020, p. 347). It is this desire to live with values and behaviors consistent to one's chosen moral principles that enlivens this concept as character is about "ultimately who we are expressed in action, in how we live, in what we do" (Coles, 1997, p. 7) and our "relations to other people in the social world" (Tirrell, 2021, p. 3).

Ethics

In common practice, the terms moral and ethical often are used interchangeably as "ethics deals, amongst other things, with right and wrong, ought and ought not, good and evil" (Mahoney, 2009, p. 283). Frequently, however, scholars describe *morality* and *ethics* as being entwined but note that these concepts are somewhat or even very different from each other.

Definitions of Ethics

The fundamental definition of ethics is a system or code of moral principles that are conscious, articulated, and "govern a person's or group's behavior" (Hobson, 2004). Also, ethics may be described as "defining the specific values by which we live" and "informing us of the overall goals and ideas which set the stage for our every action" (Solomon, 1992, p. 3).

Moreover, ethics refers to a branch of philosophy that systematically investigates key questions and issues. Although there are various taxonomies, the field of ethics may be divided into several categories which pose different questions: *normative ethics* asks "how should people act?"; *descriptive ethics* considers "what do people think is right?"; *meta-ethics* investigates values, asking "what does 'right' even mean?"; and, *applied ethics* deals with "taking moral knowledge and putting it into practice" (Mastin, 2008). In this way, "an essential part of ethics is to ask questions" such as "what actions are right?" and "what is a good person?" (Solomon, 1992, p. 3). As a field of philosophical study, ethics requires complex understanding of its nature and relevance to conduct.

Ethics also refers to "adopted principles or rules of organizational conduct, often referred to as an ethics code." This characterization of ethics is "more rule-oriented and less philosophical" (Ray, 1996, p. 48) than ethics as a field of moral philosophy. Ethical codes of conduct govern professions including medicine, law, and education. As well, governmental bodies and professional organizations have ethics committee that attempt to ensure suitable moral conduct. For the teaching profession, ethical codes serve several purposes: "to declare itself publicly accountable and to provide a framework for sanctions and the disciplining of members" and "to act as a resource and guide for teachers struggling with ethical issues and dilemmas in the context of their daily practice" (Campbell, 2000, p. 212). Therefore, such codes provide an ideal set of values as guidelines and, at the same time, can be catalysts for discussion of how professionals live and work according to ethical standards.

Ethics and Morality

One way of viewing the relationship between these two concepts is that ethics is an overarching structure of which morality is a part—as ethics "is the study of a way of life . . . its values, its rules and justifications" (Solomon, 1992, p. 1). Viewed from this perspective, "metaphorically, if one views ethics as a wall, morals are the building blocks and philosophy is the mortar" (Ray, 1996, p. 49). This description focuses more on the integral links rather than the separation between morality and ethics.

Notwithstanding, a number of scholars draw distinctions between morality and ethics akin to definitions of customary and reflective morality. Primarily, "ethics is a conscious stepping back and reflecting on morality" (Hinman, 2012, p. 361); in this way, morality may be referred to as "first-order beliefs" and ethics as "second-order reflective consideration of our moral beliefs and practices" (p. 363). Similarly, ethics "is asking us to reflect on what is important to us, on what the ultimate questions are and trying to get standards that help us make decisions" (Singer, 2009, p. 64). Most of all, ethics involves multifaceted and profound reflection:

> Ethics, derived by persons wrestling with what might be good and true on as wide a basis as possible derives principles that require deeper reflection on the what as well as the how of the substance of principles and the complexity of their application (Reardon, 2015, p. 52)

Besides the idea of reflecting on morality, ethics means that people will perceive and decide if they want to follow "aspects of morality stipulated by society" or the "norms of action and exemplification within a community"

(Mullerat, 2013, p. 179). Such reflection allows individuals to become conscious of customary morality and eventually to make judgments about previously unexamined moral beliefs.

Thus, ethics involves distancing from and scrutiny of moral beliefs sanctioned by institutions and culture and engaging in "disinterested reflection" through "an inner dialogue" (Wilson, 1993, p. 241). Ethics then is "a kind of stepping-away" so that "people become reflective and reflexive about their moral world and moral personhood and what they must do, say or think. . . ." (Zigon, 2009, p. 261). Vigorous self-examination is required when individuals attain an ethical stance and ethics requires continuous scrutiny and "calling into question your tacit assumptions and unarticulated presuppositions" (West, 2009, p. 3). For this reason, we might consider ethics as a process of questioning and not just arriving at an ultimate set of moral values and feeling self-satisfied with the results. As philosopher Avital Ronell (2009) cautions, "anyone who's sure of themselves, of their morals and intentions, is not truly ethical" (p. 41).

Moral Imagination

Finally, a powerful theory that affirms and expands various definitions and interpretations of morality and ethics is *moral imagination.* A number of scholars who conceptualize moral imagination insist that it is not enough to affirm people's moral beliefs and intentions (Abowitz, 2007); rather, they picture moral imagination as a guide to live in this world with ethical knowledge, personal integrity, and "moral artistry" (Fesmire, 2003, p. 5)—with enhanced sensitivity to the needs and feelings of others. They write that moral imagination involves a holistic intermingling of heightened cognitive and affective abilities (Joseph, 2003) and a "dynamic interplay of perception, reasoning, and feeling" (Fesmire, 2003, p. 146). Individuals with moral imagination are "engaged in critical, creative, and imaginative searches into moral situations" and critically reflect on their own beliefs and behaviors along with the "social and cultural contexts that shape who they are and how they live" (Abowitz, 2007, p. 298). Once more, some authors view moral imagination as the ability to envision ideals and possibilities (Babbit, 1996; Kekes, 2006; Pardales, 2002) including alternative, non-dominant worldviews (Joseph & Mikel, 2014). Thus, individuals with moral imagination conceive of profoundly different values and actions that lead them toward the development of moral agency.

Components of Moral Imagination

A way to understand the complex concept of moral imagination is to explain its interrelated fundamental components: *Moral emotions* include feelings that permit sympathetic and empathic connection with others and the desire to take moral action; *moral perception* is the ability of people to become aware of others and their needs, hopes, and potentials and to perceive the moral nature of situations and experiences; *ethical reasoning* refers to realistic understanding of situations calling for moral response and approaching situations with a moral standpoint; *critical reflection* means the continuous scrutiny of personal beliefs and actions and examination of immorality and injustice in existing social-political conditions; and, *visioning* in moral imagination refers to the ability to transcend status-quo thinking and to envision possibilities for the actualization of ideal moral values and a better society or world (see Table 1.1; Babbitt, 1996; Kim, 2009; Moberg & Seabright, 2000; Pardales, 2002).

Moral Emotions

Moral imagination involves feelings that spur attentiveness to others' needs. It is the amplification of sympathetic and empathic feelings that connect individuals to others and bring about "sensitivity to situations that we might be callous to otherwise" (Pardales, 2002, p. 431). Scholars understand the imaginative quality of these feelings and, at the same time, the interwoven relationship between imagination and moral feelings. In that

TABLE 1.1 Components of Moral Imagination

Component	Description
Moral Emotions	Moral feelings leading to attentiveness and sensitivity to others' needs; amplification of sympathetic and empathic feelings that connect individuals to others.
Moral Perception	The ability of people to become aware of others and their needs, desires, interests, wishes, hopes, and potentials and to discern a moral situation.
Ethical Reasoning	Realistic understanding of situations calling for moral judgment and response with knowledge of the particular issues and problems at stake.
Critical Reflection	Continual examination of beliefs and actions leading to knowledge of self, including blind spots, and consideration of judgments and action affect other people.
Visioning	Imaginative understanding of moral agency by challenging customary values and actions and envisioning ideal versions of ourselves and society—beyond what we currently experience in reality.

way, sympathy "is something more than mere feeling; it is a cultivated imagination for understanding what people "have in common and a rebellion at whatever unnecessarily divides them" (Dewey, 1916/1985, pp. 127–128). Respectively, moral imagination "broadens the scope of empathy, illuminating a greater number of salient particulars and increasing sensitivity toward dimensions of a situation that may otherwise go overlooked" (Fletcher, 2016, p. 148). Empathic feelings enhance moral deliberation (Noddings, 1998, p. 135), motivating moral perception and reasoning.

Moral Perception

For the most part, however, scholars portray moral imagination as an enhancement of cognition, in particular, the development of moral perception (Pardales, 2002, p. 431); "our ability to see and comprehend a moral situation encountered in experience" (Abowitz, 2007, p. 288). This acuity allows individuals to apprehend how all aspects of their lives and work have moral significance. Moral perception may also be defined as "moral wide-awakeness," defined as "attentiveness to the moral dimensions of existence," cognizance of personal values, and "breaking with the mechanical life" (Greene, 1978, pp. 46–47). Keen moral perception leads to peoples' emphatic rejection of indifference and, as a capacity of moral imagination, such perception contributes toward the development of a "full moral outlook" (You & Rud, 2010, p. 39).

Ethical Reasoning

Ethical reasoning is another cognitive capacity of moral imagination "involving the ability to understand the context of a situation that requires moral judgment," "the moral rules that come into play," and "the new possibilities one has envisioned"—allowing people to 'think more creatively within the constraints of what is morally possible" (Werhane, 2002, p. 34). Scholars who analyze the relationship between moral imagination and ethical reasoning describe how moral imagination is used for "sharpening powers of discrimination" (Johnson, 1993, p. 198) and to develop fluidity of reasoning so to "think in alternatives" (Abowitz, 2007, p. 288). Such reasoning also involves "rehearsing" possible solutions (Fesmire, 2012, p. 213), understanding the "metaphoric concepts" that underlie thinking (Kim, 2009, p. 70), and considering a variety of possibilities to evaluate their moral consequences (Biss, 2014; Moberg & Seabright, 2000; Werhane, 2002). Consequently, when people engage in ethical reasoning by considering alternatives they may realize that their former views were "narrow" or "parochial" (Fletcher, 2016, pp. 144, 147); they may not only develop different perspectives, but also reject their previous views, in essence, experiencing personal transformation (Babbitt, 1996). Ethical reasoning extends perception so that people can evaluate from "a moral point of view" (Werhane, 2002), p. 34) and become empowered to make decisions that may profoundly affect their lives and those of others.

Critical Reflection

Considering enhanced cognitive capacity on a continuum beginning with moral perception and then ethical reasoning, the next element is critical reflection. Scholars link such reflection to moral imagination because without examination of personal beliefs and deep understanding of the societal conditions, people may continue to have narrow and self-interested perspectives (Nussbaum, 1998). Critical self-reflection leads to knowledge of self (including "blind spots"), ethical understanding of "actions and outcomes" (Kim, 2009, p. 66), and critique of individuals' beliefs and actions. Such self-scrutiny helps people to contemplate if their values stem from "unexamined convention" or from "thoughtfully constructed choices" (Joseph, 2003, p. 17). Therefore, reflection becomes "the bridge between the contemporary situation and the ideal moral self" (Moberg & Seabright, 2000, p. 868) when individuals continually evaluate their choices and actions. Scholars also describe critical inquiry into social problems and how they affect human beings and the environment (Babbitt, 1996). The "coming to grips with realities of social inequality" and "understanding of complex issues" "helps activate a moral imagination" (Beyer, 1991, p. 210). But to possess moral imagination, critical reflection is not the last step.

Visioning

A number of scholars believe that holding a vision of a better world is an imperative element for cultivating moral imagination. Visioning inspires individuals to believe in the possibility of change, "to resist fatalism and cynicism and its close cousin contempt—where hopelessness and powerlessness may prevail" (Ledbetter, 2012, p. 15) and to compel moral action. They write that moral imagination is "the capacity to imagine something rooted in the challenges of the real world yet capable of giving birth to that which does not yet exist" (Lederach, 2005, p. 29) and emphasize the importance of reflecting upon an ideal (Kekes, 2006, p. 18). This means that we need "to live according to our various possibilities" (Antonaccio, 2001, p. xiv), and formulate "notions and ideals of ourselves and our worlds beyond what we currently experience or know as reality" (Abowitz, 2007, p. 288). People who possess this last component of moral imagination have faith that the world can be a better place and that they, through their individual and combined efforts, can become moral actors who challenge violence and injustice.

Importance of Moral Imagination

Scholars writing across various fields name several reasons for why moral imagination should be a goal for educating ethical individuals and professionals (Abowitz, 2007; McPhail, 2001; Moberg & Seabright, 2000; Scott, 1997; Werhane, 2002; Young & Annisette, 2009). Among the rationales set forth is the need to transcend conventional thinking, to develop individuals' moral guidelines, ideals, and visions, and to challenge societal norms that perpetuate violence and domination.

A compelling rationale for moral imagination is the necessity to confront ethically deficient organizational cultures. Moral imagination can "operate on organizational and systemic levels" (Werhane, 2002, p. 34); whether the organizations are schools or businesses, people can be "trapped within an organizational culture that creates mental habits that function as boundary conditions, precluding creative thinking" (Wehane, 2002, p. 39). Therefore, moral imagination can "serve as an antidote to decision environments that normally lead to morally defective choices" (Moberg & Seabright, 2000, p. 845). Once more, moral imagination needs to be cultivated even in young people before they enter organizational cultures as adults—"before their imaginations are shackled by the weight of daily duties and self-interested plans" (Nussbaum, 2002), p. 301).

Moral imagination also features in the discussions of ethical teachers who "critically challenge their own beliefs and thinking" (Joseph, 2003, p. 18), "see their students' potentials" (Abd-El-Fattah & Soong, 2008, p. 13), and develop moral perception and sensitivity to understand the "unique needs and desires of their students and the future of their best possibilities" (Simpson & Garrison, 1995, p. 252). Some scholars argue that moral imagination allows teachers to better perceive and question limited educational goals in educational systems that stress efficiency and standardization (Chapman et al., 2013, p. 142). Teachers who have moral imagination are not only guided by their ideals and values to challenge conventional aims and methods (Kim, 2009, p. 65), they can envision democratic schools and societies (O'Loughlin, 1995).

Lastly, moral imagination is a significant concept to scholars who write about peace, nonviolence, and ecojustice; they contend that to challenge ubiquitous violence in human interactions, discourse, and relationships with the natural world, cultivation of moral imagination is crucial. Scholars note that "violence results from a lack of imagination" (Jenkins, 2007, p. 368) because people do not critically examine its presence and even rationalize violence as morally justifiable. They furthermore discern that moral imagination has "binary characteristics—described not only as "critical consciousness of violence" but as experiencing connectedness with all of life and picturing a world of peace (Joseph & Mikel, 2014, p. 326). In this way, moral imagination stimulates "moral indignation" and a "concern for injustice" (Ledbetter, 2012, p. 16). It is moral imagination that gives people the capabilities to challenge acceptance of violence toward humans and the Earth and, alternatively, to find ways to "transcend the cycles of violence that bewitch the human community" (Lederach 2005, 29, p. 4).

References

Abd-El-Fattah, S., & Soong, L. (2008). Teachers' moral imagination: A multifaceted concept. In R. Fitzgerald & Nielsen, T. W. (Eds.) *Imaginative, practice, imaginative, inquiry: Proceedings of the Sixth International Conference on Imagination and Education* (pp. 3–14). Canberra, Australia.

Abowitz, K. K. (2007). Moral perception through aesthetics engaging imaginations in educational ethics. *Journal of Teacher Education, 58*(4), 287–298.

Aloni, N. (2020) Locally grounded, universally binding: The benefit of incorporating traditional care ethics, East and West, into current moral education. *Educational Philosophy and Theory, 52*(1), 98–105.

Antonaccio, M. (2001). The virtues of metaphysics: A review of Iris Murdoch's philosophical writings. *Journal of Religious Ethics, 29*(2), 309–335.

Appiah, K. A. (2006). *Cosmopolitanism: Ethics in a world of strangers.* WW Norton.

Assor, A., Benita, M., Yitshaki, N., Geifman, Y., & Maree, W. (2020). Sense of authentic inner compass as a moral resource across cultures: possible implications for resisting negative peer-pressure and for parenting. *Journal of Moral Education, 49*(3), 346–364.

Babbitt, S. E. (1996). *Impossible dreams: Rationality, integrity, and moral imagination.* Westview Press.

Baggini, J. (2016). *The edge of reason* (pp. 143–167). Yale University Press.

Baier, K. (1958). *The moral point of view: A rational basis of ethics.* Cornell University Press.

Barrow, R. (2006). Moral education's modest agenda. *Ethics and Education, 1*(1), 3–13.

Besser, L. L. (2020). Learning virtue. *Journal of Moral Education, 49*(3), 282–294.

Beyer, L. E. (1991). Schooling, moral commitment, and the preparation of teachers. *Journal of Teacher Education, 42*(3), 205–215.

Biss, M. (2014). Moral imagination, perception, and judgment. *The Southern Journal of Philosophy, 52*(1), 1–21.

Boehm, C. (1977). The moral system. In L. J. Stiles & B. D. Johnson (Eds.), *Morality examined: Guidelines for teachers* (pp. 25–39). Princeton Book Company.

Campbell, E. (2000). Professional ethics in teaching: Towards the development of a code of practice. *Cambridge Journal of Education, 30*(2), 203–221.

Chapman, A., Forster, D., & Buchanan, R. (2013). The moral imagination in pre-service teachers' ethical reasoning. *Australian Journal of Teacher Education, 38*(5), 131–143.

Cockburn, T. (2005). Children and the feminist ethic of care. *Childhood, 12*(1), 71–89.

Cohen, T. R., & Morse, L. (2014). Moral character: What it is and what it does. *Research in Organizational Behavior, 34*, 43–61.

Colby, A., Ehrlich, T., Beaumont, E., & Stephens, J. (2003). *Educating citizens: Preparing America's undergraduates for lives of moral and civic responsibility.* Jossey-Bass.

Coles, R. (1997). *The moral intelligence of children.* Random House.

Cuypers, S. E. (2009). Autonomy in RS Peters' educational theory. *Journal of Philosophy of Education, 43*(1), 189–207.

Dewey, J. (1908/1932). *Theory of the moral life.* Holt, Rinehart & Winston.

Dewey, J. (1916/1985). *Democracy and education.* Southern Illinois University Press.

Dewey, J. (1922). *Human nature and conduct: An introduction to social psychology.* Henry Holt.

Dewey, J., & Tufts, J. H. (1932). *Ethics* (rev. ed.). Henry Holt.

Epley, K. M. (2015). Care ethics and Confucianism: Caring through Li. *Hypatia, 30*(4), 881–896.

Fesmire, S. (2003). *John Dewey and moral imagination: Pragmatism in ethics.* Indiana University Press.

Fesmire, S. (2012) Ecological imagination in moral education, east and west. *Contemporary Pragmatism, 9*(1), 205–222.

Fletcher, N. (2016). Envisioning the experience of others: Moral imagination, practical wisdom and the scope of empathy. *Philosophical Inquiry in Education, 23*(2), 141–159.

Frankena, W. K. (1973). *Ethics* (2nd ed.). Prentice Hall.

Gilligan, C. (1998). Hearing the difference: Theorizing connection. In M. Rogers (Ed.) *Contemporary feminist theory: A text/reader* (pp. 341–346). McGraw-Hill.

Greene, M. (1978). *Landscapes of learning.* Teachers College Press.

Hamm, C. M. (1975). The role of habit in moral education. *Educational Theory, 25*(4), 417–428.

Hardy, S. A., & Carlo, G. (2011). Moral identity: What is it, how does it develop, and is it linked to moral action? *Child Development Perspectives, 5*(3), 212–218.

Harman, G. (2009). Skepticism about character traits. *The Journal of Ethics, 13*(2), 235–242.

Hare, H. M. (1966). Decisions of principles. In I. Scheffler (Ed.), *Philosophy and education: Modern readings* (2nd ed.; pp. 72–86). Allyn and Bacon.

Hinman, L. M. (2012). *Ethics: A pluralistic approach to ethical theory* (5th ed). Wadsworth.

Hobson, A. (2004). *The Oxford dictionary of difficult words.* Oxford University Press.

Jenkins, T. 2007. Rethinking the unimaginable: The need for teacher education in peace education. *Harvard Educational Review, 77*(3), 366–369.

Johnson, M. (1993) *Moral imagination: Implications of cognitive science for ethics.* University of Chicago Press.

Joseph, P. B. (2003). Teaching about the moral classroom: Infusing the moral imagination into teacher education. *Asia-Pacific Journal of Teacher Education, 31*(1), 7–20.

Joseph, P. B., & Mikel, E. (2014). Transformative moral education: challenging an ecology of violence. *Journal of Peace Education, 11*(3), 317–333.

Kegley, J. A. (2011). The "ethical subject/agent" as "rational individual" but also as so much more!. *Journal of Speculative Philosophy, 25*(1), 116–129.

Kekes, J. (2006). *The enlargement of life: Moral imagination at work.* Cornell University Press.

Kim, J. (2009). Dewey's aesthetics and today's moral education. *Education and Culture, 25*(2), 62–75.

Ledbetter, B. (2012). Dialectics of leadership for peace: Toward a moral model of resistance. *Journal of Leadership, Accountability and Ethics, 9*(5), 11–24.

Lederach, J. P. (2005). *The moral imagination: The art and soul of building peace.* Oxford University Press.

Le Grange, L. (2012). Ubuntu, ukama, environment and moral education. *Journal of Moral Education, 41*(3), 329–340.

Linton, R. (1945). *The cultural background of personality.* Appleton-Century.

Mahony, P. (2009). Should 'ought' be taught?. *Teaching and Teacher Education, 25*(7), 983–989.

Mastin, L. (2008). *The basics of philosophy.* Retrieved April 25, 2022 from https://www.philosophybasics.com/branch_ethics.html

McPhail, K. (2001). The other objective of ethics education: Re-humanising the accounting profession—A study of ethics education in law, engineering, medicine and accountancy. *Journal of Business Ethics, 34*(3–4), 279–298.

Merry, M. S., & de Ruyter, J. (2011). The relevance of cosmopolitanism for moral education. *Journal of Moral Education, 40*(1), 1–18.

Moberg, D. J., & Seabright, M. A. (2000). The development of moral imagination. *Business Ethics Quarterly, 10*(04), 845–884.

Mullerat, R. (2013). Professional ethics, what for . . . ? *Journal of Ethics, 4,* 173–199.

Musgrave, P. W. (1978) *The moral curriculum: A sociological analysis.* Methuen.

Narvaez, D., & Lapsley, D. K. (2009). Moral identity, moral functioning, and the development of moral character. *Psychology of learning and motivation, 50,* 237–274.

Neldner, K., Wilks, M., Crimston, C. R., Jaymes, R. W. M., & Nielsen, M. (2022). I may not like you, but I still care: Children differentiate moral concern from other constructs. *Developmental Psychology,* 1–18. https://dx.doi.org/10.1037/dev0001485

Niedermeyer, W. J. (2017). Why do we care?: A natural history of Noddings' ethical theory. *Between the Species, 22*(1), 185–213.

Noddings, N. (1989). *Women and evil.* University of California Press.

Noddings, N. (1992). *The challenge to care in schools: An alternative approach to education.* Teachers College Press.

Noddings, N. (1998). Thinking, feeling, and moral imagination. *Midwest Studies in Philosophy, 22*(1), 135–145.

Nucci, L. (2019). Character: A developmental system. *Child Development Perspectives, 13*(2), 73–78.

Nussbaum, M.C. (1998). *Cultivating humanity: A classical defense of reform in liberal education.* Harvard University Press.

Nussbaum, M. (2002). Education for citizenship in an era of global connection. *Studies in Philosophy and Education, 21*(4–5), 289–303.

O'Loughlin, M. (1995). Daring the imagination: Unlocking voices of dissent and possibility in teaching. *Theory into Practice, 34*(2), 107–116.

Pardales, M. J. (2002). "So, how did you arrive at that decision?" Connecting moral imagination and moral judgement. *Journal of Moral Education, 31*(4), 423–437.

Peters, R. S. (1962). Moral education and the psychology of character. *Philosophy, 37*(139), 37–56.

Ray, T. T. (1996). Differentiating the related concepts of ethics, morality, law, and justice. *New directions for teaching and learning, 1996*(66), 47–53.

Reardon, B. A. (2015). Human rights learning: Pedagogies and politics of peace. In *Betty A. Reardon: A pioneer in education for peace and human rights* (pp. 145–164). Springer International Publishing.

Ronell, A. (2009). Meaning. In A. Taylor (Ed.), *Examined life: Excursions with contemporary thinkers* (pp. 25–60). The New Press.

Scott, P. A. (1997). Imagination in practice. *Journal of Medical Ethics, 23*(1), 45–50.

Sevenhuijsen, S. (2000). Caring in the third way: the relation between obligation, responsibility and care in Third Way discourse. *Critical Social Policy, 20*(1), 5–37.

Simpson, P. J., & Garrison, J. (1995). Teaching and moral perception, *Teachers College Record, 97*(2), 252–278.

Singer, M. G. (2002). *The ideal of rational morality: Philosophical compositions.* Oxford University Press.

Singer, P. (2000). *Writings on an ethical life.* Ecco Press.

Singer, P. (2009). Ethics. In A. Taylor (Ed.), *Examined life: Excursions with contemporary thinkers* (pp. 61–86). The New Press.

Smetana, J. G. (1999). The role of parents in moral development: A social domain analysis. *Journal of Moral Education, 28*(3), 311–321.

Solomon, R. C. (1992). *Morality and the good life: An introduction to ethics through classical sources.* McGraw-Hill.

Taylor, J. (2006). Virtue and the evaluation of character. In S. Traiger (Ed.), *The Blackwell guide to Hume's Treatise* (pp. 276–295). Blackwell Publishing/Wiley.

Tirrell, J. M. (2021). Forgiveness as a character strength: Toward a developmental model and research agenda. *Journal of Moral Education,* 1–24.

Walker, D. I. (2020). Sociological contributions for researching morality and cultivating states of moral character. *Journal of Moral Education, 51*(1), 24–34.

Werhane, P. H. (2002). Moral imagination and systems thinking. *Journal of Business Ethics, 38*(1/2), 33–42.

West, C. (2009). Truth. In A. Taylor (Ed.), *Examined life: Excursions with contemporary thinkers* (pp. 1–24). The New Press.

Wilson, J. Q. (1993). *The moral sense.* The Free Press.

You, Z., & Rud, A. G. (2010). A model of Dewey's moral imagination for service learning: Theoretical explorations and implications for practice in higher education. *Education and Culture, 26*(2), 36–51.

Young, J. J., & Annisette, M. (2009). Cultivating imagination: Ethics, education and literature. *Critical Perspectives on Accounting, 20*(1), 93–109.

Zigon, J. (2009). Within a range of possibilities: Morality and ethics in social life. *Ethnos, 74*(2), 251–276.

2

Human Nature and Morality

A critical part of our morality—so much of what makes us human—emerges over the course of human history and individual development. It is the product of our compassion, our imagination, and our magnificent capacity for reason.

—Paul Bloom, 2013, Just Babies: The Origins of Good and Evil, p. 218

Underlying the concept of moral imagination is the multifaceted belief that people can attain the power of ethical reflection and strive for moral action—inspired by sensitive understanding of others and their needs. By this perspective we view humans as having "compassion, imagination, and a magnificent capacity for reason" (Bloom, 2013, p. 218). Thus, as moral educators we need to understand how we can stimulate and support young people's moral consciousness and their desire to care for others and the Earth.

And yet, "human history testifies to both the relative ease and ready motivations with which humans kill and maim each other" (Sheets-Johnstone, 2008, p. 137). So too, in the 21st century, we live in a violent world in which "humanity seems to be trapped in a deepening spiral of hatred, vengeance, and militarism" as well as the threat of "destruction of life on

Teaching for Moral Imagination, pages 23–44

www.infoagepub.com

this planet" (Miller, 2003, p. 25). Violence takes 'horrific forms" such as "ecocide, genocide, modern warfare, ethnic hatred, racism, sexual abuse, domestic violence" (Harris, 2004, p. 5) and in young people's perniciously bullying of their peers (Rosen & Rubin, 2016). How do we reconcile the faith that people can be thoughtful, just, empathic, and morally responsible with so many examples of the violent nature of humankind?

This conundrum regarding the capability for moral imagination and violence epitomizes some of the confounding questions asked over time about human nature and moral development:

- What are the deeply rooted instincts and human needs that influence moral development?
- What intrinsic assets make humans capable of moral reasoning and behavior?
- Why do some individuals go beyond a nascent level of moral functioning and live according to their ethical principles—even as they jeopardize their own security or safety to protect others from harm?
- What are the reasons for and consequences of moral dysfunction thwarting moral feelings, ethical reflection, and moral agency?

Of course, these perplexing questions do not lend themselves to unequivocal answers when we grapple with them ourselves or explore them through the works of scholars. There are human dynamics—intricate and immeasurable combinations of capabilities and traits—that influence individuals' moral beliefs and behaviors. We need to appreciate the complexity of human nature and the process of moral development, although such understanding neither will leave us with certainty nor give us lockstep strategies for helping children to become morally responsible.

Assumptions About Human Nature and Morality

Beliefs about children's moral nature have influenced educators over time. Long ago, harsh religious doctrines characterized children as born evil; such dogmas resulted in fear-inducing, punitive school practices of moral instruction. In more modern times, romantic educational philosophers posited that children are innately good and that it was the fault of school and society for corrupting their natural moral nature—casting doubt on the need for explicit moral education. More recently, teachers have rejected both stereotypes of children's natures as inherently wicked or virtuous.

Instead, many present-day educators rightfully assume that students' moral competences are profoundly affected by their caregivers, peers, and social environments—including explicit and implicit moral education taking place in classrooms and schools. While far more accurate than assuming children's natures are fixed or predetermined, current notions about influences upon students' moral development still may lead to naïve conclusions. The first inference stems from the misconception that cultural elements in children's lives unequivocally affect their moral futures and, in particular, if families, peers, and communities are anti-social influences, there is nothing that schools can do to ameliorate these experiences. The second supposition is based on the stereotype of children as blank slates or sponges who "drink in" moral teaching as though their teachers' moral values—no matter how individualistic or culturally insensitive—will easily replace students' own perceptions and experiences.

Both of the above impressions are fairly simplistic in contrast to a more complicated picture portrayed by contemporary researchers. As educational psychologist Darcia Narvaez (2019) contends, "each person is an embodied story—integrating the tale of not only human evolution but also their own lived experience" (p. 357). She describes both "horizontal influences—inherited through evolutionary processes... as well as ancestral history" and "vertical influences that shape people's lives" (p. 347) such as families and cultures—including the earliest experiences that instill moral feelings and values. Thus, from infancy through adulthood individuals construct their moral lives by making sense of moral teachings and models in light of their own instincts, personalities, and needs.

Moral Predispositions

For numerous scholars, it is a given that humans possess moral instincts and capabilities, that human beings share "a moral nature" (Appiah, 2009, p. 101), and being human is to have "a moral sense" by which "most people intuitively rely" (Wilson, 1993, p. 12). Among our "natural endowments" are:

- a moral sense—some capacity to distinguish between kind and cruel actions;
- empathy and compassion—suffering at the pain of those around us and the wish to make this pain go away;
- a rudimentary sense of fairness—a tendency to favor equal divisions of resources;
- a rudimentary sense of justice—a desire to see good actions rewarded and bad actions punished. (Bloom, 2013, p. 5)

Still, these assumptions are tempered by recognition of limitations of naturally occurring morality. The moral sense means that "humans, by their nature, are potentially good," but that "is not the same as saying that they are innately good" (Wilson, 1993, p. 12). Moreover, the moral sense "is not a strong beacon light" in view of the fact that "greed, passion, anger, self-love—are constantly at work to suppress disinterested reflection" (p. 241) and the omnipresent existence of "cruelty and combat" (p. 227).

Through an evolutionary lens, psychologists and anthropologists highlight moral predispositions of human nature—although these inclinations are not fixed but "revised by childhood experiences" (Haidt, 2012, p. 278). Psychologists write that humans are "at least innately prepared" for moral functioning (Haidt & Joseph, 2004, p. 62) and that "our primate origins have given us specific moral tendencies and capacities" (Vozzola, 2014, p. 59) allowing people to get along and care for each other. "Bonding to others in our social world, and hence caring what happens to them, is a profoundly significant feature of our nature as human animals" (Churchland, 2019, p. 68). In addition, social psychologist Jonathan Haidt (2012) notes that although selfless generosity is rare, human evolution involves "ultrasociality" that "make us adept at promoting our *group's* interest" and being "good team players" (p. 191). As well, he remarks, "human beings are the giraffes of altruism. We're one-of-a-kind freaks of nature who occasionally—even if rarely—can be as selfless and team-spirited as bees" (p. 198)

The attraction to groups "is deeply rooted in human nature" (Baumeister, 1997, p. 192). Certainly, humankind's history of cooperation illuminates our essential moral impulses. Anthropologist Joshua Greene (2014) deduces:

> From simple cells to supersocial animals like us, the story of life on Earth is the story of increasingly complex cooperation. Cooperation is why we're here, and yet, at the same time, maintaining cooperation is our greatest challenge. Morality is the human brain's answer to this challenge. (p. 59)

Greene (2014) also points out that although humans cooperate, it is not because human nature is naturally good nor seeks goodness for its own sake, but because cooperation is beneficial on various levels: "We have cooperative brains, it seems, because cooperation provides material benefits, biological resources that enable our genes to make more copies of themselves. Out of evolutionary dirt grows the flower of human goodness" (p. 65).

Why then do humans cooperate, albeit more often within their own groups, if not for altruistic or intrinsic reasons? Anthropologist Christopher Boehm (2014) asserted that although humans have "underlying generous feelings," "these innately generous tendencies are not quite up to the job" and so cultures must provide "continuous and strong positive support" (p. 273) to encourage cooperation and to reduce conflict. Boehm (1999) also stated that "cooperation is possible because human groups invariably act as *moral* communities" that develop as organizations to "suppress the aggressive egotism and dedicated nepotism that are so powerful in our nature" (p. 254).

On the other hand, evolutionary perspectives also cast light on our "innate tribalistic tendencies" (Greene, 2014, p. 69).) "Human nature inclines people to align themselves in groups that square off against each other, each group seeing itself as good and the other as bad" (Baumeister, 1997, p. 377).

> Once again, anthropological reports indicate that in-group favoritism and ethnocentrism are human universals. Young children identify and favor in-group members based on linguistic cues.... People readily favor in-group members over out-group members, even when the groups are arbitrarily defined and temporary. (Greene, 2014, p. 69)

Therefore, while group membership affords humans comfort, security, and opportunities to care for others, viewing others not in one's own group as non-human—even as "forces of evil" (Baumeister, 1997, p. 377)—also is a feature of human history.

Another human predisposition is rationality, described as "having reason," "the ability to use knowledge to attain goals" (Pinker, 2021, p. 36), "possession of the power to reason" (Baier, 1982, p. 85), and to be aware of and in control of one's thinking processes (Moshman, 2009, p. 11). Modern and ancient philosophers as well as more contemporary psychologists assert that rationality, an essential prerequisite of morality, is "the study of reality—observation and development of understanding about the world as it is" (Johnson, 2013, p. 36)—requiring people to be empiricists. Reality, although never free from subjectivity, is ascertained through demonstrable evidence, multiple perspectives, and analytical inquiry into shared perceptions. This entails having enough understanding of the environment to be able to see the relationship between actions and consequences.

Being reasonable obliges people to engage in dialogue and to look at situations "from the point of view of others"—discounting one's own particular biases and predilections" (Peters, 1975, p. 102). "It is through our power of reason that we grasp situations calling for moral action and "make further deductions and inferences about that situation" (Blackburn, 2000, p. 240). For example, "ridding prejudice from our shores is an example of rationality defeating basic instinctual ideas such as a basic fear of outsiders" (Johnson, 2013, p. 46). Likewise, "reason forces people to acknowledge inconsistencies between their deepest values and how they were acting" (Baggini, 2016, p. 156). It is through rational thinking that people can resist accepting unfounded prejudices and conspiracies, and endeavor to "distinguish what is true from what we want to be true" (Pinker, 2021, p. 2021).

Paradoxically, we may better understand the concept of rationality and its relationship to morality by exploring what it means to be irrational.

> What we do, believe, or feel is called irrational if it is the case not only that there are conclusive or overwhelming reasons against doing, believing, or feeling these things, but also that we must know there are such reasons and still persist in our action, belief, or feelings. (Baier, 1958, pp. 315–316)

This definition of the irrational suggests that two events occur when cognitively capable people are irrational: They ignore empirical evidence and they allow their feelings to rule their judgments and actions. Individuals or groups who reject scientific data may do so because of their strong and persistent emotions that obstruct cognitive functioning when they deny overwhelming reasons even to themselves. The tenacious denial of climate change or belief in unsubstantiated conspiracy theories are examples of irrationality. We consider people to be irrational when they cannot consolidate information about real situations and act accordingly, e.g., imagining unfounded dangers and acting out by harming their imagined attackers or persecutors. Or, for example, when by believing in the inferiority of people other than from one's own ethnic or racial group, "prejudice is an arbitrary deviation from rationality" (Johnson, 2013, p. 45).

Yet, rationality and irrationality both are aspects of human nature. Psychologist Steven Pinker (2021) explains that our species has a "mindset" that can be based on "fallacies, biases, and indulgence in mythology" (p. 317). He writes "the function of these beliefs is to construct a social reality that binds the tribe or sect and gives is moral purpose (p. 300). He declares that "the paradox of our species" is that we can be "both so rational and irrational" as "our powers of reason are guided by our motives and limited by our points of view"—at times preventing us from thinking impartially and acting morally (p. 317).

Psychologist Paul Bloom (2013) concludes that even very young children have "certain capacities for judgment and feeling"—and that "these capacities are natural in the sense that they are a legacy of our evolutionary history, not cultural inventions" (p. 99). Morality seen through an evolutionary perspective reveals that humans are naturally capable of sympathetic moral feelings as well as prejudice and aggression—especially when others are perceived as different from those in one's own group. Moreover, humans develop social systems to sanction morality—to provide inducements for being good and prohibitions for immoral behavior. So too, humans also are endowed with the ability for reason, even though they may abandon rational thinking for irrational under the sway the desire to belong to a group and the necessity to then adopt the group's belief systems. Overall, by being moral and cooperative, humans fulfill certain basic needs—such as for survival, attachment, connection, and community.

Dependency and Attachment

Evolutionary theories only partially explain human's moral instincts; we must also attribute moral predispositions to the particular circumstance of human development in which "our moral sense is essentially connected to early ties of dependency between the children and their caregivers" (Govrin, 2014, p. 1). "Humans have the longest childhoods of any creature" (Bloom, 2013, p. 173), "are born highly immature compared to other hominids," and "child well-being requires an intense level of support on the part of the mother and community" (Narvaez, 2019, p. 350). The "evolved nest" of primary caregivers (mothers, fathers, and others)

> influence all that the child becomes, from physiology to sociality and morality, largely not only because humans are so immature at birth but also because humans are much more shapeable than any other animal through general plasticity and multiple epigenetic effects. (Narvaez, 2019, p. 353)

Dependency includes all means of survival and gratification, continuing to a great extent long after infancy, and the dependent relationship is the foundation for moral development. As helpless babies experience caring and tenderness, they become acutely sensitive to their caregivers as they seek comfort and receive approval and love. This intense relationship stimulates young children's emotional ties to their caregivers and their desire to learn from their nurturers—supporting the development of morality encompassing caring and compassion into adulthood.

The early experiences of dependency and care lead to "the special affective relationship that forms between infants and their primary caretakers" (Berkowitz & Grych, 1998, p. 373) known as attachment—"an intense and enduring emotional bond that is rooted in the function of protection of infants from danger" (Palm, 2014, p. 283). According to attachment theory (Ainsworth, 1982; Bowlby, 1969), this profound relationship occurs when caregivers respond sensitively and empathically to infants and young children and, consequently, a "warm, intimate, and continuous relationship" develops (Bretherton, 1992, p. 761). "Responsive care is considered fundamental to the development of a secure attachment style" (Gleason & Narvaez, 2019, p. 62) and thus the caregiver as an "attachment figure" becomes a "secure base from which an infant can explore the world" (Bretherton, 1992, p. 759).

Although cross-cultural studies on attachment focus primarily on the relationship between infants and their mothers (Bretherton, 1992), researchers also document bonds with fathers, grandparents, and non-parental caregivers (Cummings & Warmuth, 2019; Ebbeck, & Yim, 2009; Poehlmann, 2003). So too, investigations of communal child-rearing efforts, such as in the kibbutzim of Israel, depict how adults and other children provide a sense of belonging and nurturance to children in created familial systems (Bettelheim, 1969; Palm, 2014; Van Ijzendoorn, Sagi, & Lambermon, 1992); in such situations, "relationships with a group can also function as an attachment relationship" as children experience the group as "source of security, support, and comfort in times of distress" (Sidi & Shafran, 2020, p. 3).

The "attachment system is more than food and warmth; it is also about care and emotional security" (Deneault & Hammond, 2021, p. 8). In "the context of a warm, mutually responsive orientation of cooperative, reciprocal, and with shared positive affect" (Sengsavang & Krettenauer, 2020, p. 7), child and caregiver become acutely sensitive to one another. These "first relationships are dynamic and have enduring characteristics that profoundly influence later development" (Palm, 2014, p. 283). This connection that develops between the vulnerable infant and nurturing caregiver fundamentally is a moral bond of mutual belongingness and love that promotes moral development because children emerge from these early experiences "oriented to the human dimensions of moral behavior" (Sengsavang & Krettenauer, 2020, p. 7).

In various ways researchers illustrate how attachment relationships are crucial to moral development:

- "Highly responsive caregiving practices" reduce or alleviate stress" (Bland & DeRobertis, 2020, p. 941) and allow for the development of emotional wellbeing "based in appropriate physiological and emotional regulation"; "such capacities thus afford the ability to focus on others and be concerned for their wellbeing "(Gleason & Narvaez, 2019, p. 60).
- "In the context of attachment, the child discovers the patterns of human interaction and observes the ways in which people care for and hurt one another; the experience of attachment

profoundly affects the child's understanding of how one should act toward other people and the child's knowledge of human feelings" (Gilligan & Wiggins, 1987, p 280).

- "Secure attachment in children... has been associated with behaviors reflecting empathic concern for others, such as offering comfort to distressed peers" (Skoe, 2010, p. 204).
- Children who are loved and cared for in early childhood "identify with their nurturers" and "with their comforters"; such identification "allows them to identity with victims and feel pity and compassion"; "children's desire to give back love and nurturance eventually generalizes to others beyond their families (Vozzola, 2014, p. 13).
- Secure attachment bonds lead to "more harmonious interactions with peers" in early childhood and have been found "to predict successful relationships throughout life" (Berkowitz & Grych, 1998, p. 373).
- "Stable attachment relationships are likely to be important in building the resilience that may reduce the risk of adverse outcomes in adulthood in an individual subjected to adversity in childhood" (Rasmussen & Storebø, 2019, p. 1286).

Yet for some children, a secure bond with a caregiver does not take place or fully develop. An upbringing lacking secure attachment is detrimental to children's development and affects their capacity for moral feelings; "poor parental bonding seems to have its greatest effect on emotional development, and thus on psychopathic traits such as emotional detachment and lack of remorse and shame" (Churchland, 2019. p. 136). Children who do not experience care, security, and attachment, "will carry a sense of scarcity, of deep need, feeling the world is fundamentally unsafe" (Narvaez, 2020a, p. 400). Such children show behaviors that "represent malformed stress response, displayed in aggression or withdrawal" (Narvaez, 2020b, p. 4) and whereas "abused infants often respond to peers with anger, securely attached infants exhibit attention and empathy" (Decety & Howard, 2013, p. 50). For some children however, attachment may not be completely absent but incomplete or tenuous. "Insecure attachment" ensues "when a caregiver is emotionally unavailable or only intermittently responsive" whereas "disorganized attachment" arises when the caregiver seems "frightened or frightening" and so children "both crave and fear" the caregiver and "express contradictory and disorganized behavior toward the attachment figure" (Zilberstein & Messer, 2010, p. 86). Research on child development confirms that "attachment insecurity and poor parental bonds have been linked to conduct problems and delinquency in samples of children ranging from toddlers to young adults" (Savage, 2014, p. 165), is a "risk factor in the development of serious antisocial behaviour" (Van IJzendoorn, 1997, p. 720), and "may be related to greater involvement in bullying" (Murphy et al., 2017, p. 1389).

It is important to note that not all attachment breakdowns stem from cruelty or lack of love—as there may be other reasons why the bond between child and caregiver is missing or inadequate. Sometimes the attachment relationship becomes difficult when caregivers become discouraged if they are not able to sooth infants who are "irritable or unresponsive" and when, for example, interactions are "compromised due to a medical condition"; likewise, it may be difficult to engage "in a supportive caregiving relationship" in a family that is experiencing violence in the home or in the community (Perry, 2001, p. 5). So, too, caregivers' own early traumas (Shapiro, 2009) as well as feelings of overwhelming depression "diminish parents' abilities to listen and empathize" with their children (Weissbourd, 2009, p. 106). Without "healing interventions," individuals who suffer from lack of love and caring in their own childhoods "often make poor parents themselves and can pass on primal wounds to their children" (Narvaez, 2020b, p. 3)

Experiences from infancy and early years influence the development of moral emotions and this means that educators will meet children who have benefitted from optimal situations and are able to engage in prosocial and empathic behavior; likewise, there will be children who knew a "degraded nest" (Narvaez, 2020b) and feel stressed, angry, and emotionally withdrawn. But rather than simply assuming a dichotomy of consequences, "the impact of impaired bonding in early childhood varies" (Perry, 2001, p. 4):

> With severe emotional neglect in early childhood the impact can be devastating. Children without touch, stimulation and nurturing can literally lose the capacity to form any meaningful relationships for the rest of their lives. Fortunately, most children do not suffer this degree of severe neglect. There are, however, many millions of children who have some degree of impaired bonding and attachment during early childhood. The problems that result from this can range from mild interpersonal discomfort to profound social and emotional problems. In general, the severity of problems is related to how early in life, how prolonged and how severe the emotional neglect has been. (p. 4)

As follows, it is not a surety that children who have experienced emotional neglect "have no hope to develop normal relationships" (Perry, 2001, p. 4). Intensive and prolonged therapeutic interventions with families of young children have proven helpful in regenerating attachment bonds (Perry, 2001; Zilberstein & Messer, 2010). Some researchers also view the later development of attachment "with extended family members, teachers, and therapists" as helping children to feel secure (Rasmussen & Storebø, 2019, p. 1286) and write about the importance of developing consistently safe and trusting relationships with teachers (Keller, 2011; Brunzell et al., 2016).

Ongoing Human Needs and Moral Capacity

Essential needs are a crucial aspect of human nature well beyond the dependent state of infancy. Psychologist Abraham Maslow's (1954) classic depiction—still relevant in contemporary scholarship (see Bland & DeRobertis, 2020; Johnson, 2013)—helps us to understand this aspect of human nature from birth, childhood, and throughout adulthood. Maslow's theory of needs "is, primarily, a theory of motivation" because humans "feel constantly in need of things, whether it be food, love or the realization of their talents" (Johnson, 2013, p. 49). Moreover, Maslow viewed human needs as "a holistic process" (Bland & De Robertis, 2020, p. 937) of "continuous improvement and ongoing integration, organization, and self-consistency" (p. 936) and notes that "healthy children enjoy growing and moving forward, gaining new skills, capacities and powers," evolving into "authentic selfhood" (Maslow, 1999, pp. 30,).

These necessities of human development are characterized originally in a five-stage model that Maslow (1954) delineated as a hierarchy but, over the years, cautioned not to think of in a rigid order (Maslow, 1987; see Table 2.1). Maslow called the first four survival needs or "deficiency needs" and the fifth as a "growth or being need" (McLeod, 2018, p. 2). In all, these needs are: (a) physiological: biological requirements for human survival,

TABLE 2.1 Maslow's Hierarchy of Needs

Stage	Human Needs	Motivating Goals
Six	Self-Transcendence	Seeks to further a cause beyond the self and to experience a communion beyond the boundaries of the self through peak experience.
Five	Self-Actualization	Seeks fulfillment of personal potential.
Four	Esteem Needs	Seeks esteem through recognition or achievement.
Three	Belongingness and Love Needs	Seeks affiliation with a group.
Two	Safety Needs	Seeks security through order and law.
One	Physiological (Survival) Needs	Seeks to obtain the basic necessities of life.

Source: Adapted from Koltko-Rivera, 2006, p. 303

such as food, shelter, sleep; (b) safety: the desire for security (emotional and physical), stability, and well-being; (c) love and belongingness: social wants for friendship, intricacy, trust, acceptance, and love; (d) esteem: the desire for independence, achievement, and dignity as well as respect from others; and (e) self-actualization: the desire to flourish and to reach one's potential (McLeod, 2018). Eventually, Maslow (1969) named a higher being need of (f) self-transcendence: "seeking a benefit beyond purely personal" and toward "communion with the transcendent" (Koltko-Rivera, 2006, p. 306).

Numerous researchers write about human needs and the relationship of needs to moral functioning. In essence, when individuals flourish—are physically and emotionally strong and whole—they are more capable of prosocial feeling and behavior. Moreover, people motivated by the need for self-actualization may have a strong sense of moral responsibility and desire to cultivate a principled moral identity. Conversely, when basic survival and psychological needs are unfulfilled, people experience moral deficits in their reasoning, emotions, and behaviors.

Survival needs that begin at birth are biological requirements for existence. This "extended period of serious vulnerability" means that survival needs must be satisfied by the caregivers for infants to flourish who will "develop moral faculties only if in their experience someone else responds to their needs, takes care of them, and protects them at some level" (Govrin, 2014, p. 3). Gradually—by feeling secure, cared-for, and loved—children become more capable of moral feelings and reasoning and more able to attend to the needs of others. Such attainments result from caregivers who fulfill children's need for esteem and who do so by accepting children for who they are, even when children fail (Brummelman & Sedikides, 2020, p. 86). Understandably, such children feel secure and comfortable with their identities; they are less inclined to achieve identity only through peer group association or to become bullies. After these essential needs are met, children will not need continual adult support for their emotional security and may risk themselves in situations that call for sympathetic involvement.

Yet, we must take care not to oversimplify the relationship between fulfillment of survival needs and attainment of morality. Maslow (1987) noted that "healthy growth and development involves not only gratification of the basic needs but also the ability to withstand reasonable deprivation" (Bland & DeRobertis, 2020, p. 940). Tolerance of deprivation stems from the security instilled in early experience, as developmental psychologist Erik Erikson (1959/1994) explained: "a developmental task of infancy is to establish confidence in one's caregivers to eventually attend to one's needs even if caregivers are unable to drop what they are doing the moment one expresses a need" (Bland & DeRobertis, 2020, p. 941). So, despite encountering hardships, when infants and young children know that they are loved they still can become psychologically sound and resilient.

Transcendent Human Needs: Moral Agency and Identity

As Maslow continued to refine his ideas about human needs, he focused on the individuals who satisfied their survival needs "for security, belongingness, esteem and respect" and then became motivated by the being needs of self-actualization (Hoffman, 2020, p. 909). Although people's motivation for flourishing and achieving their potentials may take various forms (such as through creative arts), some individuals have compelling moral aspirations. As they are "able to reach beyond gratification of existence needs," they are motivated to realize their full potential, "shifting from self-interest to selflessness" (D'Souza & Gurin, 2016, p. 210). Researchers suggest that "characteristics associated with principled moral reasoning are consistent with how Maslow represented the characteristics of self-actualizers," among which are "autonomy, openness to experience, imagination and unconventional thought processes, lack of dogmatism, and detachment from conventional morality" (Daniels, 1984, p. 27).

Maslow "regarded self-actualizing people as guided by highly benevolent motivation: that is, the desire to help others and make a better world" (Hoffman, 2020, p. 925) and "tied individual well-being to the well-being of others and, ultimately, to society" (Johnson, 2013, p. 59). According to Maslow (1971), "self-actualizing people are, without a single exception, involved in a cause outside their own skin, in something outside of themselves. . . ." (p. 42). In later years, Maslow (1969) considered self-actualization as having several dimensions including self-transcendence (D'Souza, J., & Gurin, 2016, p. 210)—"the universal human drive to transcend selfishness and engage in altruistic behavior" (p. 212) and eventually thought of self-transcendence as a separate and highest being need.

> Maslow (1969) noted that some individuals have gone beyond even self-actualization as a salient motivation. Such individuals arrive at the top of Maslow's new hierarchy of motivation with a strong motive toward self-transcendence. That is, such individuals seek a benefit beyond the purely personal and seek communion with the transcendent, perhaps through mystical or transpersonal experiences; they come to identify with something greater than the purely individual self, often engaging in service to others. (Koltko-Rivera, 2006, p. 306)

People motivated to fulfill the self-actualization need through altruism demonstrate crucial components of high moral functioning: agency and identity. Moral agents not only have ethical values, they act on their reasoning and principles "even under pressure to behave otherwise" (Bandura, 2018, p. 132); they are empathic and "feel responsible and accountable for their actions" (Gutzwiller-Helfenfinger, 2018, p. 297). So too, scholars link moral agency with moral self-concept so that "being a moral person is important to an individual's identity" (Hardy & Carlo, 2011, p. 212). Moral identity is "the source of a moral imperative—an inner need to do the morally right thing" (Mustakova-Possardt, 2004, p. 254). Individuals motivated by moral identity can feel "self-betrayal" when they undermine their core moral values (Jeong & Han, 2013, p. 48).

Such is the case of moral exemplars for whom the need for self-actualization is expressed as the desire to "live up to... profoundly self-attributed moral principles or goals" (Gibbs, 2008, p. 180) and "feel that they can do no other" as "the thought of betraying these principles is aversive" (Hardy & Carlo, 2005, p. 240). Moral exemplars are people "who have shown long-standing commitment to moral purposes," "labor to make the world a better place," and are willing to "risk one's self-interest for the sake of one's moral values" (Colby & Damon, 1992, pp. 27, 29).

> The great difference between moral exemplars and most people is that exemplars act without equivocation about matters that go well beyond the boundaries of everyday moral engagement. They drop everything not just to see their own children across the street but to feed the poor children of the world, to comfort the dying, to heal the ailing, or to campaign for human rights. It is not so much that the exemplar's orientation to moral concerns is unusual but that the range of their concerns and the extensiveness of their engagement is exceptionally broad. (Colby & Damon, 1992, p. 303)

Moreover, "among the exemplars there [is] a common sense of faith in the human potential to realize its ideals" (Colby & Damon, 1992, p. 311). Portrayals of moral exemplars include individuals—working together or in collaboration with others—who endanger their own lives to protect children and adults from genocide. Clearly, these individuals illustrate how self-transcendence involves encountering deprivation and danger "with serenity" (Winston, 2016, p. 158) and forgoing satisfaction of survival needs "for a higher cause" (p. 178).

Survival Needs and Moral Dysfunction

Nevertheless, a great deal of research on satisfaction of survival needs pertains not to moral capacity but to deficits and moral dysfunction. A harmful path of needs deprivation can begin in early life, when neglected children experience "toxic stress," "survival systems are enhanced and become dominant, while prosociality networks are underdeveloped" (Narvaez, 2019, p. 354).

> Survival systems kick in under stress and promote things such as territoriality, imitation, deception, struggles for power, maintenance of routine, and following precedent.... When survival systems take over the mind, they change perception of what seems good in the moment... and if they trump other values and guide behavior, we can call them a self-protectionist ethic.... Protectionist ethics indicate a hierarchical orientation (dominance or submission) to which survival systems are oriented to promote self-safety. (pp. 354–355).

Likewise, "physically abused and neglected children's future development may be impaired because of a lack of internal regulation."... hence, the emotional needs of neglected children may overpower their ability to inhibit amoral behavior" (Koenig, Cicchetti, and Rogosch, 2004, p. 100). Early experience of neglect not only negatively affects "how well children understand and regulate their own emotions" but "their ability to emphasize with others" (Decety & Howard, 2013, p. 50). For instance, psychoanalysts have long noted that lack of moral development in juvenile delinquents stems from an unsatisfied "need for tenderness" (Aichhorn & Redl, 2012, p. 21).

In this way, children and adolescents can be so wrapped up in the pursuit of satisfying emotional or psychological deprivations that they lose their ability to reason and to act morally. As adults, such people may remain on a primitive level of morality, dominated by self-interest or pleasure (Garbarino & Bronfenbrenner, 1976, p. 73). As well, Maslow (1987) attended to "the phenomenon of failing to count one's blessings" as a "form of pathology." He explains that when survival needs are fulfilled, some people are not mindful of the abundances in their lives but "even devalue, mock, or destroy them" (p. 75). As follows, Maslow considered such an individual a "spoilt brat... for whom gratification is unhealthy because he or she has lost the capacity to appreciate gratification" (Winston, 2016, p. 157).

Lack of security, love, and esteem can influence moral capacity into adulthood. Interpreting Maslow's theory, researcher Mathew Johnson (2013) identifies how deficit needs lead to psychological and moral dysfunction:

- Without safety, humans become neurotic, like fearful children wishing, desperately, to control contingency through any number of pathological superstitious beliefs, obsessive compulsive behaviors and autocratic political systems. (p. 54)
- The thwarting of the need for love leads, in Maslow's view, to the most common and serious forms of psychopathology and maladaptation, leaving individuals stunted and desperate, open to exploitative relationships and pursuing needs through indirect or self-defeating avenues. Those relationships which do satisfy the need for love enable a need for self-esteem to develop. (p. 54).
- Deprived of esteem, humans may pursue the ends of others or attempt to become something not in conformity with their innate traits or interests, leaving them somewhat empty and perpetually uncertain of their true value in the world. [However, satisfaction of this need must be based on] genuine, worthy capacities [and not from] flattery for the purposes of exploitation. (p. 55)

Johnson (2013) also notes that "Maslow ties well-being to the performance of society" and considers how fulfillment of needs will depend on "societies' provision of goods in order to realize potential and reach a higher state of being" (p. 51). Accordingly, some societies provide safety and security so that caregivers are able to meet their infants' and children's survival needs whereas life can be very difficult in societies that do not support children's and familes' thriving.

Researchers underscore other dangerous consequences of needs deficiencies. In particular, psychoanalyst and philosopher Erich Fromm's influential theories (see Cheliotis, 2011; Itzkowitz, 2017) center on needs deprivation as catalysts for aggression, conformity, and domination. Fromm (1966) viewed such immoral behaviors as stemming from "the inability of the isolated individuals to stand alone and [their] need for a symbiotic relationship that overcomes this aloneness" (p. 155). Such individuals feel inferior, powerless, and insignificant and thus try to fulfill themselves by submitting compulsively to a leader or a group (p. 246). In this way, deprivation of needs in childhood contributes to the adult pattern of unprincipled morality, a morality based on hedonism or conformity. Fromm (1973) also proposed the idea that when the environment does not meet psychological needs, one way of satisfaction is through malignant aggression. He hypothesized reasons why people do not function rationally or morally in his description of narcissism—a concept that contemporary researchers also explore.

One of the most important sources of aggression is narcissism. Whereas, self-esteem "is the belief believe that one is of high value," "narcissism is a belief that one is superior and requires admiration and special recognition" (Golec de Zavala & Lantos, 2020, p. 273). As well, narcissistic individuals will not develop the capacity to care about others, except to the extent that others serve their own interests. Fromm (1973) described narcissism as a state of experience in which individuals and everybody and everything pertaining to them are experienced as fully real. Such people need to hold on to their narcissistic self-image—since their sense of worth as well as their sense of identity are based on it. Threats to this image may create intense anger or rage and such persons will never forgive someone who has wounded their narcissistic image and often desire vengeance. Still, this personality disorder deprives narcissists of contentment; "although narcissists feel superior to others and feel entitled to privileges, they are not necessarily satisfied with themselves as a person" (Brummelman et al., 2015, p. 3660).

But the theory of deficient survival needs alone is not the only explanation for the development of narcissism. Parents who satisfy their children's survival needs nevertheless can create conditions conducive to the development of narcissism "by cultivating fragility" when they want their child to be remarkable, not ordinary; "when the child is just 'regular', overvaluing parents may become disappointed or even hostile." As a result, children feel that their self-worth depends only on meeting their parents' inflated goals for them (Brummelman & Sedikides, 2020, p. 86). Fromm (1973) also emphasized how cultures can foster narcissism, for example, those that prize the values of individualism and competition can spur narcissistic rather than cooperative feelings.

A final concept for understanding needs deficits and moral dysfunction is the phenomenon of group or collective narcissism that Fromm (1973) and others explain as one of the most important sources of human aggression. "Collective narcissism is not just a positive belief about one's own group. It is a belief that the group is unique and exceptional, and therefore, entitled to privileged treatment" (Golec de Zavala & Keenan, 2020, p. 4).

> Whatever the reason to demand the privileged status, the collective narcissistic belief expresses the desire for one's own group to be noticeably distinguished from other groups and the concern that the fulfilment of this desire is threatened. Therefore, central to collective narcissism is the resentment that the group's exceptionality is not sufficiently visible to others. (Golec de Zavala & Keenan, 2020, p. 4)

As well, "collective narcissists are likely to encourage violent and antisocial behaviors "in reaction to perceived group-based deprivation" and are interested in privilege, not justice or equality" (Golec de Zavala & Lantos, 2020, p. 275). To collective narcissists, the assertion that the group (or my nation or religion) is the most wonderful, the most cultured, the most powerful, the most peace-loving, etc. does not sound outrageous at all: it sounds like the expression of patriotism, loyalty, and faith as group members continually bolster these beliefs. Fromm (1973) postulated that group narcissism gives feelings of identity and worth to its individual members, consequently, the degree of group narcissism is commensurate with the lack of real satisfaction in life. Nonetheless, some contemporary studies of group narcissism suggest that individuals' needs for esteem, belonging, and identity may not really be satisfied through group narcissism and that "the frustrated desire for personal recognition in collective narcissism is futile and, indeed damaging" as it "fuels a vicious circle of intergroup hostility" (Golec de Zavala & Lantos, 2020, p. 276).

When people choose hate over love and fill "psychic needs through destruction" (Fromm, 1973, p. 218), they live lives of aggression and discontent. Such dysfunction impedes basic moral capacity as well as desire for and attainment of moral agency and identity. Overall, this scholarship illustrates that maladaptive gratification of deficit needs leads to detrimental outcomes for individuals, the people around them, and for society.

References

Aichhorn, A., & Redl, F. (2012). A dialogue on reclaiming troubled youth. *Reclaiming Children & Youth, 20*(4), 18–22.

Ainsworth, M. D. S. (1982). Attachment: Retrospect and prospect. In C. M. Parkes & J. Stevenson-Hinde (Eds.), *The place of attachment in human behavior* (pp. 3–30). Basic Books.

Appiah, K. A. (2009). Cosmopolitanism. In A. Taylor (Ed.), *Examined life: Excursions with contemporary thinkers* (pp. 87–113). New Press.

Baggini, J. (2016). *The edge of reason* (pp. 143–167). Yale University Press.

Baier, K. (1958). *The moral point of view: A rational basis of ethics.* Cornell University Press.

Baier, K. (1982). The conceptual link between morality and rationality. *Nous,* 78–88.

Bandura, A. (2018). Toward a psychology of human agency: Pathways and reflections. *Perspectives on Psychological Science, 13*(2), 130–136.

Berkowitz, M. W., & Grych, J. H. (1998). Fostering goodness: Teaching parents to facilitate children's moral development. *Journal of Moral Education, 27*(3), 371–391.

Bettelheim, B. (1969). *The children of the dream.* Simon and Schuster.

Blackburn, S. (2000). *Ruling passions: A theory of practical reasoning.* Clarendon Press.

Bland, A. M., & DeRobertis, E. M. (2020). Maslow's unacknowledged contributions to developmental psychology. *Journal of Humanistic Psychology, 60*(6), 934–958.

Bloom, P. (2013). *Just babies: The origins of good and evil.* Crown/Random House.

Boehm, C. (1999). *Hierarchy in the forest: The evolution of egalitarian behavior.* Harvard University Press.

Boehm, C. (2012). *Moral origins: The evolution of virtue, altruism, and shame.* Basic Books.

Bowlby, J. (1969). *Attachment and loss.* Basic Books.

Bretherton, I. (1992). The origins of attachment theory: John Bowlby and Mary Ainsworth. *Developmental Psychology, 28*(5), 759.

Brummelman, E., & Sedikides, C. (2020). Raising children with high self-esteem (but not narcissism). *Child Development Perspectives, 14*(2), 83–89.

Brummelman, E., Thomaes, S., Nelemans, S. A., De Castro, B. O., Overbeek, G., & Bushman, B. J. (2015). Origins of narcissism in children. *Proceedings of the National Academy of Sciences, 112*(12), 3659–3662.

Brunzell, T., Stokes, H., & Waters, L. (2016). Trauma-informed positive education: Using positive psychology to strengthen vulnerable students. *Contemporary School Psychology, 20*(1), 63–83.

Baumeister, R. F. (1997). *Evil: Inside human cruelty and violence.* W. H. Freeman.

Cheliotis, L. K. (2011). Violence and narcissism: A Frommian perspective on destructiveness under authoritarianism. *Canadian Journal of Sociology, 36*(4), 337–360.

Churchland, P. (2019). *Conscience: The origins of moral intuition.* WW Norton & Company.

Colby, A., & Damon, W. (1992). *Some do care: Contemporary lives of moral commitment.* The Free Press.

Cummings, E. M., & Warmuth, K. A. (2019). Parenting and attachment. In M. H. Bornstein (Ed.), *Handbook of parenting* (pp. 374–400). Routledge.

Daniels, M. (1984). The relationship between moral development and self-actualization. *Journal of Moral Education, 13*(1), 25–30.

Decety, J., & Howard, L. H. (2013). The role of affect in the neurodevelopment of morality. *Child Development Perspectives, 7*(1), 49–54.

Deneault, A. A., & Hammond, S. I. (2021). Connecting the moral core: Examining moral baby research through an attachment theory perspective. *Social Cognition, 39*(1), 4–18.

D'Souza, J., & Gurin, M. (2016). The universal significance of Maslow's concept of self-actualization. *The Humanistic Psychologist, 44*(2), 210.

Ebbeck, M., & Yim, H. Y. B. (2009). Rethinking attachment: Fostering positive relationships between infants, toddlers and their primary caregivers. *Early Child Development and Care, 179*(7), 899–909.

Erikson, E. H. (1959/1994). *Identity and the life cycle.* Norton.

Fromm, E. (1966). *Escape from freedom.* Avon Books.

Fromm, E. (1973). *The anatomy of human destructiveness.* Holt, Rinehart and Winston.

Garbarino, J., & Bronfenbrenner, U. (1976). The socialization of moral judgment and behavior in cross-cultural perspective. In T. Lickona, *Moral development and behavior: Theory, research, and social issues* (pp. 70–83). Holt, Rinehart and Winston.

Gibbs, J. C. (2008) Reflections on a rescue: What is primary in moral motivation. In D. Fasko Jr., & W. Willis, W. (Eds.) *Contemporary philosophical and psychological perspectives on moral development and education* (pp. 167–184). Hampton Press.

Gilligan, C., & Wiggins, G. (1987). The origins of morality in early childhood relationships. In J. Kagan & S. Lamb (Eds.), *The emergence of morality in young children* (pp. 277–305). University of Chicago Press.

Gleason, T., & Narvaez, D. (2019). Beyond resilience to thriving: Optimizing child wellbeing. *International Journal of Wellbeing, 9*(4), 59–78.

Golec de Zavala, A., & Keenan, O. (2020). Collective narcissism as a framework for understanding populism. *Journal of Theoretical Social Psychology,* pp. 1–11. https://doi.org/10.1002/jts5.69

Golec de Zavala, A., & Lantos, D. (2020). Collective narcissism and its social consequences: The bad and the ugly. *Current Directions in Psychological Science,* 29(3), 273–278.

Govrin, A. (2014). The ABC of moral development: An attachment approach to moral judgment. *Frontiers in Psychology,* 5 (6). https://doi.org/10.3389/fpsyg.2014.00006

Greene, J. (2014). *Moral tribes: Emotion, reason, and the gap between us and them.* New York, NY: Penguin Press.

Gutzwiller-Helfenfinger, E. (2018). Not unlearning to care: Positive moral development as a cornerstone of nonkilling. *Journal of Peace Education, 15*(3), 288–308.

Harris, I. (2004). Peace education theory. *Journal of Peace Education* 1(1), 5–20.

Haidt, J. (2012). *The righteous mind: Why good people are divided by politics and religion.* New York, NY: Pantheon Books/Random House.

Haidt, J., & Joseph, C. (2004). Intuitive ethics: How innately prepared intuitions generate culturally variable virtues. *Daedalus, 133*(4), 55–66.

Hardy, S. A., & Carlo, G. (2005). Identity as a source of moral motivation. *Human Development, 48*(4), 232–256.

Hoffman, E. (2020). The social world of self-actualizing people: Reflections by Maslow's biographer. *Journal of Humanistic Psychology, 60*(6), 908–933.

Itzkowitz, S. (2017). Erich Fromm: A psychoanalyst for all seasons. *Psychoanalytic Perspectives,* 14(1), 81–92.

Jeong, C., & Han, H. (2013). Exploring the relationship between virtue ethics and moral identity. *Ethics & Behavior, 23* (1), 44–56.

Johnson, M. T. (2013). *Evaluating culture: Well-being, institutions and circumstance.* London: Palgrave Macmillan.

Keller, L. E. (2011). Repairing links: Building attachments in the preschool classroom. *Journal of the American Psychoanalytic Association, 59*(4), 737–763.

Koenig, A. L., Cicchetti, D., & Rogosch, F. A. (2004). Moral development: The association between maltreatment and young children's prosocial behaviors and moral transgressions. *Social Development, 13*(1), 87–106.

Koltko-Rivera, M. E. (2006). Rediscovering the later version of Maslow's hierarchy of needs: Self-transcendence and opportunities for theory, research, and unification. *Review of General Psychology, 10*(4), 302–317.

Maslow, A. H. (1954). *Motivation and personality.* Harper and Row.

Maslow, A. H. (1969). The farther reaches of human nature. *Journal of Transpersonal Psychology, 1*(1), 1–9.

Maslow, A. H. (1971). *The farther reaches of human nature.* Viking.

Maslow, A. H. (1987). *Motivation and personality* (3rd ed.). Harper & Row.

Maslow, A. H. (1999). *Toward a psychology of being* (3rd ed.). New York, NY: Wiley.

McLeod, S. A. (2020). Maslow's hierarchy of needs. *Simply Psychology, 1.* http://www.simplypsychology.org/maslow.html

Miller, R. (2003). Education for a culture of peace. *Encounter, 16*(1), 25–30.

Moshman, D. (2009). The development of rationality. In H. Siegel (Ed.), *Oxford handbook of philosophy of education* (pp. 145–161). Oxford University Press.

Murphy, T. P., Laible, D., & Augustine, M. (2017). The influences of parent and peer attachment on bullying. *Journal of Child and Family Studies, 26*(5), 1388–1397.

Mustakova-Possardt, E. (2004). Education for critical moral consciousness. *Journal of Moral Education, 33*(3), 245–269.

Narvaez, D. (2019). Moral development and moral values. In D. P. McAdams, R. L. Shiner, & J. L. Tackett, *Handbook of personality development,* (pp. 345–363). Guilford.

Narvaez, D. (2020a). Ecocentrism: Resetting baselines for virtue development. *Ethical Theory and Moral Practice, 23*(2), 391–406.

Narvaez, D. (2020b). Moral education in a time of human ecological devastation. *Journal of Moral Education,* 1–13.

Palm, G. (2014). Attachment theory and fathers: Moving from "being there" to "being with." *Journal of Family Theory & Review, 6*(4), 282–297.

Perry, B. D. (2001). Bonding and attachment in maltreated children. *The Child Trauma Center, 3,* 1–17.

Peters, R. S. (1975). Subjectivity and standards in the humanities. In D. Nyberg (Ed.), *The philosophy of open education* (pp. 91–109). Routledge.

Pinker, S. (2021). *Rationality: What it is, why it seems scarce, why it matters.* Viking.

Poehlmann, J. (2003). An attachment perspective on grandparents raising their very young grandchildren: Implications for intervention and research. *Infant Mental Health Journal: Official Publication of the World Association for Infant Mental Health, 24*(2), 149–173.

Rasmussen, P. D., & Storebø, O. J. (2019). Attachment as a core feature of resilience: A systematic review and meta-analysis. *Psychological Reports, 122*(4), 1259–1296.

Rosen, L. H., & Rubin, L. J. (2016). Bullying. In Naples et al. (Eds.), *Wiley Blackwell encyclopedia of gender and sexuality studies.* Wiley-Blackwell. https://doi.org/10.1002/9781118663219.wbegss431

Savage, J. (2014). The association between attachment, parental bonds and physically aggressive and violent behavior: A comprehensive review. *Aggression and Violent Behavior, 19*(2), 164–178.

Sengsavang, S., & Krettenauer, T. (2020). Moral development in the family. In S. Hupp & J. D. Jewel (Eds.), *The encyclopedia of child and adolescent development* (pp. 1–11.). John Wiley.

Shapiro, V. (2009). Reflections on the work of Professor Selma Fraiberg. *Clinical Social Work Journal, 37*(1), 45–55.

Sheets-Johnstone, M. (2008). *The roots of morality.* Pennsylvania State University Press.

Sidi, R., & Shafran, D. A. (2020). Effects of kibbutz communal upbringing in adulthood: trait emotional intelligence and attachment patterns. *Heliyon, 6*(12), 1–11.

Skoe, E. E. A. (2013). *The ethic of care: Theory and research.* In B. J. Irby, G. Brown, R. Lara-Alecio, & S. Jackson (Eds.), *The handbook of educational theories* (pp. 615–628). IAP Information Age Publishing.

Van IJzendoorn, M. H. (1997). Attachment, emergent morality, and aggression: Toward a developmental socioemotional model of antisocial behaviour. *International Journal of Behavioral Development, 21*(4), 703–728.

Van Ijzendoorn, M. H., Sagi, A., & Lambermon, M. W. (1992). The multiple caretaker paradox: Data from Holland and Israel. *New Directions for Child and Adolescent Development, 1992*(57), 5–24.

Vozzola, E. C. (2014). *Moral development: Theory and applications.* Routledge.

Weissbourd, R. (2009). *The parents we mean to be.* Houghton Mifflin Harcourt.

Wilson, J. Q. (1993). *The moral sense.* Free Press.

Winston, C. N. (2016). An existential-humanistic-positive theory of human motivation. *The Humanistic Psychologist, 44*(2), 142–163.

Zilberstein, K., & Messer, E. A. (2010). Building a secure base: Treatment of a child with disorganized attachment. *Clinical Social Work Journal, 38*(1), 85–97.

3

Becoming Moral

Emotions and Reasoning

It does not follow that emotion is uniformly hostile to cognitive endeavors, nor may we properly conclude that cognition is, in general, free of emotional engagement. Indeed, emotion without cognition is blind and cognition without emotion is vacuous.

—Israel Scheffler, 1977, "In Praise of the Cognitive Emotions," p. 172

There is a rich field of moral development scholarship that can deepen our understanding of how children gain the attributes of moral imagination and for living ethical lives. But because moral development appears as an intricate process with a "maddening number of variables" (Sherblom, 2012, p. 118), the complexity of this field may seem overwhelming. Therefore, it not surprising that researchers customarily study distinct areas of moral development so that they can focus more completely on specific aspects of thought, feelings, and experience. Two such areas are emotions and reasoning. To clarify the multitude of variables revealed in moral development research, these fundamental questions are particularly relevant:

Teaching for Moral Imagination, pages 45–67

- How do emotions influence moral sensitivity and capability for moral action?
- What is the relationship between cognition and moral development?

These two perspectives cast light on the social-emotional prerequisites that must be met for children to be capable of the moral emotions of empathy and compassion and for the developmental process of moral reasoning and reflection. Once more, unlike other explanations for moral development, affective and cognitive development theories embody moral philosophies, affirming that the ultimate aims of moral development are, respectively, the ethic of care and rational morality (see Table 3.1).

Moral Emotions

To understand the complexity of moral development, an apt starting point is the study of moral emotions. We begin here from the perspective that "the building blocks of human morality are emotional" (Haidt, 2007, p. 998); well before young children are capable of reflecting on ethical ideals or can grasp cultural values, they embark on their moral journey by experiencing feelings of caring as well as distress.

TABLE 3.1 Theories of Moral Development: Affect and Cognition

Theory	Emphases
Social-Emotional Prerequisites	Social-Emotional Needs Attachment Nurturing
Affective Development	Inter-Dependence Caring and Connectedness Empathy and Compassion
Psychoanalytic Theory	Identification Shame and Guilt Conscience Impulse Control
Cognitive Moral Development	Rationality and Reasoning Perspective Taking Autonomy and Character Justice

> The capacity for reason takes time to emerge, so that the moral life of a baby is necessarily limited. A baby will possess inclinations and sentiments; he or she might be motivated to soothe another in pain or to feel angry at a cruel act or to favor someone who punishes a wrongdoer. But a lot is absent; most of all, the baby lacks a grasp of impartial moral principles—prohibitions or requirements that apply equally to everyone within a community. (Bloom, 2013, p. 211)

"From infancy, empathic concern is evident" and forms a basis of prosocial behavior by caring for and helping others. But eventually further forms of moral feelings emerge, including sympathy and guilt (Malti & Dys, 2018, p. 47). Even when children are not yet ready to act on their emotions to ease others' distress, such emotions inspire a nascent from of morality. Beyond early childhood, moral emotions still are fundamental to moral sensibility and are "all essential parts of our moral reactions to situations" (Damon, 1990, p. 13).

Another compelling reason to firstly attend to the affective realm is because emotions are utterly central to moral functioning by stimulating moral responses and the desire to live morally. Psychologists conclude that moral feelings "contribute to the long-term development of moral values" (Damon, 1990, p. 13), "shape and influence social relationships" (Lefebre & Krettenauer, 2019, p. 445), and "are key to understanding why individuals adhere to or fail to adhere to their own moral standards" (Gutzwiller-Helfenfinger, 2018, p. 291). Moreover, moral disengagement—a lack of moral emotions such as empathy and failure to anticipate guilt or shame—contribute to aggression and bullying behaviors (Campaert, et al., 2017; Hymel & Bonanno, 2014; Rieffe & Camodeca, 2016).

Moral emotions "motivate moral behavior" and "respond to moral violations" (Haidt, 2003, p. 853). These wide-ranging feelings include sympathy, empathy, compassion, righteousness, remorse, outrage, disgust, shame, and guilt (Turner & Stets, 2006). Broadly, moral emotions can be categorized dualistically: *positive feelings* that spur moral behavior and *negative emotions* that thwart misbehavior or immoral actions (Damon, 1990; Haidt, 2003; Malti & Dys, 2015). Key positive moral feelings are empathy, sympathy, and compassion whereas shame and guilt are primary negative emotions. Despite the usefulness and clarity of this binary classification, we must take care not to mischaracterize positive and negative moral feelings as good or bad—as both contribute to moral functioning.

Ideas about positive moral feelings have changed over time. Since the Middle Ages, people believed in *pity* as an important moral emotion—"sorrow felt for another's suffering or misfortune"; yet, in the current day we are apt to interpret pity as a "condescending, or contemptuous form of feeling sorry for someone, often directed at people who are perceived as pathetic or having brought about their own misery" (Gerdes, 2011, p. 233). Another affective response, *sympathy*, also has been in use for hundreds of years. Sympathy's original meaning related to the "sharing of emotion and mutual affection" and has come to mean "expression of concern or sorrow about distressful events in a person's life" (p. 233). Nonetheless, scholars do not depict sympathy as an empathic response as a sense of sympathy is "not similar to the other person's feeling" (Gutzwiller-Helfenfinger, 2018, p. 292).

Very germane to people's desire to care about others is the crucial emotion of *empathy*. This concept entered into societal and scholarly discourse in the 20th century. Empathy signifies "feeling and perceiving the world from the perspective and subjective experience of another person" (Gerdes, 2011, p. 233) and is "an affective response to the apprehension of another person's emotional state or condition" (Gutzwiller-Helfenfinger, 2018, p. 292). Although empathy appears to be a "spontaneous response" to the suffering of others and "allows us to "grasp what another is living through," we are more able to empathize because "we have ourselves grown in life experiences" (Sheets-Johnstone, 2008, p. 226) and when we have had "direct exposure to another's emotion" (Eisenberg et al., 2014, p. 409). Unlike young children's feelings of distress, empathy is a more sophisticated emotion comprising insight and not just emotional reaction.

But empathy has limitations as a moral emotion because it may be selective, erratic, or lead to misunderstandings. Bluntly stated, "You can be mistaken in your empathy. You think you understand what the other is going through, and you could be dead wrong" (Noddings in Kawamura & Eisler, 2013, p. 6). Researchers also note the existence of an "empathy bias" because people tend to "empathize more with people they like, are more similar than strangers, and who are present and not absent" or far away (Hoffman, 1993, p. 173). Another problem with empathy is that as individuals feel empathy towards one person or group of people, they seem incapable of feeling concern for others (Bregman, 2019, p. 215). An even more critical concern is that "empathy makes us less forgiving, because the more we identify with victims, the more we generalize about our enemies" and fail to grasp their perspectives (p. 216). So too, empathy may be fleeting. "Most of us do not have an infinitely large capacity for empathy; we falter under empathy fatigue" (Churchland, 2019, p. 102) and whereas empathy "is an important motivating force," it "can be exploited to motivate us to do things that do not help" (Bloom, 2017, p. 27).

Instead of empathy, some scholars choose to highlight *compassion* as the most vital of positive moral emotions. Compassion "embraces empathic concern for others" and is "the thoughtful feeling that begets caring actions" (Schubert & He, 2020, p. 2). Empathy affords sensitivity to others' distress, but compassion also encompasses the desire to relieve suffering and to help others (Bregman, 2019; Goetz et al., 2010). Specifically, compassion "consists of three facets: noticing, feeling, and responding" (Strauss et al., 2016, p. 17) and it is "part of the care-giving system that has evolved to nurture and protect the young" (p. 16). Moreover, "most of the world's religious traditions place compassion at the center of their belief systems" (p. 16).

Nevertheless, the negative emotions also promote morality. Feelings of shame and guilt are "central to moral regulation" (Sheikh & Janoff-Bulman, 2010, p. 213) by creating discomfort when committing transgressions—inducing loss of self-esteem and even fostering self-reflection. Both shame and guilt "involve a sense of responsibility and the feeling that one has violated a moral standard" and "both can arise from concerns about the effects of one's behavior on others" (Eisenberg, 2000, p. 668). These negative emotions are alike in some ways and also different from each other (Leach, 2017). Many researchers see them as "two distinct emotions and that an important difference between them is the degree of focus on the self" (Eisenberg, 2000, p. 267). Shame and guilt "engage distinct action tendencies to hide or amend"; "shame motivates denial, withdrawal, and escape from the shame-inducing event" while "guilt motivates reparative actions, including apology, confession, and prosocial actions" (Sheikh & Janoff-Bulman, 2010, p. 214).

Shame can be a problematic emotion because it primarily centers on individuals' feelings of humiliation and inadequacy rather than on the effect of their misdeeds upon others. Shame experiences include "feelings of being weak, small, inhibited, and confused" (Elison, 2005, p. 18) in which "the entire self feels exposed, inferior, and degraded" (Eisenberg, 2000, p. 667). Because shame is "rooted in early experiences of humiliation" (Weissbourd, 2009, p. 13), psychologists caution that when people compensate for their disgraceful feelings of inferiority, shame can be a harmful emotion that exacerbates narcissistic tendencies as well as violent acting-out behaviors spurred on by "humiliated fury." Likewise, "feeling worthless and flawed is so painful that it is easier to shift the blame outward and feel angry towards others" (Silfver-Kuhalampi et al., 2015, p. 214). However, shame also can have an important pro-social role. As people experience this emotion as discomfort and embarrassment, they feel that "their own behavior is contemptible in the eyes of others" (Damon, 1990, p. 22) and thus they become concerned about how their communities will regard them. Because people "feel self-conscious and fear scorn" (Eisenberg, 2000, p. 667), shame "serves as an adaptive signal to the self, warning of diminished social rank" (Elison, 2005, p. 17). Historian Ruger Bregman (2019), commenting on "the audacious behavior" of leaders who feel no shame, asks us to "imagine what society would be like if shame didn't exist" and answers: "that would be hell" (p. 239).

On the other hand, guilt—a cousin to shame" (Hacker, 2017, p. 218)—is defined as "regret over wrongdoing" (Eisenberg, 2000, p. 667) and its "focus is outward, on how the other person is feeling"; moreover, guilt leads to taking some kind of action, e.g., "apologizing, offering to make reparation and amends, vowing to change future behavior, confessing, asking for forgiveness, seeking to restore balance in the relationship, and offering to help others in need" (Dempsey, 2017, p. 2). There is a strong relationship between guilt and empathy with "empathic concern as a precursor to guilt" (Malti & Dys, 2018, p. 47) and guilt and remorse as "highly correlated with empathy and instrumental acts of reparation" (Elison, 2005, p. 22). In psychoanalytic theory, guilt results from violation of one's conscience—the inner sense of right and wrong—imagined as a self-regulating mechanism stemming from internationalization of parental dictates and values (Berkowitz & Grych, 1998; Dempsey, 2017). Even so, guilt as a damaging emotion has been a serious concern when excessive guilt leads to neuroticism (Dempsey, 2017, p. 1). Also, survivor guilt—"felt not for something one has done, no matter whether intentionally or unintentionally; nor is it for something one allowed to be done to one"—is a painful reaction for those who lived through horrific experiences in which their family members or comrades have died (Hacker, 2017, p. 222). But contemporary psychologists also are likely to understand guilt positively—considering it "the more autonomous and effective of the two morally constraining emotions" of shame and guilt (Damon, 1990, p. 22). Accordingly, guilt is viewed as significant moral feeling that supports caring and compassion.

The Ethic of Care

A central theme in the scholarship of moral philosophy and moral development relates to the circumstances that make human beings capable of care and love—emotions necessary to moral functioning throughout childhood and adulthood. Caring relationships are vital to children's moral development because children become cognizant of being cared for and what it means to care for others. Through infancy and early childhood, the relationship between the "one-caring and the cared for" (Niedermeyer, 2017, p. 186) means that adults have the responsibility of caring for the young. But eventually children become more than "simply the recipients of care" but "active agents within this relationship" as they become carers themselves (Cockburn, 2005, pp. 73, 74). These relationships are reciprocal as "both parties must contribute something, or the connection will be broken and caring cannot occur" (Vozzola, 2014, p. 45). This dynamic creates "a very different awareness of self—as capable of having an effect on others, as able to move others and to be moved by them" (Gilligan & Wiggins, 1987, p. 280).

Psychologist Carol Gilligan (1998) and philosopher Nel Noddings (2002) defined such mutual responsiveness and feelings as the *ethic of care* which "develops from the person's early childhood experiences of attachment to others and reflects an ideal of love, connection and mutual responsiveness" (Skoe, 2013, p. 615). This ethic does not call for total self-sacrifice; care-based moral development involves a progression from self-concern to concern for others and then to a "balanced self-and-other concern" (Skoe, 2010, p. 193). The ethic of care, originally characterized as the feminist ethic of care, focuses on the voices of women and their experiences as "nurturers, caretakers, and helpmates and weavers of networks of relationships" (Gilligan, 1982, p. 17) at a time in which moral development research centered on the male perspective of justice as the moral ideal and when "women have often been judged inferior to men in the moral domain" (Owens & Ennis, 2005, p. 399). In particular, Gilligan (1998) critiqued the concept of the separate, autonomous "rational man" and the "disconnection from emotions and a blindness to relationships" in moral reasoning (p. 342). "Conversely, the ethic of care takes the idea of self in relationship as the point of entry for thinking about obligations and responsibility" (Sevenhuijsen, 2000, p. 10).

Studies comparing moral reasoning by gender generally demonstrate that women emphasize relationships and caring more than men or, at the very least, approach moral quandaries differently. Noddings noticed that, "faced with a moral dilemma, women often ask for more information, needing to talk to the participants, to see their eyes and facial expressions, to receive what they are feeling" (in Owens & Ennis, 2005, p. 399). Similarly, in Gilligan's research it was found that "women can and do give reasons for their acts, but the reasons often point to feelings, needs, impressions, and a sense of personal ideal" (Owens & Ennis, 2005, p. 399). More recent studies also suggest that women somewhat more than men hold "values, attitudes, and outlooks that emphasize and facilitate establishing and maintaining connections to others" (Forsyth, 2019, p. 53). However, the characterization of substantially different moral orientations according to gender has not been confirmed (Jaffee & Hyde, 2000; Juujärvi et al., 2012). In fact, other variables may influence people's approach to moral problems—including "age, class, ethnicity," and experiences of "marginalization" (Garrod & Beal, 1993, p. 60).

Many scholars believe that people use a combination of the ethic of care and moral principles of justice when they consider moral dilemmas (Skoe, 2013, Walker, 2006). Noddings (2002) contended that care is a basic life process and that both men and women often express "natural caring" (p. 2). Psychologist William Damon (1990) writes that "no one can dispute that men can value caring just as women can value justice" although "the vagaries of social experience may orient girls towards one and boys towards the other, particularly in cultural settings that establish more nurturant roles and expectations for girls" (p. 102). But in the last several decades, cultural roles have been in flux as caring opportunities have become more balanced among genders (Sevenhuijsen, 2003, p. 182) as women "increasingly have been relocating their activities to the public sphere" and "men are contributing more to the daily care of children, partners and family members" (p. 181). Certainly, there is benefit in not just waiting for cultural shifts but for parents and teachers to cultivate in all children appreciation for both the principles of justice and caring so to "expand their moral horizons to the full limits of human potential" (Damon, 1990, pp. 102–103).

Moral Reasoning

Moral development as a cognitive activity "has been the dominant focus in the last two centuries" (Sherblom, 2012, p. 129) with *moral cognitive developmental theory* still influencing moral development research in contemporary studies (Carpendale, 2009; Lapsley, 2006; Sherblom, 2012; Snarey & Samuelson, 2008). Cognitive developmental theorists (Kohlberg 1969; Piaget, 1932/1965) viewed moral development as "the development of moral reasoning ability"—leading to the attainment of ethical understanding and principled judgment. This rationalist theory is based on the assumption that how people think about moral issues will strongly influence how they will make decisions and take subsequent actions and that "cognition, and particularly reasoning, is the main driver of moral decisions" (Garrigan et al., 2018, p. 82).

> Proponents of the rationalist perspective have maintained that moral reasoning is the basis for moral judgments, and by extension, moral behavior. People make moral decisions based on a deliberative, rule-based cognitive process in which information in a situation is gathered and analyzed, and a correct or appropriate moral evaluation is made following particular moral principles. (Stets, 2016, p. 348)

Or, another way to characterize cognitive moral development as the process of realizing "moral intelligence"—the ability "to reflect upon what is right and wrong" (Coles, 1997, p. 3).

Cognitive moral development is explained as the construction of morality over time as children learn from social interactions, rather than through adult persuasion or coercion, about how to act in moral situations. This viewpoint challenges the notions that "morality is imposed on children by adults" and that children then "passively adopt and follow social norms" (Carpendale, 2009, p. 271). Instead, the theory highlights "perspective taking as important for moral development, allowing for the thoughts and feelings of others to be taken into account when making moral decisions" (Garrigan, et al., 2018, p. 89). Researchers note that opportunities for perspective taking take place through interaction with multi-layered social world that includes peers; in fact, this theory suggests that "interactions with peers are more potent and significant in stimulating moral growth than interactions with parents" (Walker et al., 2000, p. 1033). As well, moral reasoning can be stimulated by exposure to higher-level thinking and experiencing of perplexity or disequilibrium—"a state of cognitive conflict that challenges current ways of thinking and stimulates development toward higher level reasoning" (p. 1034).

The "pioneering" researcher and theorist of cognitive moral development (Lapsley, 2006; Turiel, 2015), psychologist Jean Piaget, challenged the commonplace view that children primarily internalize moral values passed on by parents or adult authority and instead insisted that "children acquire moral values by constructing them from within, through interactions with their environment" (Kamii, 1984, p. 112). Piaget became interested in "children's practical moral activity" (Carpendale, 2009), p. 281) and his research on how children use and understand rules as they played games formed the basis of his ground-breaking book, *The Moral Judgment of the Child* (1932/1965). Piaget realized that far more important to children than playing by the rules of the game—which they eventually came to view as subjective rather than inviolate—are their "concerns about fairness" and how to "find solutions all will accept as fair" (Skitka et al., 2016, pp. 407–408).

Although Piaget (1932/1965) acknowledged that children do learn cultural values from their parents, whose authority they accepted at the beginning of the moral socialization process, he declared that "moral socialization does not end there" (Lapsley, 2006, p. 42):

> Children eventually engage in new forms of social relationships that are reciprocal and equal, where relationships are balanced and in stable equilibrium, and where rules take on new meaning. In the context of peers, for ex-

> ample, one constructs ideas about fairness, justice, and moral responsibility, and about the function of rules in social life, that are at once different and developmentally advanced over the sort of moral understandings coerced by the huff and puff of adult authority. (p. 42)

Piaget became convinced that "from the ages of about six or seven, children's opportunities for peer co-operation facilitate the development of mutual respect and so they move away from egocentric thought"—concern only for their own perspectives (Garrigan et al., 2018, p. 82). Furthermore, he wrote that moral life develops through "democratic cooperation" (Lapsley, 2006, p. 43) and reciprocal understanding of viewpoints; in relationships of cooperative interaction, an "interchange of thoughts occurs" (Carpendale, 2009, pp. 278, 279) and children "sort out the benefits and burdens of cooperation in ways that are judged fair and equitable" (Lapsley, 2006, p. 43).

Piaget described moral learning through experiences of relationships among children and others. He named the experiences of learning by reciprocal understanding as the *morality of cooperation*, explaining that "morality develops as children are able to take the perspectives of others" (Carpendale, 2000, p. 192). Conversely, Piaget conceived of the *morality of constraint* as the relationships in which children conform to adult authority. Because of the inequality in adult-child relationships, "joint construction of rules in that relationship" cannot take place (Langdale, 1993, p. 32) and children's "understanding of justice cannot develop, as they cannot fully understand the other perspectives involved" (Carpendale, 2009, p. 279). But although constraint and cooperation seem to be a "dichotomy," Piaget realized "that most relationships consist of some mixture of the two types and the proportions will vary" as some parents establish cooperative relationships with their children while others are more authoritarian (Carpendale, 2000, p. 192).

Also important to Piaget's theory relating to constraint and cooperation are the concepts of *heteronomy* and *autonomy*. In the morality of constraint, a "heteronomous orientation emerges" in which "a young child has unilateral respect for the power and magnificence of adults," "adheres to fixed rules," and obeys adults and does not question their authority. Through the morality of cooperation, "the autonomous orientation emerges within a peer society of equals, and yields a morality of cooperation that makes possible a more equilibrated understanding of justice" (Lapsley, 2006, p. 42). Piaget concluded that "the development of autonomous moral thinking involves a differentiation of justice from adult authority and the force of custom" and that "the highest-level moral judgments are autonomous in that individuals participate in the elaboration of norms; they construct judgments, with understandings of fairness, equality, and the need for co-operation" (Turiel, 2015, pp. 505–506). In this way, Piaget understood the development of *rational morality* as "moving away from external imposition of inviolable injunctions, sacred laws, or the strictures of elders or of tradition, away from heteronomy and unilateral respect, to autonomy, mutual respect, and democratic cooperation" (Lapsley, 2006, p. 43).

The other preeminent cognitive moral development researcher and theorist, psychologist Lawrence Kohlberg, equated moral development with "the development of moral reasoning ability" (Schinkel & de Ruyter, 2017, p. 129) and, additionally, focused on the educational experiences necessary for fostering moral development. As did Piaget, Kohlberg interpreted moral development as "a constructive process stemming from children's interactions in a multifaceted social world" (Turiel, 2015, p. 504) and connected "the moral domain with the concept of justice" (Langdale, 1993, p. 32). But whereas Piaget centered on children's moral development, Kohlberg also considered moral development in adolescents and adults (Garrigan et al., 2018) and gave greater emphasis to the idea of sequential stages, noting that "there is a parallel between an individual's logical stage and his or her moral stage" (Kohlberg, 1984, p. 171).

Kohlberg posited that children move from the preconventional level in which their own needs take precedence, to a conventional level emphasizing rewards and punishments as well as respect for following the rules, to a post-conventional level in which individuals begin to identify moral principles that will guide their reasoning and actions. In his delineation of six stages of moral progression, he portrayed "a developmental sequence of increasing maturity or sophistication of judgment about difficult moral questions," the attainment of "moral reflection" (Colby, 2002, p. 132), and autonomous reasoning so that individuals are "not driven by emotions" nor are their actions "determined by conventions of society and tradition" (Schinkel & de Ruyter, 2017, pp. 129–130).

Cognitive developmental moral research became extremely influential, but was not unchallenged. In particular, critics raise objections relating to methodology: Kohlberg's studies of moral reasoning based on hypothetical moral quandaries is deemed problematic as "these dilemmas may be far removed from the situations in individuals experience" (Stets, 2016, p. 348). Also, "both Piaget and Kohlberg encountered problems when they applied their developmental models to girls and women" (Langdale, 1993, p. 32) and neither of these researchers contemplated that there was "a problem with male-based theory" (p. 33).

Another concern about cognitive moral developmental theory is that there is insufficient attention to culture as "the type of moral reasoning individuals use is highly sensitive to the context and content of the dilemmas" (Jaffee & Hyde, 2000, p. 721) and disregard to moral development as "specific to unique social, cultural, and historical contexts" (Tappan, 1997, p. 95). As Jonathan Haidt (2012) cautions, "morality can't be entirely self-constructed by children based on their growing understanding of harm. Cultural learning or guidance must play a larger role than rationalist theories had given it" (p. 26). Other scholars doubt the idea of moral autonomy because humans are so culturally bound, it would be unrealistic to imagine people totally autonomous in choosing moral principles and acting according to them. Behaviors "designated as moral, their relative importance, and the sanctions linked to them are culturally situated" (Bandura, 2006, p. 171) and therefore the range of moral possibilities would depend on the nature of moral rules and responses to transgressions that shape human beings from childhood to adulthood. Furthermore, depending upon the societies in which people live, autonomous belief and action might be acceptable or, conversely, could be severely "punished or censored by a collective silence" (Bowers, 2012, p. 306).

Scholars also criticize cognitive moral development theory's emphasis on rational thinking as the decisive factor in moral existence as "despite the undeniable importance of moral judgment, it represents only one part of morality" (Colby, 2002, p. 134) and thus does not offer "a fully comprehensive theory of morality or moral development" (Rest et al., 2000, p. 384). For instance, "the Piaget-Kohlberg model does not at all incorporate the irrational aspect of human existence" (Cuypers, 2021, p. 126) as "the principle that we are, or even can be, entirely rational beings does not stand the test of time" (Alderice, 2021, p. 15). As well, lacking from cognitive moral development theory are "implicit or unconscious schemes or habits of interpretations" (Colby, 2002, p. 134), dispositional factors (Narvaez & Lapsley, 2009, p. 241), and empathy (Stets, 2016, p. 348). Moreover, "reasoning can be argued to be a part of almost all of our means of moral knowing, but in precious few cases can it be said to work in isolation from other means of knowing" (Sherblom, 2012, p. 129).

Once more, scholars question aspects of Piaget's and Kohlberg's stage theories as well as the relevance of these theories for real-life application. Recent research "calls into question the description of children's early moral reasoning as primarily based on authority, existing social rules, or avoidance of punishment" (Helwig & Chang, 2019, p. 2).

> Like adults, children are reflective creatures who make moral judgments about their social world, which includes evaluations of the behaviors of other children and adults, the social organizational institutions and rule systems in which they grow up, and everyday struggles with how to balance their own interests with those of others in situations of conflict. (p. 9)

Current-day researchers also critique moral development characterized as consistent and "sequential stages" and "that higher stages of reasoning replace immature stages wholly separate cognitive stages" because "individuals are not consistent in their stage of reasoning... suggesting that immature stages can co-exist alongside mature stages" (Garrigan et al., 2018, p. 85). Also, although Kohlberg (1975) acknowledged that people may believe in moral principles but still may not "live up" to them (p. 672), recent scholars also express concern about the disconnection between moral reasoning and action and stress that "there is only a weak link between moral reasoning and moral action" and "the disparity between knowing and doing has become increasingly evident across psychological fields" (Narvaez, 2008, p. 311). Lastly, moral development researchers instead propose that several "components of the moral life represent a process that includes moral sensitivity, judgment, motivation and character" and that "we should think of moral development as growing complexity and integration along multiple vectors rather than as a unilinear movement through fixed stages" (Strain, 2005, pp. 64–65).

Rational Morality and the Ethic of Justice

Embedded in the cognitive moral development perspective are the entwined philosophies of *rational morality* and the *ethic of justice*. Scholars realize that cognitive moral theory does not just describe a developmental process but also articulates certain ethical goals. "Moral psychologists adopted the 'rationalist' position that conscious reasoning about harm, welfare, and rights is the core process involved in moral judgments" (McAuliffe, 2019, p. 207) leading to a widening understanding of justice (Garrigan et al., 2018, p. 82). The ultimate outcome of moral development is to become a "just person, someone who autonomously subscribes to and acts in accordance with the principle of justice" (Schinkel & de Ruyter, 2017, p. 129). Rational moralist philosophers (Baier, 1958; Peters, 1962) believed that individuals can and should make conscious and reasoned choices, resist purely emotional instincts, and live according to ethical principles and obligations. From this perspective, "the moral life is largely a matter of rational judgment" (Bailey, 1980, p. 114) and that "a world with no creatures capable of judgment and reflection would not be an immoral world—it would simply be a world without a moral dimension" (p. 115).

Likewise, Kohlberg (1975) delineated an ethical aim in his final stage of moral development: the "universal-ethical-principle orientation" guided by "abstract and ethical principles" that are "are universal principles of justice, of the reciprocity and equality of human rights, and of respect for the dignity of human beings as individual persons" (p. 671). Kohlberg affirmed that "moral principles are ultimately principles of justice" and "central to justice are the demands of liberty, equality, and reciprocity" (p. 673). As follows, the philosophy of rational morality rests on the notion that "human beings are above all reasoning beings" (Nussbaum, 1999, p. 71) and that individuals can and should make moral decisions based on reasoning and reflection—informed by the principle of justice—rather than persuasion or coercion.

In cognitive moral theory, the goal of rational powers is to learn more about reality—about the situation of others, the environment, and, above all, the relationship between actions and consequences. Consequently, rational morality necessitates that individuals approach moral situations with awareness of verifiable evidence and act congruently with realistic perceptions. As Dewey (1922) explained, "intelligent action is not concerned with the bare consequences of the thing known, but with consequences to be brought into existence by action conditioned on the knowledge" (p. 299). Rational morality also depends upon knowledge of oneself and how one's behavior affects other people—self-awareness with "critical self-honesty" (Sherblom, 2012, p. 130) and "self-reflective capacity" to "examine one's own desires and to form judgments with respect to them" (Narvaez & Lapsley, 2009, p. 239).

A corresponding tenet of rational morality is how reasoning allows people to become autonomous (Johnson, 2013, p. 11). As "people "stand back from the positive (or social) concept of morality and try to make up [their] minds whether to accept or reject some part of it," independent or autonomous morality results (Cooper, 1966, p. 23). Moreover, if individuals come to understand that the beliefs of their society are immoral because of prejudicial and unjust treatment of certain people, they then see that "this conventional morality ought to change and that the change ought to be in the direction of a more rational, equitable, justified arrangement" (Singer, 2002, p. 7).

Yet, philosophers are circumspect about the concept of autonomy construed as unconditional liberty to choose and act on moral values. They note that "to be autonomous is not to act without constraint" and that "the development of autonomy is accompanied by increasing recognition of, and respect for, the autonomy of others" (Moshman, 2009, p. 155) and "recognition of each other's dignity" (Morse, 1997, p. 40). Hence, autonomous morality—the removal of unquestioning obedience to authority—is not always synonymous with rational morality. Although autonomy means freedom to choose, the individual's action is not necessarily right (Frankena, 1958, p. 308) and "there is nothing necessarily open-minded about being idiosyncratic; individuals may have a set of moral beliefs that are peculiar to themselves and yet have closed minds" (Barrow, 1975, p. 211). Therefore, whereas reflection leads to autonomous morality, resulting personal values may not be particularly rational or moral. From this viewpoint, rational morality provides a degree of "moral freedom where each person must decide individually what to do" (Singer, 2002, p. 13). But clearly, this philosophy does not suggest accepting any or all moral beliefs.

The most significant differences between rational morality and other moral orientations are the matter of examination of beliefs and autonomous moral reasoning. Whereas more traditional moralities praise the quality of faith (even when exercised blindly), rational morality invites questioning, as philosopher Kurt Baier (1958) declared:

> We could not properly speak of morality as opposed to a system of conventions, customs, or laws, until the question of the correctness or incorrectness, truth or falsity, of the rules prevalent in a community is asked, until, in other words, the prevalent rules are subjected to certain tests. It is only when the current rules are no longer regarded as sacrosanct, as incapable of alteration or improvement, only when the current rules are contrasted with other possible, improved ideal rules, that a group can be said to have a morality as opposed to a mere set of taboos. (p. 174)

Reasoning allows for "a change of mind on a moral matter" so that people thus say to themselves, "I used to think that was all right, and now I see that it is wrong" (Singer, 2002, p. 7). In sum, a major theme of rational morality is the belief in the power of reflective thinking which enables people to rationally adopt ethical codes and adapt moral rules to changing situations.

But for rational moralists, reasoning is not merely a cognitive activity; using reason means striving to make moral decisions with the goal of improving the human condition. As psychologist Steven Pinker (2021) insists, rationality is "not just a cognitive virtue but a moral one" (p. 317). Rational moralists write that although autonomy is instrumental in creating rational morality, it is not an end in itself. To the contrary, rational moralists embrace justice as the ultimate goal of moral deliberation and conduct

(Singer, 2002), believing that rational morality resides in the ethic of justice: "individuals acting as autonomous, objective and impartial agents," "ethical decisions made on the basis of universal principles and rules," and the goal of "ensuring the fair and equitable treatment of all people" (Botes, 2000, p. 1072).

Integrating Heads and Hearts

Although perceived as "hostile worlds apart" (Scheffler, 1977, p. 171) or as dichotomies of "heads and hearts" (Joseph, 1990), scholars in various fields discuss how emotion and reasoning are interconnected and that both are essential to moral functioning. Developmental researchers maintain that emotion and cognition "work together to process information and execute action" (Bell & Wolfe, 2004, p. 366) and that "ordinary moral concepts and moral emotions are linked in multifaceted ways" (Malti & Ongley, 2014, p. 165). Even researchers and theorists who focus on cognitive moral development and rational morality do not unequivocally reject the role of affect. "Emotion is not completely absent from moral judgments given the rationalist perspective" (Stets, 2016, p. 348):

> A situation may elicit emotional arousal (for example, sympathy or indignation in terms of how another is being treated), which may call attention to the moral relevance of the situation. In turn, this can activate moral reasoning. Here, moral reasoning remains central to moral judgments because it determines what moral action is most appropriate given the emotion that is aroused. (p. 348)

Indeed, Piaget (1968) attended to "powerful moral feelings of the child" (p. 57) and Kohlberg (1986) included the influence of positive and negative emotions in his conceptualization of stages of moral motivations, discerning a correspondence between moral feelings and cognition and making clear that people do not function only on an intellectual level. Eventually, research "enlarged the social cognitive domain" and demonstrated that the ethic of care "could exist alongside his justice domain" (Jorgensen, 2006, p. 187).

Feeling for others and desiring their well-being encourages people to use their intellectual capacities to develop moral insight, "the imaginative realization of the feelings of our neighbors" (Frankena, 1966, pp. 242–243). Yet, when we consider the ethic of care and how this view of morality impels us to do something about others' distress, having feelings of concern is not enough; we also need to have realistic perceptions of the nature and cause of suffering. "We actually want to involve our reason, we want to think about what is the best thing to do in these circumstances" (Singer, 2009, p. 66) so that individuals become more capable of consistent and effectual moral action. Thusly, major components of moral imagination evince the cognitive realm—of perception, reasoning, critical reflection, and transcendence of customary thinking.

But whereas some scholars equate rationality with morality so that individuals master their passions through intelligent perception and self control (Pinker, 2021; Rieff, 1959), others conclude that feelings must support rational ethical decisions (Ellett, 1986; Rawls, 1971). A number of moral philosophers critique the viewpoint that moral development is singularly cognitive. R. S. Peters (1962) pointed out that sympathy is the quality missing in malevolent people:

> The wicked man could be almost described as the man who feels too little remorse or guilt about his actions which he knows to be wrong. Remorse is usually felt for actions which have dire consequences for others; the capacity for feeing remorse therefore presupposes that we have sympathy for them. (p. 53)

Dewey and Tufts (1932) regarded the capacity for moral action as situated in the affective domain. They cautioned that that reflection alone may not encourage morality or realistic perception of a moral problem; if people are "antipathetic or indifferent" to situations that they should care about, "they will not be stirred to action" (p. 296). Moreover, Maxine Greene (1988) doubted that "reasoning is enough when it comes to acting in a resistant world, or opening fields of possibilities among which people may choose to choose" (p. 199).

In conclusion, emotion and cognition go hand in hand; both "are very important to the early development of moral action tendencies" and "moral competence" (Malti & Latzko, 2010, pp. 2, 5). Thereby, "emotion and thought are two interrelated features of individuals' orientations related to morality" and "influence each other in bi-directional ways" (Turiel & Dahl, 2019, p. 266). As important as reasoning is to morality, "emotions help children and adolescents anticipate the outcomes of sociomoral events and adjust their moral action tendencies accordingly" (Malti & Ongley, 2014, p. 164). Consequently, raising children to become moral human beings requires knowledge of an integrated moral development theory for understanding childrearing practices and moral education.

References

Alderdice, J. (2021). Morality, complexity and relationships. *Journal of Moral Education, 50*(1), 13–20.

Baier, K. (1958). *The moral point of view: A rational basis of ethics.* Cornell University Press.

Bailey, C. (1980). Morality reason and feeling. *Journal of Moral Education, 9*(2), 114–121.

Bandura, A. (2006). Toward a psychology of human agency. *Perspectives on Psychological Science, 1*(2), 164–180.

Barrow, R. (1975). *Moral philosophy for education.* George Allen and Unwin.

Bell, M. A., & Wolfe, C. D. (2004). Emotion and cognition: An intricately bound developmental process. *Child development, 75*(2), 366–370.

Berkowitz, M. W., & Grych, J. H. (1998). Fostering goodness: Teaching parents to facilitate children's moral development. *Journal of Moral Education, 27*(3), 371–391.

Bloom, P. (2013). *Just babies: The origins of good and evil.* Crown/Random House.

Bloom, P. (2017). Empathy and its discontents. *Trends in Cognitive Sciences, 21*(1), 24–31.

Botes, A. (2000). A comparison between the ethics of justice and the ethics of care. *Journal of Advanced Nursing, 32*(5), 1071–1075.

Bowers, C. A. (2012). Questioning the idea of the individual as an autonomous moral agent. *Journal of Moral Education, 41*(3), 301–310.

Bregman, R. (2019). *Humankind—A hopeful history.* Little Brown and Company.

Campaert, K., Nocentini, A., & Menesini, E. (2017). The efficacy of teachers' responses to incidents of bullying and victimization: The mediational role of moral disengagement for bullying. *Aggressive Behavior, 43*(5), 483–492.

Carpendale, J. I. (2000). Kohlberg and Piaget on stages and moral reasoning. *Developmental Review, 20*(2), 181–205.

Carpendale, J. I. (2009). Piaget's theory of moral development. In U. Müller, J. I. Carpendale, & L. Smith (Eds.), *The Cambridge companion to Piaget* (pp. 270–286). Cambridge University Press.

Churchland, P. (2019). *Conscience: The origins of moral intuition.* WW Norton & Company.

Cockburn, T. (2005). Children and the feminist ethic of care. *Childhood, 12*(1), 71–89.

Colby, A. (2002). Moral understanding, motivation, and identity. *Human Development, 45*(2), 130–135.

Coles, R. (1997). *The moral intelligence of children.* Random House.

Cooper, N. (1966). Two concepts of morality. *Philosophy, 41*(155), 19–33.

Cuypers, S. E. (2021). RS Peters' philosophy of moral education in relation to his Freudian psychology. *Journal of Moral Education, 50*(2), 122–139.

Damon, W. (1990). *The moral child: Nurturing children's natural moral growth.* New York, NY: Free Press.

Dempsey, H. L. (2017). A comparison of the social-adaptive perspective and functionalist perspective on guilt and shame. *Behavioral Sciences, 7*(4), 1–19.

Dewey, J., & Tufts, J. H. (1932). *Ethics* (rev. ed.). Henry Holt.

Eisenberg, N. (2000). Emotion, regulation, and moral development. *Annual Review of Psychology, 51*(1), 665–697.

Eisenberg, N., Spinrad, T. L., & Taylor, Z. E. (2014). Sympathy. In S. van Hooft (Ed.), *The Handbook of Virtue Ethics* (pp. 417–425). Acumen Publishing.

Elison, J. (2005). Shame and guilt: A hundred years of apples and oranges. *New Ideas in Psychology, 23*(1), 5–32.

Ellett, Jr., F, S. (1986). Research on emotion: How can it be done? *Educational Theory, 36*(2), 115–124.

Forsyth, D. R. (2019). *Making moral judgments: Psychological perspectives on morality, ethics, and decision-making.* Routledge.

Frankena, W. K. (1958). Toward a philosophy of moral education. *Harvard Educational Review, 28*(4), 300–313.

Frankena, W. K. (1966). Toward a philosophy of moral education. In I. Scheffler (Ed.), *Philosophy and education: Modern readings* (2nd ed.). Allyn and Bacon.

Garrigan, B., Adlam, A. L., & Langdon, P. E. (2018). Moral decision-making and moral development: Toward an integrative framework. *Developmental Review, 49,* 80–100.

Garrod, A., & Beal, C. R. (1993). Voices of care and justice in children's responses to fable dilemmas. In A. Garrod (Ed.), *Approaches to moral development: New research and emerging themes* (pp. 59–71). Teachers College Press.

Gerdes, K. E. (2011). Empathy, sympathy, and pity: 21st-century definitions and implications for practice and research, *Journal of Social Service Research, 37*(3), 230–241.

Gilligan, C. (1982). *In a different voice: Psychological theory and women's development.* Harvard University Press.

Gilligan, C., & Wiggins, G. (1987). The origins of morality in early childhood relationships. In J. Kagan & S. Lamb (Eds.), *The emergence of morality in young children* (pp. 277–305). University of Chicago Press.

Gilligan, C. (1998) "Hearing the difference: Theorizing connection." In M. Rogers (Ed.) *Contemporary feminist theory: A text/reader* (pp. 341–346). McGraw-Hill.

Goetz, J. L., Keltner, D., & Simon-Thomas, E. (2010). Compassion: An evolutionary analysis and empirical review. *Psychological Bulletin, 136*(3), 351–374.

Greene, M. (1988). *The dialectic of freedom.* Teachers College Press.

Gutzwiller-Helfenfinger, E. (2018). Not unlearning to care—Positive moral development as a cornerstone of nonkilling. *Journal of Peace Education, 15*(3), 288–308.

Hacker, P. (2017). Shame, embarrassment, and guilt. *Midwest Studies in Philosophy, 41,* 202–224.

Haidt, J. (2003). The moral emotions. In R. J. Davidson, K. Scherer, & H. H. Goldsmith (Eds.), *Handbook of affective sciences* (pp. 852–870). Oxford University Press.

Haidt, J. (2007). The new synthesis in moral psychology. *Science,* 316, 998–1002.

Haidt, J. (2012). *The righteous mind: Why good people are divided by politics and religion.* Pantheon Books.

Helwig, C. C., & Chang, X. M. (2019). Moral reasoning. In S. Hupp & J. D. Jewell (Eds.), *The encyclopedia of child and adolescent development* (pp. 1–11). Wiley. https://doi.org/10.1002/9781119171492.wecad144

Hoffman, M. L. (1993). Empathy, social cognition, and moral education. In A. Garrod (Ed.), *Approaches to moral development: New research and emerging themes* (pp. 157–179). Teachers College Press.

Hymel, S., & Bonanno, R. A. (2014). Moral disengagement processes in bullying. *Theory into Practice, 53*(4), 278–285.

Jaffee, S., & Hyde, J. S. (2000). Gender differences in moral orientation: A meta-analysis. *Psychological Bulletin, 126,* 703–726.

Johnson, R. (2013). *Rational morality: A science of right and wrong.* Dangerous Little Books.

Jorgensen, G. (2006). Kohlberg and Gilligan: Duet or duel? *Journal of Moral Education, 35*(2), 179–196.

Joseph, P. B. (1990). Charts and layers/heads and hearts: Toward an integrated theory of moral education. *Theory & Research in Social Education, 18*(1), 7–26.

Juujärvi, S., Myyry, L., & Pesso, K. (2012). Empathy and values as predictors of care development. *Scandinavian Journal of Psychology, 53*(5), 413–420.

Kamii, C. (1984). Autonomy: The aim of education envisioned by Piaget. *Phi Delta Kappan, 65*(6) 410–415.

Kawamura, K. M., & Eisler, R. (2013). An interview with Nel Noddings, PhD. *Cross Cultural Management: An International Journal, 20*(2), 1–6.

Kohlberg, L. (1969). Stage and sequence: The cognitive-developmental approach to socialization. In D. A. Goslin (Ed.), *Handbook of socialization theory and research* (pp. 347–480). Academic Press.

Kohlberg, L. (1975). The cognitive-developmental approach to moral education. *The Phi Delta Kappan, 56*(10), 670–677.

Kohlberg, L. (1984). *The psychology or moral development: The nature and validity of moral stages,* 2. Harper and Row.

Kohlberg, L. (1986) A current statement on some theoretical issues. In S. Modgil & C. Modgil (Eds.), *Lawrence Kohlberg: Consensus and controversy* (pp. 485–546). The Falmer Press.

Langdale, S. (1993). Moral development, gender, identity, and peer relationships in early and middle childhood. In A. Garrod (Ed.), *Approaches to moral development: New research and emerging themes* (pp. 30–58). Teachers College Press.

Lapsley, D. K. (2006). Moral stage theory. In M. Killen & J. Smetana (Eds.), *Handbook of moral development* (pp. 37–66). Lawrence Erlbaum.

Leach, C. W. (2017). Understanding shame and guilt. In L. Woodyatt, E. Worthington, Jr., M. Wenzel, & B. Griffin (Eds.), *Handbook of the psychology of self-forgiveness* (pp. 17–28). Springer.

Lefebvre, J. P., & Krettenauer, T. (2019). Linking moral identity with moral emotions: A meta-analysis. *Review of General Psychology, 23*(4), 444–457.

Malti, T., & Dys, S. P. (2015). A developmental perspective on moral emotions. *Topoi, 34*(2), 453–459.

Malti, T., & Dys, S. P. (2018). From being nice to being kind: Development of prosocial behaviors. *Current Opinion in Psychology, 20,* 45–49.

Malti, T., & Latzko, B. (2010). Children's moral emotions and moral cognition: Towards an integrative perspective. In B. Latzko & T. Malti (Eds.), *Children's moral emotions and moral cognition: Developmental and educational perspectives* (vol. 129, pp. 1–10). Jossey-Bass.

Malti, T., & Ongley, S. (2014). The development of moral emotions and moral reasoning. In M. Killen & J. Smetana (Eds.), *Handbook of moral development* (pp. 163–183). Taylor & Francis.

McAuliffe, W. H. (2019). Do emotions play an essential role in moral judgments?. *Thinking and Reasoning, 25*(2), 207–230.

Morse, J. F. (1997). Fostering autonomy. *Educational Theory, 47*(1), 31–50.

Moshman, D. (2009). The development of rationality. In H. Siegel (Ed.), *Oxford handbook of philosophy of education* (pp. 145–161). Oxford University Press.

Narvaez, D. (2008). Human flourishing and moral development: Cognitive and neurobiological perspectives of virtue development. In L. Nucci & D. Narvaez (Eds.), *Handbook of moral and character education* (2nd ed.; pp. 326–343). Routledge.

Narvaez, D., & Lapsley, D. K. (2009). Moral identity, moral functioning, and the development of moral character. *Psychology of Learning and Motivation, 50,* 237–274.

Niedermeyer, W. J. (2017). Why do we care?: A natural history of Noddings' ethical theory. *Between the Species, 22*(1), 185–213.

Noddings, N. (2002). *Educating moral people: A caring alternative to character education.* Teachers College Press.

Nussbaum, M. C. (1999). *Sex and social justice.* Oxford University Press.

Owens, L. M., & Ennis, C. D. (2005). The ethic of care in teaching: An overview of supportive literature. *Quest, 57*(4), 392–425.

Park, J., & Barron, R. W. (1977). Can morality be taught?. In L. J. Stiles & B. D. Johnson (Eds.), *Morality examined: Guidelines for teachers* (pp. 3–23). Princeton Book Company.

Peters, R. S. (1962). Moral education and the psychology of character. *Philosophy, 37*(139), 37–56.

Piaget, J. (1932/1965) *The moral judgement of the child.* Kegan Paul.

Piaget, J. (1968). *Six psychological studies.* Vintage Books.

Pinker, S. (2021). *Rationality: What it is, why it seems scarce, why it matters.* Viking Press.

Rawls, J. (1971). *A theory of justice.* Belknap Press.

Rest, J. R., Narvaez, D., Thoma, S. J., & Bebeau, M. J. (2000). A neo-Kohlbergian approach to morality research. *Journal of Moral Education, 29*(4), 381–395.

Rieffe, C., & Camodeca, M. (2016). Empathy in adolescence: Relations with emotion awareness and social roles. *British Journal of Developmental Psychology, 34*(3), 340–353.

Rieff, P. (1959). *Freud, the mind of the moralist.* Viking Press.

Scheffler, I. (1977). In praise of the cognitive emotions. *Teachers College Record, 79,* 171–186.

Schinkel, A., & de Ruyter, D. J. (2017). Individual moral development and moral progress. *Ethical Theory and Moral Practice, 20*(1), 121–136.

Schubert, W. H., & He, M. F. (2020). Practicing care and compassion. In M. F. Fang & W. Schubert (Eds.), *Oxford research encyclopedia of curriculum studies.* Oxford University Press. https://doi.org/10.1093/acrefore/9780190264093.013.619

Sevenhuijsen, S. (2000). Caring in the third way: the relation between obligation, responsibility and care in Third Way discourse. *Critical Social Policy, 20*(1), 5–37.

Sevenhuijsen, S. (2003). The place of care: The relevance of the feminist ethic of care for social policy. *Feminist Theory, 4*(2), 179–197.

Sheets-Johnstone, M. (2008). *The roots of morality.* Pennsylvania State University Press.

Sheikh, S., & Janoff-Bulman, R. (2010). The "shoulds" and "should nots" of moral emotions: A self-regulatory perspective on shame and guilt. *Personality and Social Psychology Bulletin, 36*(2), 213–224.

Sherblom, S. A. (2012). What develops in moral development? A model of moral sensibility. *Journal of Moral Education, 41*(1), 117–142.

Sherblom, S. A. (2015). A moral experience feedback loop: Modeling a system of moral self-cultivation in everyday life. *Journal of Moral Education, 44*(3), 364–381.

Silfver-Kuhalampi, M., Figueiredo, A., Sortheix, F., & Fontaine, J. (2015). Humiliated self, bad self or bad behavior? The relations between moral emotional appraisals and moral motivation. *Journal of Moral Education, 44*(2), 213–231.

Simpson, E. L. (1976). A holistic approach to moral development and behavior. In T. Lickona (Ed.), *Moral development and behavior: Theory, research and social issues* (pp. 159–170). Holt, Rinehart and Winston.

Singer, P. (2009). Ethics. In A. Taylor (Ed.), *Examined life: Excursions with contemporary thinkers* (pp. 61–86). The New Press.

Skitka, L. J., Bauman, C. W., & Mullen, E. (2016). Morality and justice. In C. Sabbagh & M. Schmitt (Eds.) *Handbook of social justice theory and research* (pp. 407–423). Springer.

Skoe, E. E. (2010). The relationship between empathy-related constructs and care-based moral development in young adulthood. *Journal of Moral Education, 39*(2), 191–211.

Skoe, E. E. A. (2013). *The ethic of care: Theory and research.* In B. J. Irby, G. Brown, R. Lara-Alecio, & S. Jackson (Eds.), *The handbook of educational theories* (pp. 615–628). IAP Information Age Publishing.

Snarey, J., & Samuelson, P. (2008). Moral education in the cognitive development tradition: Lawrence Kohlberg's revolutionary ideas. In L. Nucci & D. Narvaez (Eds.), *Handbook of moral and character education* (pp. 69–95). Routledge.

Stets, J. E. (2016). Rationalist vs. intuitionist views on morality a sociological perspective. In C. Brand (Ed.), *Dual-process theories in moral psychology* (pp. 345–366). Springer VS.

Strain, C. R. (2005). Pedagogy and practice: Service-learning and students' moral development. *New Directions for Teaching and Learning, 2005*(103), 61–72.

Strauss, C., Taylor, B. L., Gu, J., Kuyken, W., Baer, R., Jones, F., & Cavanagh, K. (2016). What is compassion and how can we measure it? A review of definitions and measures. *Clinical Psychology Review, 47,* 15–27.

Tappan, M. B. (1997). Language, culture, and moral development: A Vygotskian perspective. *Developmental Review, 17*(1), 78–100.

Turiel, E. (2015). Moral development. In R. M. Lerner (Ed.), *Handbook of child psychology and developmental science: Vol. 1. Theory and method* (7th ed., pp. 484–522). Wiley.

Turiel, E., & Dahl, A. (2019). The development of domains of moral and conventional norms, coordination in decision-making, and the implications of social opposition. In K. Bayertz & N. Roughley (Eds.), *The normative animal?: On the anthropological significance of social, moral and linguistic norms* (pp. 195–213). Oxford University Press.

Turner J.H., & Stets J.E. (2006). Moral emotions. In Stets J. E., & Turner J. H. (Eds.), *Handbook of the sociology of emotions* (pp. 544–566). Springer.

Vozzola, E. C. (2014). *Moral development: Theory and applications.* Routledge.

Walker, L. J. (2006). Gender and morality. In M. Killen & J. Smetana (Eds.), *Handbook of moral development* (pp. 93–115). Lawrence Erlbaum.

Walker, L. J., Hennig, K. H., & Krettenauer, T. (2000). Parent and peer contexts for children's moral reasoning development. *Child Development, 71*(4), 1033–1048.

Weissbourd, R. (2009). *The parents we mean to be.* Houghton Mifflin Harcourt.

4

Becoming Moral

Culture and Socialization

> *The child is inducted into a human way of living and is expected to master extraordinary subtle and complicated patterns of behavior and the beginnings of different modes of communication. Each generation of children must learn these patterns, undergo various transformations . . . striving to master what the human race has been struggling with from the beginning of human living.*
>
> —Lawrence K. Frank, 1956, "Social Systems and Culture," p. 208

Affective and cognitive theories cast light on requisites for moral development, but these perspectives alone provide an incomplete knowledge base unless we also explore the social-cultural influences upon morality and the transmission of moral codes from families and cultures to the next generation. Accordingly, this chapter considers these questions:

- How do children learn their culture's moral standards?
- How do families teach moral values and behaviors?

Teaching for Moral Imagination, pages 69–90

- In what ways do peers and media influence children's moral values and behaviors?

Research on socialization and culture informs us that children learn about moral values from various sources, in particular, through families' explicit moral teaching and reactions to children's missteps or wrongdoing—especially those digressions that flaunt deeply held cultural beliefs. Caregivers correct moral misbehaviors in diverse ways—some that encourage empathy and reflection and some that merely model power and aggression. Eventually, peers, media, and teachers convey a myriad of moral messages to children and adolescents. However, this area of scholarship—unlike the literature of affective and cognitive moral development—does not embody moral philosophies but focuses on the process of learning cultural and societal standards (see Table 4.1).

Culture and Morality

A crucial perspective on the learning of moral values is that culture profoundly influences individuals' basic orientations to life, including their interactions with others and moral decisions, and that cultural identity has "important moral dimensions" (Pillutla, 2011, p. 351). Cultural identity may stem from that of the wider culture or from subcultures (Singer, 2002, pp. 8–9) and in that respect, "culture is not synonymous with country

TABLE 4.1 Theories of Moral Development: Culture and Socialization

Theory	Emphases
Cultural-Affective Moral Learning	Childrearing Cultural Norms Affect Internalization of Values
Behaviorism	Management Self Control Rewards and Punishments
Social Learning Theory	Agents of Socialization Observing Modeling
Social Domain Theory	Social Interaction Reciprocal Relationships Complexity

or ethnicity but rather describes communities whose members share key beliefs, values, behaviors, routines, and institutions" (Jensen, 2015, p. 9). We cannot consider culture a monolithic concept nor can we assume that individuals identify with the moral values of only one culture—especially when living in diverse societies with a multitude of moral messages (Jensen, 2008, p. 307).

Influence of Culture on Values

Scholars who attend to "the wide discrepancy in the values communicated to young people in societies across the world" (Damon, 1990, p. 96) point out various examples of how cultural values influence individuals' activities. For example, cultures "suppress and repress different things and in different ways," providing assorted avenues for people to strive for contentment (Hollan, 2012, p. 380). Some cultures tend to recognize achievement according to individuals' success at warfare or by accumulation of wealth (Mead, 1971, p. 130). Cultures also channel or offer outlets for aggression but constrain violence so that it is tolerated in systems of normal behaviors. Even though a culture may define itself as peaceful, there can be less obvious outlets for aggression than physical confrontations such as gossip and slander. Correspondingly, there are cultures that tolerate children's belligerence more than others but may only approve certain kinds of aggressiveness (Hall, 1976, p. 137). Clearly, cultures "vary on the kinds of criteria they have for regarding behaviors as moral" and depending on a culture's system of ethical reasoning, people "are likely to regard a number of behaviors as moral that people who do not use [another] kind of reasoning will imbue with little or no moral significance" (Jensen, 2008, p. 304).

Another view of culture is as a selective screen—a filtering process for perceiving and dealing with reality. "Culture designates what we pay attention to and what we ignore" (Hall, 1976, p. 85). People's thought and communication systems and many of their affective responses are formed according to cultural patterns; these patterns influence beliefs and behavior. For instance, culture informs how people solve problems (Wallace, 1961, p. 6). Decision-making, including of a moral nature, draws from "knowledge about how to make decisions and what decisions to make under what circumstances" (Güss & Robinson, 2014, p. 2); judgments are not "idiosyncratic" but "depend, at least in part, on the cultural mindset accessible at that moment" (Arieli & Sagiv, 2018, p. 789). As well, moral functioning can be "considered as a form of mediated action" in which individuals as moral agents draw from "moral mediational means" including the "words, language and forms of discourse, which profoundly shape moral thinking, feeling and acting" (Tappan, 2006, p. 6). In particular, judgments about moral actions will be influenced by the culture's "view of the relationship between the individual and the collective" (Arieli & Sagiv, 2018, p. 790). As follows, decisions will be informed by beliefs about the rightness of an action for individuals or for their groups and even who should participate in the decision-making process.

More broadly, a number of anthropologists and psychologists hypothesize that an individual culture has an ethos—a shared and moral investment in certain goals and values—and that "the moral domain varies by culture" (Haidt, 2012, p. 26). Several scholars affirm three overarching themes of moral reasoning or "systems of ethics" (Jensen, 2015):

> - The *ethic of autonomy* involves a focus on the self as an individual; moral reasons within this ethic include the interests, well-being, and rights of individuals (self or other) and fairness between individuals.
> - The *ethic of community* focuses on persons as members of social groups, with attendant reasons such as duty to others, and concern with the customs, interests, and welfare of groups.
> - The *ethic of divinity* focuses on people as spiritual or religious entities and moral reasons encompass divine and natural law, sacred lessons, and spiritual purity. (Jensen, 2015, p. 3)

This "trinity of moral foundations" (Bloom, 2013, p. 175) honors the philosophy of rational morality as well as the morality of community and spirituality. Suggesting a triumvirate of ethical systems allows for appreciation of diverse perspectives and "calls into question dominant Western conceptions of moral life" (Mattingly & Throop, 2018, p. 477).

Yet, some scholars cast doubt on the existence of an unequivocal cultural ethos with "homogeneous orientations" (Turiel, 2014, p. 13) and they express concern about "downplaying differences within cultures" (Wainryb & Recchia, 2014, p. 260). This suggests that we need to consider "the possibility that individuals within a culture may develop contradictory perspectives and enter into significant conflict with each other" (p. 261).

> Rather than being products of their culture and exchangeable copies of other members of their culture, people in cultures try to make sense of their experiences, disagree with one another about the meanings and value of these experiences, assume critical roles toward them and, at times, attempt to resist or subvert their culture's norms and practices, and may even succeed in changing them. (p. 259)

Such critique rests on the viewpoint that "the individual is an active agent, rather than a passive recipient, in social and cultural processes" (Haste & Abrahams, 2008, p. 379). Therefore, we oversimplify the cultural theory of moral development if we suppose that children see no alternatives to dominant values.

Childrearing: Cultural Moral Learning

The perspective of cultural moral learning begins with the premises that "we are born into a culture and acquire its moral outlook as we acquire its language" (Singer, 2002, p. 8) and that "as soon as children can communicate with others and can make inferences about their social communications, they have already access to their culture's values and beliefs" (Damon, p. 1990, p. 3). Cultural teaching influences children's development of deeply-felt moral values as well as rules of social convention.

> Our culture strongly influences whether we regard a practice as so important and essential to membership in the group that we deem that practice as to be on the moral end of the spectrum, or whether, like table manners, the practice is regarded as toward the social-convention end of the spectrum. (Churchland, 2019, p. 175)

The socio-cultural influences on moral emotions, beliefs, and actions begin early in childhood, reflecting the ways in which parents and other significant people sanction and model certain beliefs and behaviors. These "parenting strategies reflect cultural beliefs and values" and also affect "the meaning a child attaches to socialization strategies" (Grusec et al., 2014, p. 120). As well, children learn about right and wrong—or what is deemed correct or customary—through spontaneous responses to actions and missteps. By prizing, directly teaching, and purposely or unintentionally modeling certain values, families and other participants in childrearing give considerable moral guidance to the young—even as children actively construct their own understanding of morality.

In what we may think of as the theory of cultural-affective moral learning, anthropologist Edward T. Hall (1973, 1976) described three levels of culture—the *formal, informal,* and *technical*—and observed that each level is taught to children differently. Hall's conceptualization casts light on how children learn subtle and complicated cultural norms; moreover, communication of values to children—ordinarily in instances of deviation which involve reprimand or punishment—can place a particular force or energy behind certain moral ones.

Hall (1973) determined that children learn the *formal* level of culture usually when the adult "will correct the child... using a tone of voice indicating that what you are doing is unthinkable" (p. 68). The tenets of formal learning do not have alternatives. Because formal learning is deeply ingrained and communicated to children with vehemence, "whenever violations of formal norms occur, they are accompanied by a tide of emotion" (p. 74). Sometimes formal systems are so strong that individuals think that other ways of behavior are "unnatural if not impossible" (p. 75). But when formal values are not instilled, children grow up without a deep sense of what is moral and what is not, lacking the prerequisites for the development of internal moral regulation.

Unlike formal learning, *informal* learning involves a modeling process. "Whole clusters of related activities are learned at a time, in many cases without the knowledge that they are being learned at all or that there are patterns of rules governing them" (Hall, 1973, p. 69). Hall explained that via informal learning "entire systems of behavior made up of hundreds of thousands of details are passed from generation to generation, and nobody can give rules for what is happening" and "only when the rules are broken down do we realize they exist" (p. 70). Informal learning occurs parallel to formal learning and involves the nuances of behavior, such as when to appropriately address people by their first or last names. People may experience discomfort or anxiety when there are deviations from informal rules, but not moral outrage (p. 76).

Hall's third cultural level is *technical*, occurring as adults teach the young (or each other) specific skills. Learning is explicit and conscious, and follows "a coherent outline form." Also, "one can introduce changes (on the technical level) with the greatest ease without violating the norms of the other two systems." These changes can be observed, verbalized, and transmitted to others (Hall, 1973, p. 71). Although people, especially experts, have a clear sense of how to follow technical rules—even knowing that there may be a right or wrong way for procedures—these are not moral rules.

Yet, in cross-cultural interactions, assumptions about the formal, informal, and technical levels can be fraught with difficulty as what may be an informal habit in one culture can violate the moral rules of another; or a technical rule in one culture can conflict with the religious or spiritual beliefs of another—such as the sacredness of the land. Without deep knowledge of another culture's value systems, individuals may be clueless when they cross the line and are disrespectful. Hall (1973) noted that "the whole matter of deviation from norms bristles with complexity."

> For example, children never know where the line is until they step across it. The manner in which they are reprimanded provides the glue that holds together these systems in later life. Children never know until they find out by trial and error whether they have violated a formal, informal, or technical norm. (p. 77)

For Hall, the distinction between formal and informal cultural values seems more of an unconscious phenomenon, but more recent studies suggest that even in childhood individuals learn the differences between social and moral norms. Although "kids can't talk like moral philosophers, they are busy sorting social information in a sophisticated way" and "in all cultures children still make a distinction between moral rules and conventional rules" (Haidt, 2012, p. 10). Researchers also suggest that "that construction of thinking about norms in the social realms begins in childhood and continues into adolescence and adulthood" (Turiel & Dahl, 2019, p. 200).

In sum, child-rearing practices transmit values—not only via explicit teaching but through the emotional quality of encouragements and prohibitions about moral behavior. Responses to moral transgressions vary in content and intensity and will influence the process of understanding and internalization of adults' moral teachings. On the other hand, children and adolescents are not automatons who just passively receive their cultures' dominant moral values but are capable of contemplating, affirming, or challenging them.

Moral Socialization

Socialization explains the process of how children become habituated to systems of acceptable values and approved conduct as they learn from models and interfaces with caregivers, peers, media, and teachers as well as how they make sense of these experiences. Socialization is defined as "the ways in which individuals come to behave in accord with the standards, beliefs, values, and actions of their social group" (Grusec & Davidov, 2021) and is "the process whereby new members of a social group are assisted by more experienced members" (Vinik et al., 2013, p. 475). "This process continues throughout adolescence" and extends to "emerging adulthood" as "elders" in communities and workplaces "help the novices to develop the values, behaviors, and motives necessary to becoming a part of the social community" (Arnett, 2015, pp. 97, 87). The socialization process takes time: "repeated exposure to specific social standards, rules, and values is required before these become individually engrained" (Genner & Süss, 2017, p. 1). Moreover, this is not merely a top-down value transmission process but a "dynamic system consisting of nested systems interacting" (Sherblom, 2015, p. 369). While there are various explanations for how socialization for moral development takes place, three key theories predominate: *behaviorism*, *social learning theory*, and *social domain theory*.

Key Socialization Theories

The earliest prominent socialization theory in the 20th century, *behaviorism*, had "a major impact on theories of morality" (Smetana, et al., 2019, p. 124). Behaviorism's underlying premise is that "all learning is a result of the connection between the behavior and an environmental response" (Bryant et al., 2013, p. 94). Its foremost theorist, B. F. Skinner (1953, 1971), believed that behavior is the result of "operant conditioning and the role of reinforcements or punishments in the environment to influence behavior" (Albaiz & Ernest, 2015, p. 344). Skinner offered "a strict behaviorist conception of moral acquisition" in which "morality reflects behaviors that have been reinforced (positively or negatively) with value judgments associated with cultural norms"; as such, all behaviors are the "consequence of contingencies of reinforcement" (Turiel, 2015, p. 488) and not the results from people being moral actors influenced by their principles or sympathies. Over time, scholars disparaged this explanation of socialization as a process as it "has mechanistic overtones" (Howell, 2005, p. 162), realizing that "reinforcement and punishment were too narrow to encompass the richness of human social interactions" (Grusec, et al., 2014, p. 115). Thus, despite the ever-present belief in behaviorism with its explanation of rewards and punishments to reinforce learning, this theory does not enlighten us about how to help children to become moral people and has little to do with ethics and moral imagination—with reflection, moral responsibility, or compassion.

A subsequent socialization conceptualization, *social learning theory*, does not negate the idea of behavioral reinforcement but stresses how "imitation and observation" also influence children's behavior and how children are "more likely to model and learn correct behavior from more powerful (but also more nurturant) models" (Smetana et al., 2019, p. 124). Social psychologist Albert Bandura (1977), whose influential research explored how modeling affects both pro-social and aggressive behavior, conceived of social learning as having cognitive dimensions involving several stages beginning with (a) paying attention to "a live model, or indirectly via a mediated source such as television," and then (b) to "acquiring and retaining knowledge of the observed behavior." Eventually, it is possible to (c) imitate the observed behavior but also (d) "to choose whether to accept the model's behavior" as a guide to their own actions (Kunkel et al., 2005, p. 262). In this way, learning values is not "a strictly passive process" as "children attend to conflicting information and choose which behavior or norm to adopt" based on their perceptions of both the norm itself and "the socialization agent" (Smetana et al., 2019, p. 124). But in due course scholars became critical of social learning theory for being "unidirectional and deterministic" (Kuczynski et al., 2014, p. 135) and "more explicitly acknowledged children's agency in the socialization process" (Smetana et al., 2019, p. 127).

Eventually a third socialization explanation emerged, *social domain theory* (See Nucci, 1989; Turiel, 1983), portraying moral socialization as the process of learning through "children's reciprocal relationships with adults and other children" (Turiel, 2014, p. 3). This perspective acknowledges the complexity of moral socialization by emphasizing "children's multifaceted lives and development through experience of different forms of social interaction" (Carpendale, 2009, p. 281). Besides "caregivers' feedback to moral transgressions about what constitutes moral norms and wrongness," children's social experiences and interpretations of these experiences, "lead to their construction of moral concepts" (Smetana, 1999, pp. 313–314). Children especially "construct moral understanding" from interactions with peers—both from the reactions of victims of aggression and knowledge of what it is like to be a "victim of moral transgressions" (Essler & Paulus, 2021, p. 330). Moreover, the research supporting social domain theory confirms that "individuals struggle with moral issues in their social lives" (Turiel, 2014, p. 3)—suggesting how moral learning is an ongoing and complicated phenomenon.

Childrearing: Moral Socialization

Considerable moral socialization research centers on parents' and significant caregivers' long-term goal of "assisting their children to become competent adults" (Holden, et al., 2011, p. 130) and to "internalize the values and attitudes" of their society and culture (Grusec & Davidov, 2021, pp. 3–4). Within the family, viewed as "a small social system" (Damon, 1990, p. 51), young children learn culturally pertinent values and beliefs—even though individuals are socialized into various groups throughout their lives. Studies on socialization highlight that "parents are more important than any other socialization agents" because of the early bonds between parents and children and the continuation of their relationships and interactions throughout childhood (Grusec & Davidov, 2021, p. 2). Into late childhood and even adolescence, parents can strongly influence children's moral reasoning (Caravita et al., 2014, p. 194) as relationships of mutuality within "a close family climate" promote "willingness to accept parental values" (Barni et al., 2011, p. 117). Nonetheless, although these discussions often refer to parents, "families are not homogeneous and are not structured simply" (Walker, 1999, p. 262); therefore, we need to remember that the parenting role may be performed by other people who provide love and moral guidance to children.

Socialization studies illuminate how and why parents influence moral development. Young children who experience a "harmonious parent-child relationship" become "more cooperative and responsive to the parent's socialization initiatives" (Thompson, 2014, p. 285) and are "more open to consider parental messages and others' needs" (Smetana, et al., 2019, p. 133). Researchers also note that children have "higher levels of moral reasoning, sympathy, and prosocial behavior" (Mounts & Allen, 2019, p. 4) if they experience "parental warmth, affection, and responsiveness" (Smetana, et al., 2019, p. 133). This mutually receptive relationship also stems from parents creating relationships of "respectful engagement" (Berkowitz & Grych, 1998, p. 382) cultivated when "parents are considerate of their children's wishes" (Grusec, 2019, p. 8).

Modeling also is an essential aspect of socialization, but this concept is far more complicated than merely having a parent who is role model; although parents may be good or even noble people in the eyes of society, that by itself does not foster moral development. Rather, parents are influential models as children observe them in everyday encounters, especially through "interactions with their children regarding moral issues" and when they are "nurturant and supportive," model respect and compassion towards others, express empathy, and discuss moral reasoning (Berkowitz & Grych, 1998, p. 385). Parents also "monitor their child's environment," encourage children's exposure to examples of "positive social behavior" (Grusec, 2019, p. 9), and support activities that "create opportunities for their children to manifest responsibility for others" (Berkowitz & Grych, 1998, p. 378).

Role modeling comprises a multipart process of moral socialization. Firstly, parents need to demonstrate that they really care about morality. It is "important for children to realize that adults are also concerned about 'fairness' and 'right' and 'wrong'" (Kuhmerker, 1976, p. 265). Also, studies confirm that "children model their parents and other adults' prosocial behaviors" (Eisenberg et al., 2015, p. 122); when, for example, children who view their parents as caring and engaging in "the prosocial act of volunteering," tend to become volunteers themselves in adolescence and young adulthood (Grusec et al., 2014, p. 125). Lastly, children need "to see that adults can cope with major and minor injustices around them, that adults can be angry or disappointed but not lose control, and that adults have positive ways for trying to redress injustice" (Kuhmerker, 1976, p. 264). Such parental models have "appropriate reactions to distress experienced by themselves and others" (Grusec, 2019, p. 9), demonstrating reasonableness, self control, and "appropriate conflict-resolution skills" (Mounts & Allen, 2019, p. 7).

In studies of moral socialization in childrearing, researchers highlight the significance of conversations with children and that the "long-term goal of teaching values" involves reasoning (Grusec, et al., 2017, p. 465). A paramount moral socialization practice is *induction*—"discussing consequences of children's behaviors on others"—when correcting children's behavior. Induction "focuses children's attention on the harm caused to another person" as well as "minimizing distress, making it more likely that children will focus on the content of parents' messages" (Mounts & Allen, 2019, p. 6). Through induction "parents help to promote children's caring and compassion toward the feeling states of others as well as emotional understanding and perspective-taking" (Laible et al., 2019, p. 289). Consequently, "parental induction is associated with children's moral competence, including high levels of empathy and prosocial behavior" (p. 288).

Some parents, however, model moral reasoning just to a limited extent but, at the same time, use non-coercive disciplinary approaches evincing "confrontive power that is reasoned, negotiable, outcome-oriented and concerned with regulating their children's behavior"; in this scenario, "children choose between complying, negotiating with parents a satisfactory compromise, or paying a known price for noncomplying" (Baumrind, 2012, p. 36). Certainly, in such situations in which parents are not "harsh, unresponsive, or rely on unqualified force" (p. 36), they are more "supportive and flexible" models (p. 40). In contrast to coercive power assertion, parental socialization practices to correct behavior are more effective when "moderate and appropriate levels of punishment are accompanied by reasons or explanation for why a given action is unacceptable" (Grusec, 2019, p. 13).

Because parents want children to behave cooperatively, sympathetically, or minimally, to abstain from hurting others before they fully understand reasons for good behavior, they may resort to a system of rewards and punishments. Positive inducements—such as acknowledging and praising behavior, shows of affection, or special privileges or material rewards for observed or future behaviors—reinforce good conduct. Studies suggest that praise can "facilitate internalization of prosocial behavior through the development of sympathy" but that "intrinsically motivated behavior can be undermined through the provision of material rewards" (Mounts & Allen, 2019, p. 9). But parents' reactions to a children's misconduct also can be in the form of negative reinforcements such as verbal reprimands, withdrawing children for short periods of time from situations or objects that stimulated their behavior, or denial of pleasures or privileges. Although "negative reinforcement is often confused with punishment" (Troutman, 2015, p. 4), removing miscreants from situations is quite different than angry punitive responses. Punishments might be used to "obtain immediate compliance with requests" (Grusec et al., 2017, p. 465)—as would be the case of inappropriate behavior that could harm children or others.

Scholars critical of moral socialization through rewards and punishments state several reasons for their concerns: They maintain that rewards thwart intrinsic motivation because an "overreliance on rewards and positive feedback can undermine children's moral motivation" (Nucci, 2006, p. 720). Furthermore, negative reinforcers do not allow for moral learning because such consequences may have "no logical connection to the action" and offer no opportunities for prosocial development (p. 721). Punishments, are not "inducements to moral growth" as "avoiding personal harm is not a moral reason" (Watson, 2008, p. 191) and such "practices are external to the child, and can be ineffective in cultivating an innate sense of right and wrong" (Albaiz & Ernest, 2015, p. 342). The punitive approach to discipline undermines the development of moral life through "democratic cooperation" (Lapsley, 2006, p. 43) and reciprocal understanding of viewpoints. Psychiatrist Rudolph Dreikurs (1958) argued that behaviorist discipline is an authoritarian tactic:

> Both reward and punishment are only possible in a social setting where there are superiors and inferiors. They require a person endowed with superior authority. No reward and punishment is possible unless a person has the power to decide when either is appropriate and can then mete them out. Superiority of one person over another is not "natural." It is established only socially, through an autocratic system in an authoritarian society. In a democracy, all members of the society are equal. (p. 171)

Then too, parents or significant caregivers can be negative influences by modeling "harmful or abusive behavior" toward their children or other family members (Berkowitz & Grych, 1998, p. 385). Their methods of correction involve coercive power that is "arbitrary, peremptory, concerned with retaining hierarchical status distinctions in family relationships, and gives the child no choice but to comply" (Baumrind, 2012, p. 36). Such forms of discipline may include "deprivation of privileges or psychological aggression" (p. 39)—angrily telling children that they are bad or worthless.

Children who have experienced "harsh and rejecting caregiving" and have witnessed parental aggression, including "interparental violence" are more likely to exhibit antisocial behavior (Hyde et al., 2010, p. 199) and to "imitate parental outbursts in their own behavior" (Damon, 1990, p. 55). Once more, "children who bully their peers are more likely to come from families where parents use authoritarian, harsh and punitive childrearing practices" (Georgiou & Stavrinides, 2013, p. 166). Parents "who model aggression" are not teaching children how to regulate "negative emotions such as feelings of anger and frustration" (Van IJzendoorn, 1997, p. 721).

Corporal punishment, the inflicting physical pain, is a common form of coercive discipline. Parents are more likely to use such punishment in stressful situations (Simons & Wurtele, 2010, p. 640) so that lack of control or anger spurs this disciplinary practice. Such discipline may stop children's poor conduct but can provoke their anger and resentment. On the whole, "parental power assertion—defined in terms of physical and verbal pressure by a relatively angry parent—undermines morally relevant functioning" (Smetana et al., 2019, p. 136). Various researchers conclude that spanking or hitting children is an ineffective mode of correction that may achieve short-term compliance but neither results in long-term changes of behavior nor contributes to moral learning (Gershoff, 2013; Kish & Newcombe, 2015). Additionally, children may view inflicting physical harm as acceptable because they are socialized to use hitting "to resolve conflicts with peers and siblings" (Simons & Wurtele, 2010, p. 645). Nevertheless, some cultures more routinely use corporal punishment than others but not necessarily as an angry response. In these societies, children may believe that "although the discipline is unpleasant, it is carried out in a careful manner with their best interests at heart "(Lansford, 2010, p. 96).

Finally, parents can undermine moral development by creating conditions for the development of *moral disengagement*. This can occur when parents "minimize children's transgressive behavior or respond positively" (Bussey, 2020, p. 317), encouraging children not to take responsibility for their actions. When socialized to believe that parents are not concerned about their antisocial or immoral acts, empathy development is impeded and, consequently, children may not be able to feel guilt or shame. Such parenting practices become the catalyst for the "selective disengagement of moral standards that enables the commission of immoral and antisocial behavior without feeling any remorse" (p. 307)—"turning off the internal process of self-regulation that makes people anticipate self-sanctions in case they harm somebody" (Campaert et al., 2017, p. 483). Moral disengagement is a commonality among children and adolescents who are bullies

(Bandura, 2016) as well as those who have "more passive involvement in bullying as bystanders" (Hymel & Bonanno, 2014, pp. 280–281).

Moral Socialization: Peers and Media

Parents or other significant adult family members do not remain the primary agents of socialization. As children's social worlds expand to encompass relationships with playmates and classmates, the process of moral socialization is enriched by "reciprocal relationships" with peers that involve "mutual respect and concerns with fairness, justice, and cooperation" (Turiel, 2014, p. 7). Moreover, as children transition to adolescence, strong attachments form with peers and these attachments "are important for the development of empathy and perspective taking" (Murphy et al., 2017, p. 1390)—crucial "social and cognitive skills" (Lynn et al., 2019, p. 9).

Peers become increasingly influential in early adolescence as "peer interactions become more frequent and less supervised" (Espelage et al., 2003, p. 205). Throughout adolescence young people spend more time and become closer with friends than their families (Arnett, 2015, p. 97) and "invest more in establishing their social position within their peer group" (Boniel-Nissim & Sasson, 2018, p. 177). Likewise, adolescents (albeit so do other age groups) "tend to choose friends who are similar to themselves in many ways, a process known as selective association" (Arnett, 2015, p. 97) and choices are made based on nearness in locations as well as gender and race (Espelage et al., 2003, p. 205). Research particularly confirms "the high correlations between the behaviors of people and their friends" in adolescence (Faris & Ennett, 2012, p. 371).

But to a far greater extent in adolescence, peers contribute to and reinforce identity development as "identity building is highly connected to a sense of belonging to social groups" (Genner & Süss, 2017, p. 6). Adolescents are socialized to behave akin to members of their peer groups but whereas "adolescent friends do influence one another, but those influences are complex" (Arnett, 2015, p. 97):

> Although the influence of friends in adolescence is often assumed to be negative, tending toward violations of the socialization outcomes of self-regulation and conforming to authority figures (e.g., toward illicit substance use), in fact, adolescent friends tend to reinforce their preexisting similarities.... That is, adolescent friends who have a tendency toward deviant behavior encourage each other toward such deviance, whereas adolescent friends who tend to follow the rules reinforce that tendency in each other.... (p. 97)

In the negative sense, "peers are a major influence in the development of antisocial behavior" (Sijtsema & Lindenberg, 2018, p. 140). First, peers can contribute to bullying and moral disengagement by "corroborating and reinforcing" the views of adolescents who already see "the world as a dangerous and uncaring place" (Hyde et al., 2010, p. 199). Consequently, adolescents may be drawn to friendships and cliques that enact and model aggressive behavior. "As a result, friends may resemble each other in overall levels of aggression and share targets of aggression toward specific peers"; moreover, "bullying might not only be useful for gaining status and power, but also for creating a sense of belonging between children who bully" (Salmivalli, 2010, p. 116). And yet, peers also can be positive influences, even supporting each other when standing up to and defending victims of bullying, "and might thus encourage each others' prosocial behaviors and serve as positive models to each other" (p. 116). Research simply does not support the stereotype of peer groups as only antisocial.

Along with peers, forms of media—television, video games, music, and social media—affect perceptions, emotions, beliefs, and behaviors (Prot et al., 2015, p. 276). Media influence older children's and adolescents' identity exploration and development. Social media intensify "a sense of belonging to social groups" and "peer demands" (Genner, & Süss, 2017, pp. 5, 6). In addition, there is an interrelated relationship of peers and social media and the lines between media producers and users have become increasingly blurred" (p. 3) as media experiences have become more synergistic. Yet, the role of media in socialization "depends on the interplay of a wide range of influences" including families, friends, the context, and motivations for why children and adolescents engage in media (Genner, & Süss, 2017, p. 2). Although media remains a socialization agent, some young people are "resilient" and "deal better with negative media effects" (Genner, & Süss, 2017, p. 10) whereas those who are "more socially isolated" especially turn to social media to the point of having a "behavioral addiction" (Boniel-Nissim & Sasson, 2018, p. 176) even though they do not experience emotional fulfillment by doing so (Ballarotto et al., 2021, p. 1). Notwithstanding, young people are not just passive media consumers; "they actively construct an understanding of the world through interactions with their social and cultural environment, of which media are part" (Genner, & Süss, 2017, pp. 4–5).

As in the case of peer influences, "media effects are complex" (Prot et al., 2015, p. 291) and the use of media is "associated with both prosocial and aggressive behaviors" (Padilla-Walker et al., 2020, p. 181). Prosocial media provide examples of helping behaviors and caring role models (Greitemeyer, 2022, p. 136) and contribute to non-stereotypical gender characterizations

(Prot et al., 2015, p. 287). However, a predominance of research focuses on media as a negative influence by provoking aggression and encouraging stereotypical gendered and racial views (Chakroff & Nathanson, 2008, p. 552; Prot et al., 2015, p. 283). Researchers suggest that violent television shows affect children's moral reasoning (Bajovic, 2013, p. 177) and prolonged playing of violent video games "activate one or more mechanisms of moral disengagement" (Bussey, 2020, p. 312) as young people become "desensitized to violence" and have diminished empathic responses to those in need (Brockmyer, 2013, pp. 3, 9). As noted above, moral disengagement affects the ability to care about one's victims and is a factor in bullying; but with "the possibilities of anonymity, publicity, and the mass dissemination of messages or other types of audiovisual content," cyberbullying "can contribute to certain abuses being committed that would not be committed in face-to-face situations" (Cuadrado-Gordillo & Fernández-Antelo, 2019, p. 3).

Parents also have a role to play regarding media socialization influences. When parents monitor media exposure, they can lessen modeling of aggression and encourage prosocial actions (Padilla-Walker et al., 2020, p. 181). There are, however, different types of monitoring: *restrictive* and *active*. Restrictive mediation "involves regulating children's access to certain content or limiting their time spent with media" (Meeus et al., 2018, p. 270). But as an unintended consequence, children and adolescents may "resist high levels of parental restrictions" and form "less positive attitudes" towards their parents—sometimes intensified by "a significant disparity in knowledge and practical skills between [parents] and their children when it comes to new forms of media" (p. 271). In describing active monitoring or mediation, researchers emphasize the role of parents and teachers in "fostering resilience" by attending to media's portrayal of violence and stereotypes (Genner, & Süss, 2017, p. 10) and helping young people to become "more critical consumers of media content" (Fikkers et al., 2017, p. 407). To avoid an authoritarian approach that could provoke resistance, parents and educators should ensure that young people are "actively involved in conversations regarding media use and effects" (Padilla-Walker et al., 2020, p. 195). Such conversations provide opportunities for children to develop reflective capacities and for parents and children to "practice their agency as interacting partners" (Kuczynski et al., 2014, p. 141) as they learn from each others' perspectives.

References

Albaiz, N. E., & Ernest, J. M. (2015). Between kindergartners' stickers and adolescents' fancy cars: How to build an autonomous generation. *Childhood Education, 91*(5), 342–350.

Arieli, S., & Sagiv, L. (2018). Culture and problem-solving: Congruency between the cultural mindset of individualism versus collectivism and problem type. *Journal of Experimental Psychology: General, 147*(6), 789.

Arnett, J. J. (2015). Socialization in emerging adulthood: From the family to the wider world, from socialization to self-socialization. In J. E. Grusec & P. D. Hastings (Eds.), *Handbook of socialization: Theory and research* (pp. 85–108). The Guilford Press.

Bajovic, M. (2013). Violent video gaming and moral reasoning in adolescents: Is there an association?. *Educational Media International, 50*(3), 177–191.

Ballarotto, G., Volpi, B., & Tambelli, R. (2021). Adolescent attachment to parents and peers and the use of Instagram: The mediation role of psychopathological risk. *International Journal of Environmental Research and Public Health, 18*(8). https://doi.org/10.3390/ijerph18083965

Bandura, A. (1977). *Social learning theory.* Prentice-Hall.

Bandura, A. (2016). *Moral disengagement: How people do harm and live with themselves.* Worth Publishers.

Barni, D., Ranieri, S., Scabini, E., & Rosnati, R. (2011). Value transmission in the family: Do adolescents accept the values their parents want to transmit?. *Journal of Moral Education, 40*(1), 105–121.

Baumrind, D. (2012). Differentiating between confrontive and coercive kinds of parental power-assertive disciplinary practices. *Human Development, 55*(2), 35–51.

Berkowitz, M. W., & Grych, J. H. (1998). Fostering goodness: Teaching parents to facilitate children's moral development. *Journal of Moral Education, 27*(3), 371–391.

Bloom, P. (2013). *Just babies: The origins of good and evil.* Crown/Random House.

Boniel-Nissim, M., & Sasson, H. (2018). Bullying victimization and poor relationships with parents as risk factors of problematic internet use in adolescence. *Computers in Human Behavior, 88,* 176–183.

Brint, S., Contreras, M. F., & Matthews, M. T. (2001). Socialization messages in primary schools: An organizational analysis. *Sociology of Education,* 157–180.

Brockmyer, J. F. (2013). Media violence, desensitization, and psychological engagement. In K. E. Dill (Ed.), *The Oxford handbook of media psychology* (pp. 212–222). Oxford University Press.https://doi.org/10.1093/oxfordhb/9780195398809.013.0012

Bryant, L. C., Vincent, R., Shaqlaih, A., & Moss, G. (2013). Behaviour and behavioural learning theory. In B. Irly, G. H. Brown, R. Lara-Alecio, & S. Jackson (Eds.), *The handbook of educational theories* (pp. 91–104). Information Age Publishing.

Bussey, K. (2020). Development of moral disengagement. *The Oxford handbook of moral development: An interdisciplinary perspective*, 306–326. https://doi.org/10.1093/oxfordhb/9780190676049.013.17

Campaert, K., Nocentini, A., & Menesini, E. (2017). The efficacy of teachers' responses to incidents of bullying and victimization: The mediational role of moral disengagement for bullying. *Aggressive Behavior, 43*(5), 483–492.

Caravita, S., Sijtsema, J. J., Rambaran, J. A., & Gini, G. (2014). Peer influences on moral disengagement in late childhood and early adolescence. *Journal of Youth and Adolescence, 43*(2), 193–207.

Carpendale, J. I. M. (2009). Piaget's theory of moral development. In U. Müller, J. I. M. Carpendale, & L. Smith (Eds.), *The Cambridge companion to Piaget* (pp. 270–286). Cambridge University Press.

Chakroff, J. L., & Nathanson, A. I. (2008). Parent and school interventions: Mediation and media literacy. *The handbook of children, media, and development*, 552–576.

Churchland, P. (2019). *Conscience: The origins of moral intuition.* WW Norton & Company.

Cuadrado-Gordillo, I., & Fernández-Antelo, I. (2019). Analysis of moral disengagement as a modulating factor in adolescents' perception of cyberbullying. *Frontiers in Psychology, 10*, 1–12. https://doi.org/10.3389/fpsyg.2019.01222

Damon, W. (1990). *The moral child: Nurturing children's natural moral growth.* Free Press.

Dreikurs, R. (1958). The cultural implications of reward and punishment. *International Journal of Social Psychiatry, 4*(3), 171–178.

Eisenberg, N., Eggum-Wilkens, N. D., & Spinrad, T. L. (2015). The development of prosocial behavior. In D. A. Schroeder & W. G. Graziano (Eds.), *The Oxford handbook of* prosocial *behavior* (pp. 114–136). Oxford University Press.

Espelage, D. L., Holt, M. K., & Henkel, R. R. (2003). Examination of peer–group contextual effects on aggression during early adolescence. *Child Development, 74*(1), 205–220.

Essler, S., & Paulus, M. (2021). When do caregivers begin to view their child as a moral agent? Comparing moral and non-moral reactions to young children's moral transgressions. *Journal of Moral Education, 50*(3), 330–342.

Faris, R., & Ennett, S. (2012). Adolescent aggression: The role of peer group status motives, peer aggression, and group characteristics. *Social Networks, 34*(4), 371–378.

Frank, L. K. (1956). Social systems and culture. In R. R. Grinker (Ed.), *Toward a unified theory of human behavior.* Basic Books.

Georgiou, S. N., & Stavrinides, P. (2013). Parenting at home and bullying at school. *Social Psychology of Education, 16*(2), 165–179.

Genner, S., & Süss, D. (2017). Socialization as media effect. In P. Rössler (Ed.), *The international encyclopedia of media effects.* Wiley-Blackwell. https://doi.org/10.1002/9781118783764.wbieme0138

Gershoff, E. T. (2013). Spanking and child development: We know enough now to stop hitting our children. *Child Development Perspectives, 7*(3), 133–137.

Greitemeyer, T. (2022). Prosocial modeling: person role models and the media. *Current Opinion in Psychology, 44*, 135–139.

Grusec, J. E. (2019). Domains of socialization. In D. J. Laible, G. Carlo, L. M. Padilla-Walker (Eds.), *The Oxford handbook of parenting and moral development* (pp. 72–90). Oxford University Press.

Grusec, J. E., Chaparro, M. P., Johnston, M., & Sherman, A. (2014). The development of moral behavior from a socialization perspective. In M. Killen & J. G. Smetana (Eds.), *Handbook of moral development* (pp. 113–134). Psychology Press.

Grusec, J. E., & Davidov, M. (2021). *Socializing children.* Cambridge University Press.

Grusec, J. E., Danyliuk, T., Kil, H., & O'Neill, D. (2017). Perspectives on parent discipline and child outcomes. *International Journal of Behavioral Development, 41*(4), 465–471.

Güss, C. D., & Robinson, B. (2014). Predicted causality in decision making: the role of culture. *Frontiers in Psychology, 5*(479), 1–4.

Haidt, J. (2012). *The righteous mind: Why good people are divided by politics and religion.* Pantheon Books.

Hall, E. T. (1973). *The silent language.* Anchor Press/Doubleday.

Hall E. T. (1976). *Beyond culture.* Anchor Books/Doubleday.

Haste, H., & Abrahams, S. (2008). Morality, culture and the dialogic self: Taking cultural pluralism seriously. *Journal of Moral Education, 37*(3), 377–394.

Holden, G. W., Vittrup, B., & Rosen, L. H. (2011). Families, parenting, and discipline. In M. K. Underwood & L. H. Rosen (Eds.), *Social development: Relationships in infancy, childhood, and adolescence* (pp. 127–152). Guilford Press.

Hollan, D. (2012). Cultures and their discontents: On the cultural mediation of shame and guilt. *Psychoanalytic Inquiry, 32*(6), 570–581.

Howell, C. (2005). Democratic education and social learning theory. *Philosophy of Education 2005*, 161–170.

Hyde, L. W., Shaw, D. S., & Moilanen, K. L. (2010). Developmental precursors of moral disengagement and the role of moral disengagement in the development of antisocial behavior. *Journal of Abnormal Child Psychology, 38*(2), 197–209.

Hymel, S., & Bonanno, R. A. (2014). Moral disengagement processes in bullying. *Theory into Practice, 53*(4), 278–285.

Jensen, L. A. (2008). Through two lenses: A cultural–developmental approach to moral psychology. *Developmental Review, 28*(3), 289–315.

Jensen, L. A. (2015). Theorizing and researching moral development in a global world. In L. A. Jensen (Ed.), *The Oxford handbook of human development and culture: An interdisciplinary perspective* (pp. 1–19). Oxford Library of Psychology.

Kish, A., & Newcombe, P. (2015). "Smacking never hurt me!" Identifying myths surrounding the use of corporal punishment. *Personality and Individual Differences, 87,* 121–129.

Kuczynski, L., Parkin, C. M., & Pitman, R. (2014). Socialization as dynamic process. In J. E. Grusec & P. D. Hastings (Eds.), *Handbook of socialization: Theory and research* (pp. 135–157). Guilford Publications.

Kuhmerker, L. (1976). Social interaction and the development of a sense of right and wrong in young children. *Journal of Moral Education, 5*(3), 257–264.

Kunkel, A., Hummert, M. L., & Dennis, M. R. (2005). Social learning: Modeling and communication in the family context. In D. O. Braithwaite & L. A. Baxter (Eds.), *Engaging theories in family communication: Multiple perspectives* (pp. 260–275). Sage.

Laible, D. J., Karahuta, E., Van Norden, C., Interra, V., & Stout, W. (2019). The socialization of children's moral understanding in the context of everyday discourse. *The Oxford handbook of parenting and moral development* (pp. 287–300). Oxford University Press.

Lansford, J. E. (2010). The special problem of cultural differences in effects of corporal punishment. *Law and Contemporary Problems, 73*(2), 89–106.

Lapsley, D. K. (2006). Moral stage theory. In M. Killen & J. Smetana (Eds.), *Handbook of moral development* (pp. 37–66). Lawrence Erlbaum.

Lynn, S., Carroll, A., Houghton, S., & Bower, J. M. (2019). Emotion socialization in peer groups. *The encyclopedia of child and adolescent development* (pp. 1–12). Wiley.

Mattingly, C., & Throop, J. (2018). The anthropology of ethics and morality. *Annual Review of Anthropology, 47,* 475–492.

Mead, M. (1971). Guilt, ritual, and culture: Some anthropological considerations concerning guilt. In R. W. Smith (Ed.), *Guilt: Man and society* (pp. 117–134). Doubleday.

Meeus, A., Beyens, I., Geusens, F., Sodermans, A. K., & Beullens, K. (2018). Managing positive and negative media effects among adolescents: Parental mediation matters—but not always. *Journal of Family Communication, 18*(4), 270–285.

Mounts, N. S., & Allen, C. (2019). Parenting styles and practices. In D. J. Laible, G. Carlo, & L. M. Padilla-Walker, *The Oxford handbook of parenting and moral development.* Oxford University Press. https://doi.org/10.1093/oxfordhb/9780190638696.013.4

Murphy, T. P., Laible, D., & Augustine, M. (2017). The influences of parent and peer attachment on bullying. *Journal of Child and Family Studies, 26*(5), 1388–1397.

Nucci, L. P. (1989). Challenging conventional wisdom about morality: The domain approach to values education. In L. P. Nucci (Ed.), *Moral development and character education: A dialogue* (pp. 183–203). McCutcheon.

Nucci, L. (2006). *Classroom management for moral and social development.* In C. M. Evertson & C. S. Weinstein (Eds.), *Handbook of classroom management: Research, practice, and contemporary issues* (pp. 711–731). Lawrence Erlbaum.

Padilla-Walker, L. M., Stockdale, L. A., Son, D., Coyne, S. M., & Stinnett, S. C. (2020). Associations between parental media monitoring style, information management, and prosocial and aggressive behaviors. *Journal of Social and Personal Relationships, 37*(1), 180–200.

Pillutla, M. M. (2011). When good people do wrong: Morality, social identity, and ethical behavior. *Social Psychology and Organizations,* 353–368.

Prot, S., Anderson, C. A., Gentile, D. A., Warburton, W., Saleem, M., Groves, C. L., & Brown, S. C. (2015). Media as agents of socialization. In J. E. Grusec, & P. D. Hastings (Eds.), *Handbook of socialization: Theory and research* (2nd ed.; pp. 276–300). Guilford Press.

Salmivalli, C. (2010). Bullying and the peer group: A review. *Aggression and Violent Behavior, 15*(2), 112–120.

Sherblom, S. A. (2015). A moral experience feedback loop: Modeling a system of moral self-cultivation in everyday life. *Journal of Moral Education, 44*(3), 364–381.

Sijtsema, J. J., & Lindenberg, S. M. (2018). Peer influence in the development of adolescent antisocial behavior: Advances from dynamic social network studies. *Developmental Review, 50,* 140–154.

Simons, D. A., & Wurtele, S. K. (2010). Relationships between parents' use of corporal punishment and their children's endorsement of spanking and hitting other children. *Child Abuse & Neglect, 34*(9), 639–646.

Singer, M. G. (2002). *The ideal of rational morality: Philosophical compositions.* Oxford University Press.

Skinner, B. F. (1953). *Science and human behavior.* Free Press.

Skinner, B. F. (1971). *Beyond freedom and dignity.* Knopf.

Smetana, J. G. (1999). The role of parents in moral development: A social domain analysis. *Journal of Moral Education, 28*(3), 311–321.

Smetana, J. G., Ball, C. L., & Yoo, H. N. (2019). Parenting and moral development. In M. H. Bornstein (Ed.) *Handbook of parenting, Vol 5: The practice of parenting* (3rd ed.; pp. 122–155). Routledge.

Tappan, M. (2006) Moral functioning as mediated action, *Journal of Moral Education, 35*(1), 1–18.

Thompson, R. A. (2012). Whither the preconventional child? Toward a life-span moral development theory. *Child Development Perspectives, 6*(4), 423–429.

Troutman, B. (2015). Viewing parent-child interactions through the lens of behaviorism. In B. Troutman (Ed.), *Integrating behaviorism and attachment theory in parent coaching* (pp. 3–20). Springer.

Turiel, E. (1983). *Development of social knowledge.* Cambridge University Press.

Turiel, E. (2014). Morality: Epistemology, development, and social opposition. In M. Killen & J. G. Smetana (Eds.), *Handbook of moral development* (2nd ed.; pp. 3–22). Psychology Press.

Turiel, E. (2015). Moral development. In R. M. Lerner, W. F. Overton, & P. C. Molenaar (Eds.), *Handbook of child psychology and developmental science* (7th ed., pp. 484–522). Wiley.

Turiel, E., & Dahl, A. (2019). The development of domains of moral and conventional norms, coordination in decision-making, and the implications of social opposition. In N. Roughley & K. Bayertz (Eds.), *The normative animal? On the anthropological significance of social, moral, and linguistic norms* (pp. 195–213). Oxford University Press.

Van IJzendoorn, M. H. (1997). Attachment, emergent morality, and aggression: Toward a developmental socioemotional model of antisocial behaviour. *International Journal of Behavioral Development, 21*(4), 703–728.

Vinik, J., Johnston, M., Grusec, J. E., & Farrell, R. (2013). Understanding the learning of values using a domains-of-socialization framework. *Journal of Moral Education, 42*(4), 475–493.

Wainryb, C., & Recchia, H. (2014). Moral lives across cultures: Heterogeneity and conflict. In M. Killen & J. G. Smetana (Eds.), *Handbook of moral development* (2nd ed.; pp. 259–278). Psychology Press.

Walker, L. J. (1999). The family context for moral development. *Journal of Moral Education, 28*(3), 261–264.

Wallace, A. F. C. (1961) *Culture and personality*. Random House.

Watson, M. (2008). Developmental discipline and moral education. In L. P. Nucci, & D. Narvaez (Eds.) *Handbook of moral and character education* (pp. 175–203). Routledge.

5

Moral Socialization and School Culture

The notion of culture as shared ways of making sense reveals the action patterns and underlying assumptions in the conduct of educational practice that otherwise might go unnoticed, or they might be dismissed as trivial because they are so commonplace.

—Frederick Erickson, 1987, "Conceptions of School Culture: An Overview," p. 23

Although the family is the primary moral teacher with peers and media contributing to the development of moral beliefs and behaviors, schooling also has a role in moral socialization. Schools overtly promote values that involve "judgments based on a notion of what is good and what is bad" (Veugelers & Vedder, 2003, p. 379) as is deemed right and proper by culture and society—exposing students to notions of morality throughout their daily experiences. As well, there are cultural patterns of beliefs and behaviors that may be implicit, deeply ingrained, and unquestioned.

Moral socialization in schools is a process for transmitting "moral and ethical traits and standards" (Zajda, 2014, pp. 836). Schools cultivate moral values, those that provide "a prescriptive understanding of how individuals

Teaching for Moral Imagination, pages 91–114

ought to behave toward each other" (Smetana, 1999, p. 312), through moral instruction and school culture (Brint et al., 2001; Cohen et al., 2009; Jackson, Boostrom, & Hansen, 1993). Scholars write that "one cannot involve children in schooling from the time they are six until they are 17 or 21 and not affect the way they think about moral issues and the way they behave" (Purpel & Ryan, 1975, p. 662). Likewise, educators "cannot help influencing moral growth and it is absurd to insist that we should not do what we cannot help doing" (Barrow, 1975, p. 199).

To interrogate purposeful as well as inadvertent classroom and school practices that contribute to moral socialization, we turn primarily to the fields of curriculum studies, educational psychology, anthropology, and sociology to explore these questions:

- How does moral socialization take place in classrooms and schools?
- What is the role of discipline in moral socialization?
- In what ways do school cultures convey values and norms?

Such questions allow us to contemplate the myriad of moral messages and standards upheld by teachers and administrators as well as the moral repercussions of adults' relationships with students, students' interactions with each other, and the social environments of classrooms and schools. However, as required for moral imagination, we need to reflect critically about how socialization efforts and school cultures can impede moral development if we are to envision classrooms and schools as moral communities.

Moral Socialization and Schooling

Studies of moral socialization in schooling inform us that "education has always been about more than simply the development of students' basic academic knowledge and skills" (Battistich, 2010, p. 115) and that major purposes of schooling include the transmission of cultural "attitudes, beliefs, and behaviors" through "direct and overt and/or subtle, insidious, and unconscious" means (Saldana, 2013, p. 228). Through the socialization process, schools may impart "national identity and culture" (O'Flaherty & Mccormack, 2022, p. 6), national values such as "individualism and achievement" (Brint et al., 2001) or "social harmony" (Yang, et al., 2013), as well as beliefs about codes of conduct. Researchers posit that schools validate "behavior that is permissible and desirable" (Brint et al., 2001, p. 161), "existing patterns of social relations" (Johnson, 1982, p. 32), and political socialization for citizenship (Althof & Berkowitz, 2006; Wiseman et al., 2011).

Scholars emphasize that moral socialization, "a multifaceted process" for transmitting social norms (Zajda, 2014, pp. 835), is "a largely covert operation" (Kapferer, 1981, p. 258) taking place "through the natural and everyday features of school life" (Margolis et al., 2001, p. 7). "Embedded in the curriculum and teachers' activities with students," moral values are not always explicit (Veugelers, 2021, p. 113) but implicitly "imparted by the classroom and school environment" (Cornbleth, 1984, p. 29) and through "interaction in the classroom" (Brint et al., 2001, p. 161). This implicit curriculum expresses "both social and cultural norms" and is "replicated from one generation to the next" (Brownwell, 2017, p. 211).

Moral socialization in schooling often is described as "teaching children how to behave, work together cooperatively, and to have important prosocial or morally acceptable attitudes" (Copp, 2016, p. 156). Such studies depict children's school experience as a transition between the world of childhood and working adulthood, "beginning with children just leaving their (particularistic) families and ending with the (universalistic) preparation of adults just ready to participate in our industrial, bureaucratic sociocultural system" (Johnson, 1982, p. 33).

> For most children, entry into school marks the initial encounter with large and complex social organizations, with their attendant rules, norms, and procedures; where most people are strangers (at least initially); and where relationships are based largely on social roles and pursuit of common goals rather than affective bonds. (Battistich, 2010, p. 115)

In that way, "school settings are relatively unique in their focus on specific skills that are central to children's future roles as citizens and workers" (Wentzel, 2015, p. 251). From this viewpoint, children also learn that cooperation is necessity for achievement and productivity, but this aim conveys a social rather than a moral value as it has little to do with caring and empathy.

When investigating socialization messages in elementary schools, researchers find that teachers frequently tell students to "stay on task, finish on time, work faster, and the like"; these classroom communications echo the "strong cultural norm of schooling as preparation for the workplace" (Joseph et al., 2011, pp. 44–45) and "support the conclusions of sociologists who have argued that schools as performance-oriented bureaucracies have fundamental interests in order and effort" (Brint et al., 2001, p. 161). The values taught in a preponderance of schools "overlap nicely with the requirements of an economic system that values a compliant and industrious work force" (Purpel, 1999, p. 89), emphasizing "an achievement value orientation" (Johnson, 1982, p. 33) and accepting "as proper and normal for schools to train individuals for competition and to foster their sense of worth within a system of rewards" (Joseph, et al., p. 45). Therefore, scholars question schooling as a moral influence for cooperative and sympathetic behavior when achievement is the dominant motif (Stewart, 1974).

In the literature about school socialization, one viewpoint is that schools may lack a conscious "clearly defined set of socialization goals," especially in public schools "that cater to heterogenous groups" holding different values and goals for education; at times then, socialization efforts can be "haphazard, uncoordinated, and unfocused" (Kapferer, 1981, p. 259). By contrast, studies of religious schools illustrate "moral socialization as an unequivocal goal" (Tuastad, 2016, p. 70) as they aim to "'socialize students into the conventions, values, attitudes and ways of perceiving the world that are shared by one's family, faith community, society and culture" (Johnson & Johnson, 2010, p. 827). In faith-based schools, explicit instruction draws from sacred texts and traditional practices with the intention of transmitting moral beliefs and practices from generation to generation (Boland, 2000; Woocher & Woocher, 2014) and to "provide an environment in which [religious] practices and teachings... could be incorporated into everyday learning" (Hussain & Read, 2015, p. 558). A key rationale for parents in choosing a faith-based school for their children is religious socialization and the maintenance of religious identity (Hussain & Read, 2015, p. 561; Samson, 2018, p. 233; Woocher & Woocher, 2014) as parents want schools "to provide an education congruent with their beliefs" (Carper & Layman, 2002). Religious schools allow for "coherence between the tradition in which the children are nurtured in the family and in which they are taught in school" (De Ruyter, 1999, p. 223). Moreover, these schools may also accentuate "character building" (Bryk et al., 1993, p. 134) or "concern about the kind of person that each student becomes" (p. 97) and desire "to translate the knowledge of morality into daily life" (Efron, 1996, p. 6). But despite the emphasis on religion, studies of faith-based schools suggest that socialization efforts are more expansive; children in religious schools also are socialized to live in the wider society and for citizenship (Cross et al., 2018, p. 28; Hussain & Read, 2015, p. 566; Tuastad, 2016, p. 66).

Still, scholars critique aspects of school socialization theories for "not explaining how individuals learn what" (Bowles & Gintis, 2002, p. 12). For example, the process of socialization for citizenship and "how this actually happens through schools is still not well understood" despite a great deal of studies that demonstrate that "citizenship production is a central task of nation-states" (Wiseman et al., 2011, p. 562). Also, as schooling is just one agent of socialization and the values emphasized in schooling may or may not coincide with parents' morality, researchers inform us that schooling's sway over students' attitudes, beliefs, and behaviors should not be viewed in isolation from family and peers. To what extent schooling "refines and reinforces skills and values learned at home" cannot be determined (Wentzel, 2015, p. 266) nor do researchers fully understand the role of peers in the schooling socialization process (p. 267).

Finally, an insightful criticism of school socialization theory is that it places "the individual in an entirely passive role" (Bowles & Gintis, 2002):

> a mere receptacle of the content of socialization, rather than an active participant in the process. For this reason, socialization theory appears to be incompatible with widely accepted notions of human agency that stress our rationality, intelligence, and capacity to make choices that are informed by knowledge of the consequences of such choices for achieving goals. (p. 12)

But research also suggests that conformity to dominant social values is not necessarily the outcome of schooling. "Individuals with more schooling are substantially more likely to hold liberal values than those with less schooling" (Pallas, 2000, p. 517) because "schooling is a broadening activity," encouraging students to consider a wider range of values "beyond those observed in their own families of immediate surroundings" (p. 518). Schools also can socialize students to become more accepting and tolerant and "less prejudiced against ethnic minorities" (Hello et al., 2004, p. 253). Besides, inculcation of values is not a certainty because "students may also actively accommodate and sometimes resist learning" (Orón Semper & Blasco, 2018, p. 482).

Undoubtedly, there are numerous avenues for studying moral socialization and schooling, but we should not to be content with simplistic explanations. Rather, we need to be aware of the multitude of values children and adolescents encounter in the process of moral socialization—some complementary and some discordant with families' values—and that young people become increasingly capable of critically reflecting on values and forging their own moral identities.

Moral Socialization and Discipline

A significant element of moral socialization in schooling is discipline. By analyzing the role of discipline in moral socialization efforts, we gain insight into beliefs about how schools can influence or control students' values and behavior. Moreover, as we discern rationales for discipline in classrooms and schools, we might question if scholarship on moral development and socialization informs educators' practices or if discipline stems from a "folk pedagogy" (Bruner, 1996, p. 49)—"deeply embedded cultural knowledge about education" (Joseph, 2011, p. 9)—that leads to acceptance of commonplace and deeply ingrained notions about children's needs and capabilities.

In a pragmatic sense, schools construct systems of discipline because "sheer numbers of children as well as their levels of immaturity make it necessary for teachers to exert control" (Watson, 2008, p. 183) and, for various reasons, misbehavior occurs (p. 189). But first and foremost, scholars contend that discipline supports moral socialization efforts and establishes the authority of adults (Arum & Way, 2005, p. 168). "Regulating pupils' behavior is an essential part of every day school life" by helping students to "acquire moral and social skills and teaching them to be good citizens" (Thornberg, 2009, p. 245). In fact, students themselves "expect schools to have rules governing moral transgressions" and "argue that it is wrong for schools or teachers to permit behaviors that result in harm to people" (Nucci, 2009, p. 66).

Schools create processes and rules to "limit the possibility of misbehavior or increase the probability of desired behavior" (Watson, 2008, p. 183). Rules define "appropriate behavior" including what it means to be a "good pupil" (Thornberg, 2009, pp. 251–252) and reflect "the social etiquette of the dominant culture which includes knowing what and when to raise particular issues" such as challenges to discrimination or racism (Castagno, 2008, p. 325). But scholars discern differences between rules and misconduct that "offend the core of school (and society's) moral foundations" and those that "are merely instrumental to an institution's smooth functioning" (Goodman, 2006, p. 214). In other words, discipline may either be related to moral socialization or to "serving school routines" (p. 219). However, when schools impart moral significance to all misbehavior, truly injurious conduct becomes equated with breaches that merely are inconsiderate or interfere with school routines (Boostrom, 1991, p. 221).

> When every rule is a moral obligation and every infraction elicits moral blame, students are poorly equipped to differentiate amongst wrongs—the administratively efficient from the morally injurious—and, in any case, will have little motivation to try, for morality is trivialized when so extended. (Goodman, 2006, p. 227)

By muddling violations of social norms and moral transgressions, rules and sanctions do not contribute to students' moral awareness.

So too, whereas educators have available a number of theoretical bases to draw from as foundations for systems of discipline in classrooms and schools, behaviorist theory can broadly influence schooling—leading educators to believe that they must exercise power over children by using rewards and punishments (Kamii, 1984, p. 12). "Most American schools marinate students in behaviorism" (Kohn, 1999, p. 91) as behaviorist beliefs and strategies are "rampant" in education and particularly in special education (Althoff & Berkowitz, 2013, p. 571); as well, "behavioral approaches" have been "widely employed and supported in the UK education system" (Woods, 2008, p. 182). In contrast, in Asian countries pupils tend to respect their teachers and educators there do not use behaviorist discipline and are not focused on "motivating their pupils and making them aware and attentive" (Postholm, 2013, p. 395).

Some scholars over time have taken a nuanced stance about rewards and punishments. For instance, moral philosopher, R. S. Peters (1962), asserted that children have "to learn to regulate their impulses" and "to understand that there are reasons for doing so" as they "develop a moral code of their own." The difficulty is that "in the early stages" of their moral learning, they are "incapable of appreciating what the real reasons for this are" (p. 49). He addressed this dilemma by examining the dichotomy between reason and habit, concluding that moral habits, such as adherence to rules such as prohibitions against harming others, lying, or stealing, ought to be impressed upon children because of the beneficial aspect of habits, especially when children are too little to understand reasons. Peters believed that eventually intrinsic, instead of extrinsic motivations will have the larger effect on the development of morality. For example, children who are persuaded to do the right thing because of a material reward or punitive action will eventually discover their own rewards for good deeds. Yet, he contemplated a paradox: Can intrinsic motivations develop without extrinsic motivations? Conversely, will moral development. become stunted at lower levels of moral functioning when children become dependent on extrinsic motivations?

Child psychoanalyst Bruno Bettelheim (1970) similarly recognized the problem to which Peters referred: how to teach children to become moral although they may be cognitively unprepared to understand reasons for morality. He explained that without the ability to postpone pleasure, children will not be particularly moral or have the motivation for learning. When children stay on the level of egotism, their self-interest alone is not enough to inspire learning, so caregivers must offer compelling incentives (p. 87). As caregivers and teachers, we want children to behave cooperatively, sympathetically, or minimally—to abstain from hurting others before they fully understand reasons for good behavior. Such positions imply that rewards and punishments may be resorted to only as temporary measures but cannot be the mainstay of discipline for moral socialization.

Nonetheless, behaviorist discipline is the most compatible with the experiences and training of teachers in school systems in which there are incentives for teachers to be "in control" and because "controlling teachers are considered more competent than autonomy-supportive teachers"; "accordingly, educators are not challenged to develop nor prepared to use forms of instruction that appeal to students' sense of autonomy and self-determined motivation" (Althoff & Berkowitz, 2013, p. 571). But while some research concludes that "behavioral approaches seem to increase on-task behavior among children with social, emotional and behavioral difficulties or with attention deficit hyperactivity disorder," the "benefits may quickly be lost once the intervention has ended" (Woods, 2008, p. 182).

Educators influenced by behaviorism often affirm "a basic principle that organisms tend to repeat behaviors that are followed by positive outcomes" so "rewards and praise are frequently used by teachers as a form of proactive control" (Watson, 2008, p. 186) in the belief that calling attention to prosocial behavior will encourage moral development. Schools employ rewards through the use of "stickers, candy, treats, additional privileges" (Moberly et al., 2005, p. 260) or tickets or tokens "that can be exchanged for tangible rewards or privileges" (Bear, 2013, p. 319). Positive reinforcement need not be expressed only by material rewards; teachers communicate their awareness of good behavior to students through compliments.

Some studies indicate that "there are few if any drawbacks from external reinforcement, particularly when it is verbal and linked to pupil competence" (Postholm, 2013, p. 392) while other research suggests that praise can "harm children's intrinsic motivation" and can "create pressure to continue performing well, discourage risk taking, and reduce perceived autonomy" (Henderlong & Lepper, 2002, p. 776). Some scholars view praise as manipulative—and perceived by students thusly—when used for "obtaining student compliance to adults' rules and behavioral expectations" (Bear et al., 2017, p. 77). Critics of behaviorism argue that praise and rewards "discourage children from judging for themselves what is right or wrong" (Kamii, 1984, p. 12) and warn that "moral actions must be done for moral reasons" as "praise deprives students of the opportunity to behave in positive ways because they understand that those ways are more helpful, more considerate, or more fair" (Watson, 2008, p. 187). Moreover, if educators' goals are to encourage students to create community and care about each other, giving rewards can mean that "children must compete for limited prizes" turning classmates into "rivals" (Watson, 2008, p. 187). Certainly, it is a very narrow view of human motivation to believe that children (or the adults they will become) will engage in prosocial or kind actions only to gain rewards (Kohn, 1999, p. 25).

The other facet of behaviorism is negative reinforcement or punishment. One thought-provoking definition of punishment is "harm purposefully done to someone who has caused harm as a response to the harm." As such, "its purpose may be retaliation, retribution, or to teach a lesson and thus reduce the probability of the person causing harm in the future" (Watson, 2008, p. 191). Sometimes a negative reinforcement involves penalties (such as demerits for lateness or fines for overdue library books) but many such sanctions "are administered for non-moral wrongs" and do not evoke "moral condemnation" (Goodman, 2006, p. 223). At other times, punishments are imposed in response to "moral violations" with the hope that "the recipient acknowledges culpability and experiences remorse" although some students may not care about censures and even "take pride in disobedience" so discipline has "a punitive intent, but no punitive effect" (p. 222).

Stemming from behaviorism, a disciplinary system adopted widely by classroom teachers in the United States, is *assertive discipline* (Moberly et al., 2005). This tactic accentuates both explicit instruction on expected behaviors and the consequences for misconduct: most likely "a maximum of five consequences beginning with a warning, followed by a timeout, and eventually calls to the parents and removal of students to the principal's office" (Canter, 1989, p. 58). Critics of assertive discipline note this system allows "no flexibility for children" who may need "encouragement rather than punishment' and that teachers become engaged in "manipulative relationships [with students] to meet [teachers] needs" (Robinson & Maines, 1994, pp. 198–199); they also point out the lack of systematic research about this method (Render et al., 1989, p. 616)

There are, however, other ways to view discipline. Psychologist Jean Piaget (1932/1965) delineated two types of discipline: *expiatory punishment* and *punishment by reciprocity*. Expiative forms of punishment are negative reinforcements such as traditional penalties for wrongdoing, e.g., detention or writing a phrase over and over. Such punishments "have no logical connection to the action and therefore provide little by way of information that would contribute to student social development" (Nucci, 2006, p. 721). Instead, Piaget preferred reciprocal punishment as it "has a natural or logical connection to the misdeed" (Barchard & Atkins, 1991, p. 109) by focusing on "restorative aspects of punishment and putting right what was done wrong" (Leman & Björnberg, 2010, p. 959); as a result, students can help repair inflicted damage or gain understanding of the consequences of their behavior.

Another established form of punishment is *exclusionary discipline*—considered a normal aspect of childrearing and schooling in Western nations but "not commonly used in all cultures" (Prochner & Hwang, 2008, p. 522). Exclusionary discipline in schools aims to isolate or "keep misbehaving students out of the classroom... or out of the school altogether" through in-school suspensions and expulsions (Perguero & Bracy, 2015, p. 414). These disciplinary practices, such as a time-out, have been considered a "safety net" for removing children from a fraught situation until they can regain self control or reflect on the consequences of their behavior. Yet, exclusionary discipline has painful repercussions: it "isolates children who have misbehaved and deprives them of peer interaction" (Goodman, 2006, p. 223); for adolescents, "being a recipient of school discipline may actually set students on a path toward educational disengagement and failure as a consequence of being disconnected from legitimate paths to success" (Perguero & Bracy, 2015, p. 414). "Most children seem to dislike enforced isolation—the forced withdrawal of social contact for a period of time"; it is "a kind of mock abandonment/banishment, teaching children that adults can regulate their relationship and arouses strong feelings in children" (Prochner & Hwang, 2008, p. 522).

Educators may see exclusionary discipline as a behavioral technique and even commonsensical—viewing isolation within and removal from the school as a natural consequence of misbehavior that affords safety for other students and educators. For these reasons, exclusionary punishment has become a mainstay of zero tolerance policies that operate regardless of students' "extenuating circumstances" or teachers' discretion (Walker & Snarey, 2004, p. 113). These policies "were initially implemented to respond to violent and serious behavioral issues" but have increasingly been applied to "even minor behavior infractions" (Hwang et al., 2022, p. 3). Once more, "zero tolerance policies do not offer students the strategies and services necessary to teach and promote school appropriate behavior" (Kline, 2016, p. 99). Overall, it is apparent that exclusionary discipline is extremely punitive and irrelevant to moral development.

Finally, *corporal punishment*—"the use of physical force with the intention of causing a child to experience bodily pain or discomfort so as to correct or punish a child's behavior" (Straus, 1994, p. 4)—generally remains outside of behaviorist learning theory. Rather, it "is deeply rooted in culture and religion" and "perceived as an acceptable and effective method of disciplining in order to teach children right from wrong" (Atiles et al., 2017, p. 9). Although illegal or discouraged in many contemporary schools and "despite research demonstrating that this means of discipline is not effective, it remains a common practice" (Albaiz & Ernest, 2015, p. 342)—allowed in more than one-third of nations (Gershoff, 2017, p. 225) and in more than one-third of schools in the United States, primarily in Southern and rural areas (Font & Gershoff, 2017, p. 408). Because of its widespread use and negative consequences, corporal punishment "has been the focus of increasing concern from researchers and policymakers around the world" (Gershoff, 2017, p. 224).

Corporal punishment is "a form of institutionalized violence against children" (Heekes et al., 2022, p. 52) manifest through hitting students with hands, wooden boards, and sticks on "every part of their bodies" (Gershoff, 2017, p. 224) and by "being forced to stand in painful positions, carry heavy objects, to kneel on small objects such as stones or rice, and to exercise excessively without rest or water—among other torments" (p. 225). Such discipline "has no long-term benefits" (Kaltenbach et al., 2018, p. 37) and "may interfere with children's learning" as "children avoid or dislike school because it is a place where they are in constant fear of being physically harmed by their teachers" (Gershoff, 2017, p. 232). Even when negative reinforcers halt misbehavior, there may be "long term consequences of punishment such as alienation from school, damage to self-esteem, and an increase in future misbehavior" (Althoff & Berkowitz, 2013, p. 571). More alarming, corporal punishment "carries multiple risks of harm" including "depressive disorders, suicide attempts, aggression, antisocial behavior, and substance abuse" and "may aggravate rather than eliminate behavioral problems in children" (Heekes et al., 2022, p. 52).

Additionally, from the perspective of constructivist learning theory, punitive discipline is detrimental to rational moral development.

> Piaget warned parents and teachers against the use of coercion and indoctrination as a means of moral education. Indoctrination reinforces the young child's natural tendency toward a heteronomous reliance on external regulation. Coercion can lead to rebellion, mindless submission, or calculation (where children are obedient and follow adult rules only when the adult is watching). (Hildebrandt & Zan, 2014, p. 355)

All in all, effective discipline involves "legitimacy and moral authority" and "what gives school discipline its efficacy is the degree to which students internalize rules as fair and just" (Arum & Way, 2005, p. 159).

However, disavowing conventional discipline strategies in no way means that educators relinquish their responsibility for responding to misconduct. While refraining from punitive and manipulative discipline, teachers would instead view discipline as a feature of the developmental process of moral socialization and understand their role in providing guidance; they would help students learn not only about the unacceptability of misbehavior but the consequences of "the harm they have caused" (Watson, 2008, p. 192). Furthermore, educators can still establish their moral presence and even convey "genuine moral outrage" (p. 194) so that students see them as human beings hurt or offended by cruel behavior and compassionate toward those who are harmed.

Scholars who write about growing children's moral understanding emphasize the concept of *induction*, involving "empathy, moral reasoning, and moral instruction" by "letting the misbehaving student try to repair harm caused" (Watson, 2008, p. 194). *Developmental discipline* is a related "conceptual framework" that respects children's need for autonomy (Flicker & Hoffman, 2002, p. 87) and rests on the principle that "when adults minimize the exercise of unnecessary authority, it opens up more possibilities for children to construct their own reasons and feelings of necessity about rules and other social relationships" (Hildebrandt & Zan, 2014, p. 355).

> Involving students in determining the guidelines and structures that, once established, will exert control is ideal from a developmental perspective. When students are involved in creating structures that facilitate the smooth functioning of the classroom their autonomy is honored and they are helped to understand why the rules and structures are necessary. (Watson, 2008, p. 184)

Although with very young children, teachers may need to "take full control in some areas in order to make room for autonomous learning in others" (Watson, 2008, p. 184), they gradually can share moral authority and decision-making—thereby empowering young people to take responsibility for their conduct (Arum & Way, 2005, p. 165). With the goal of moral development rather than control, rebuke, and retribution, educators can recast discipline as an opportunity for moral learning.

Culture and Schooling

For a more holistic understanding of moral socialization and schooling, we need to grasp the anthropological perspective that "education is deeply rooted in culture" (Hall, 1976, p. 205) and to "bother with the notion of culture when thinking about schools" (Erikson, 1987, p. 23). Researchers employ ethnographic methods to study intentional teaching of morality and to investigate the implicit curriculum of moral socialization, trying "to make these hidden values explicit and to analyze how they contribute to students' moral learning" (Veugelers, 2021, p. 113). "The concept of culture can be helpful as one tries to gain new and deeper understanding about the nature of daily life and instruction in schools" and culture affords a "a set of interpretative fames for making sense of behavior" (Erickson, 1987, p. 13).

But not only can we view moral socialization as an aspect of culture, scholars interpret schools as cultures. School culture refers to:

> . . . the underground stream of norms, values, beliefs, traditions, and rituals that has built up over time as people work together, solve problems, and confront challenges. This set of informal expectations and values shapes how people think, feel and act in schools. This highly enduring web of influence binds the school together and makes it special. (Glover & Coleman, 2005, p. 260)

These "shared beliefs and values closely knit a community together" and become "the lens through which participants view themselves and the world" (Schoen & Teddlie, 2008, p. 132). Scholars portray school culture as "the character of the school," an "unwritten curriculum" (Barr & Higgins-D'Alessandro, 2007, p. 234), and "the way we do things here" (Glover & Coleman, 2005, p. 260). In this vein, the transmission of values reflects the "normative structures, organizational processes, and nature of interpersonal relationships that characterize the school as a social organization" (Battistich, 2010, p. 115).

Another important construal of school culture is that it is not "a homogeneous or holistic entity that pervades and influences everyone within a school" but "the result of multiple interaction of sub-cultures" and "two-way interaction between school culture and sub-cultures" (Prosser, 1999, p. 14). Thus, school culture can be conceptualized as a "complex and dynamic set of relationships" (Glover & Coleman, 2005, p. 260) among various people, but is especially "associated with interpersonal relationships between teachers and students" (Barr & Higgins-D'Alessandro, 2007, p. 234). Likewise, as students participate in school culture, "they jointly and actively shape that culture" (Veugelers & Vedder, 2003, p. 382).

The idea of school culture "has its roots in anthropology and sociological traditions" (Prosser, 1999, p. 13). First, anthropological (or ethnographic) studies center on "knowledge, beliefs, values, customs, morals, rituals, symbols and language of a group" (Hargreaves, 1995, p. 25) and the "deep patterns of . . . traditions that have been formed over the course of [the school's] history" (Deal & Peterson, 1990, p. 7). Through cultural artifacts (Stoll, 1998, p. 10), educators "send strong signals about vision and values" (Jerald, 2006, p. 6). Second, researchers focus on schools as social organizations, the behaviors of people therein (p. 11), and the "micropolitics" involved in their interactions (p. 4). School culture, portrayed as organizational culture, refers to "the social glue that holds organizations together" or is "an umbrella term for inter-related subcultures" (p. 10). Some scholars believe that understanding of school culture is necessary for school reform (Erickson, 1987; Higgins-D'Alessandro & Sadh, 1998) as change is impossible without becoming aware of deeply ingrained values and patterns of behavior.

Studies of schooling also disclose various explicit and implicit moral socialization efforts. The landmark observational study, *The Moral Life of Schools* (Jackson, Boostrom, & Hansen, 1993), provides a guide for "looking for the moral" by illustrating occurrences of moral socialization in religious and public schools—ranging from explicit moral curriculum to visual displays in signs, posters, and showcases, to rituals and ceremonies within school culture. As well, this research takes into account teachers' spontaneous communication of values through interactions with students. Finally, this study encompasses values reflected in choices of curricular content—what is included and emphasized or excluded and ignored (see Table 5.1).

Another powerful way to gain insight into the culture of a school is to examine its rules and enactments of discipline for regulating student behavior, thereby exposing beliefs about the purposes of moral socialization as well as other values and norms of school culture.

TABLE 5.1 Looking for the Moral in Schooling

Explicit and Implicit Curriculum	Examples
Moral instruction as a formal part of the curriculum	Deliberate attempts to promote moral instruction through classes in religion and moral choices guided by religious doctrine
Moral instruction within the regular classroom	Lessons decidedly moral in tone, often dealing with real or legendary characters or role models
Rituals and ceremonies	Religious and civic rituals, assemblies, special programs, daily welcoming of students
Visual displays with moral content	Value-laden signs, decorations, posters, banners, bulletin boards, showcases
Classroom rules and regulations	Rules on conduct made by teachers or collaboratively with students, rewards for moral conduct, and punishments for ignoring rules
Spontaneous interjection of moral commentary into ongoing activity	Teachers responding to a breach of moral conduct, taking notice of good behavior, communicating judgments
Expressive morality	Responses to students' behavior through nonverbal communication, facial expressions of emotions and attitudes, gestures, body language
The morality of the curricular substructure	The organizing principal of curricular content, what becomes content and what is excluded, what is important, worthwhile, or fair and what is not

Source: Adapted from Jackson, Boostrom, Hansen, 1993, *The Moral Life of Schools*)

> The rules of the classroom embody a way of life. They put abstract aims of schooling into concrete patterns of daily activity. They are embraced as the way of school, so that to reject them is to reject the whole educational enterprise, and to contravene them is to move outside the pale.... This structuring is needed by all students, so that rules are not just for the unruly; they are a statement of obligations that hold for everyone. (Boostrom, 1991, p. 214)

By interviewing educators and students, ethnographers illuminate teachers' intentions behind their moral instructions (Thornberg, 2008, p. 53) and how students "make meaning of rules and teachers' expectations of appropriate behavior" (p. 58).

Such research often depicts the school as a "culture of control" (Welsh & Little, 2018, p. 766), interpreting it "as a key institution of social control" (Mowen et al., 2020, p. 740). While schools "ensure order and efficiency," they retain "an important custodial function, exercising considerable authority over students" even "suspending many of students' basic civil rights" (Saldana, 2013, p. 229). Portrayals of schools as cultures of control (historically and in contemporary times) likewise reveal control over teachers, enforcement of dominant societal norms, and political acquiescence. Although researchers note that in various nations, "teachers' perceptions of their relationship with the state are complicated" (Zhao, 2014, p. 161), analyses of the teaching profession illustrate that "teachers have only limited power and control over key decisions" including curricula and discipline policies (Ingersoll & Collins, 2017, pp. 80, 83). The "idea of an autonomous profession has been at odds with the model of the teacher as an obedient servant of authority" (Connell, 2009, p. 215). Additionally, the recent era of high-stakes testing and accountability has meant "greater control of teachers" (Osborn, 2006, p. 243) and "students and teachers being surveilled through test scores... promoting teaching and learning under constant threat and fear" (Au, 2020, p. 108).

So, too, numerous studies portray schools as "cultures of aggression" (Harger, 2019). Such cultures are hostile, prejudiced environments characterized by harsh and disproportionate punishment. In recent times, scholars "have documented that school discipline has become increasingly punitive" and refer to the "criminalization of school discipline" (Hirschfield, 2008) through exclusionary punishment and zero tolerance policies. Researchers also note that "intensification of disciplinary strategies may counterproductively increase offending behaviors" (Mowen et al., 2020, pp. 741) and that "school environments that are perceived as excessively punitive or unfair are more prone to disorder" (Preiss et al., 2016, p. 236). Such practices also lead to "deterioration in the broader school climate" and students' "heightened levels of anxiety and stress" (Mowen et al., 2020, pp. 739, 754). Moreover, "school suspension and exclusion can have a negative impact upon students' sense of social belonging and on their trust in school authority figures" (Graham et al., 2022, p. 2).

Cultures of aggression especially affect the lives and school experience of "students with disabilities, non-heterosexual youth, low-socioeconomic-status students, low-performing students, Black, Latinx, and male students" as it is these students who receive exclusionary punishment at higher rates than their peers (Rodriguez & Welsh, 2022, p. 1). Scholars conclude that "disparities in disciplinary outcomes are fairly consistent across all settings and grades… starting as early as preschool" (Welsh & Little, 2018, p. 752). In particular, high rates of disproportionality for African American students "have been widely documented" (Welsh & Little, 2018, p. 756) as have higher rates of receiving corporal punishment (Font & Gershoff, 2017, p. 413). So too, students from marginalized groups also are punished for non-serious offenses (Nese et al., 2021, p. 302).

Another reason for disproportionate discipline is that educators are likely to interpret student conduct through their own cultural lens and misread students' behaviors and intentions (Welsh & Little, 2018, p. 766). "Disparities in disciplinary outcomes may be better explained by the behavior of teachers and principals in schools rather than student characteristics such as misbehavior, poverty, or race" (Nese et al., 2021, p. 758). School leadership is another factor in disciplinary disparity and "rates of suspension are linked to principals' disciplinary philosophies" (p. 770). However, some current studies suggest that there has been growing awareness of the misuse of exclusionary punishment which has led to decreased rates of exclusionary discipline in United States schools (Hwang et al., 2022).

Some schools sanction aggression whether or not they emphasize punitive punishment; rather, they exist as "bullying cultures" (Migliaccio & Raskauskas, 2015). Bullying—described as physical or verbal assaults—is a "vicious kind of aggressive behavior distinguished by repeated acts against weaker victims" and "is characterized by a power imbalance" (Espelage & Hong, 2019, p. 47). Although the potent psychological factors of moral disengagement (Hymel & Bonanno, 2014) and prejudice (Thornberg, 2018) serve as catalysts for individuals to become bullies and to remain bystanders, schools can provide conditions that reinforce bullying—contributing to "the normalization" of aggression and domination (Harger, 2019, p. 1107).

> Bullying is larger than just the relationship between bully and victim. That relationship is embedded within layers of social forces that create the culture that generates the opportunity for bullying to occur. These social forces work together to produce, and reproduce a bullying culture by defining

and maintaining paths to power among students. (Migliaccio & Raskauskas, 2016, p. 30)

Although educators may intervene in various ways to halt instances of bullying and pervasive bullying, research suggests that their responses may be inconsistent and interventions may not be timely or morally instructive (Gutzwiller-Helfenfinger & Perren, 2022, p. 443).

When educators accept that bullying is a normal activity in school culture, "moral corrosion has definitely set in"—leaving teachers feeling "morally numb" and victimized students experiencing emotions of "helplessness and despair" (Gutzwiller-Helfenfinger & Perren, 2022, p. 445). In addition, researchers describe some schools as "toxic cultures" in which school leaders promulgate and tolerate "workplace incivility and bullying" (Mannix-McNamara et al., 2021, p. 12) that includes administrators' harassment of teachers and teacher-to-teacher bullying. As well, there are reports from various nations that show bullying of teachers by parents increasingly occurring in both public and private schools (Evans & Thompson, 2016; Henebery, 2019; Twemlow & Sacco, 2013). Clearly, cultures of aggression in schooling affect both children and adults.

In conclusion, educators need to examine existing moral socialization practices to discern if their efforts foster or hinder students' moral understanding and conduct. But not until they apprehend the potent force of culture can they create and sustain moral school environments. Formidable cultures of schooling—controlling, aggressive, and discriminatory—can abrogate the sincere attempts of individuals to nurture students' moral development and to develop moral communities. The first step for envisioning moral classrooms and schools is to become aware of existing patterns of culture and how they affect individuals, practices, and policies. By making culture "visible," it is possible that "what people have made they can change" (Erickson, 1987, p. 24).

References

Albaiz, N. E., & Ernest, J. M. (2015). Between kindergartners' stickers and adolescents' fancy cars: How to build an autonomous generation. *Childhood Education, 91*(5), 342–350.

Althof, W., & Berkowitz, M. W. (2006). Moral education and character education: Their relationship and roles in citizenship education. *Journal of Moral Education, 35*(4), 495–518.

Arum, R., & Way, S. (2005). School discipline and youth socialization. In R. Arum (Ed.), *Judging school discipline: The crisis of moral authority* (pp. 159–187). Harvard University Press.

Atiles, J. T., Gresham, T. M., & Washburn, I. (2017). Values and beliefs regarding discipline practices: How school culture impacts teacher responses to student misbehavior. *Educational Research Quarterly, 40*(3), 3–24.

Au, W. (2020). Testing for whiteness? How high-stakes, standardized tests promote racism, undercut diversity, and undermine multicultural education. In H. P. Baptiste & J. H. Writer (Eds.) *Visioning multicultural education: Past, present, future* (pp. 99–113). Routledge.

Barchard, K., & Atkins, C. (1991). Children's decisions about naughtiness and punishment: Dominance of expiatory punishments. *Journal of Research in Childhood Education, 5*(2), 109–115.

Barr, J. J., & Higgins-D'Alessandro, A. (2007). Adolescent empathy and prosocial behavior in the multidimensional context of school culture. *The Journal of Genetic Psychology, 168*(3), 231–250.

Barrow, R. (1975). *Moral philosophy for education.* George Allen & Unwin.

Battistich, V. (2010). School contexts that promote students' positive development. In J. L. Meece & J. S. Eccles (Eds.), *Handbook of research on schools, schooling, and human development* (pp. 111–127). Routledge.

Bear, G. G. (2013). Teacher resistance to frequent rewards and praise: Lack of skill or a wise decision?. *Journal of Educational and Psychological Consultation, 23*(4), 318–340.

Berkowitz, M. W. (2011). What works in values education. *International Journal of Educational Research, 50*(3), 153–158.

Bettelheim, B. (1970). Moral education. In N. F. Sizer & T. R. Sizer (Eds.), *Moral education/Five lectures.* Harvard University Press.

Boland, P. (2000). Catholic education in the 21st century. *Catholic Education: A Journal of Inquiry and Practice, 3*(4), 508–520.

Boostrom, R. (1991) The nature and functions of classroom rules. *Curriculum Inquiry, 21*(2), 193–216.

Bowles, S., & Gintis, H. (2002). Schooling in capitalist America revisited. *Sociology of Education, 75,* 1–18.

Brint, S., Contreras, M. F., & Matthews, M. T. (2001). Socialization messages in primary schools: An organizational analysis. *Sociology of Education, 74,* 157–180.

Brownell, C. J. (2017). Starting where you are, revisiting what you know: A letter to a first-year teacher addressing the hidden curriculum. *Journal of Curriculum and Pedagogy, 14*(3), 205–217.

Bruner, J. (1996). *The culture of education.* Harvard University Press.

Bryk, A. S., Lee, V. E., & Holland, P. B. (1993). *Catholic schools and the common good.* Harvard University Press.

Canter, L. (1989). Assertive discipline: More than names on the board and marbles in a jar. *Phi Delta Kappan, 71*(1), 57–61.

Carper, J. C., & Layman, J. (2002). Independent Cristian day schools: The maturing of a movement. *Journal of Catholic Education*, 5 (4), pp. 502–514.

Castagno, A. E. (2008). "I don't want to hear that!": Legitimating whiteness through silence in schools. *Anthropology & Education Quarterly*, *39*(3), 314–333.

Cohen, J., McCabe, E. M., Michelli, N. M., & Pickeral, T. (2009). School climate: Research, policy, practice, and teacher education. *Teachers College Record*, *111*(1), 180–213.

Copp, D. (2016). Moral education versus indoctrination. *Theory and Research in Education*, *14*(2), 149–167.

Cornbleth, C. (1984). Beyond hidden curriculum?. *Journal of Curriculum Studies*, *16*(1), 29–36.

Cross, G., Campbell-Evans, G., & Gray, J. (2018). Beyond the assumptions: Religious schools and their influence on students' social and civic development. *International journal of Christianity & Education*, *22*(1), 23–38.

De Ruyter, D. J. (1999). Christian schools in a pluralistic society?. *Interchange*, *30*(2), 213–233.

Deal, T. E., & Peterson, K. D. (1990). *The principal's role in shaping school culture*. U.S. Department of Education, Office of Educational Research and Improvement.

Efron, S. G. (1996). Jewish moral education and character education: A comparison. *Journal of Jewish Education*, *62*(1), 4–13.

Erickson, F. (1987). Conceptions of school culture: An overview. *Educational Administration Quarterly*, *23*(4), 11–24.

Espelage, D. L., & Hong, J. S. (2019). School climate, bullying, and school violence. In M. J. Mayer & S. R. Jimerson (Eds.), *School safety and violence prevention: Science, practice, policy* (pp. 45–69). American Psychological Association.

Evans, R., & Thompson, M. G. (2016). Parents who bully the school. *Independent School*, *75*(3). https://www.nais.org/magazine/independent-school/spring-2016/parents-who-bullyschool/

Flicker, E. S., & Hoffman, J. A. (2002). Developmental discipline in the early childhood classroom. *Young Children*, *57*(5), 82–89.

Font, S. A., & Gershoff, E. T. (2017). Contextual factors associated with the use of corporal punishment in US public schools. *Children and Youth Services Review*, *79*, 408–418.

Gershoff, E. T. (2017). School corporal punishment in global perspective: prevalence, outcomes, and efforts at intervention. *Psychology, Health & Medicine*, *22* (sup1), 224–239.

Glover, D., & Coleman, M. (2005). School culture, climate and ethos: interchangeable or distinctive concepts?. *Journal of In-service Education*, *31*(2), 251–272.

Goodman, J. F. (2006). School discipline in moral disarray. *Journal of Moral Education*, *35*(2), 213–230.

Graham, L. J., Gillett-Swan, J., Killingly, C., & Van Bergen, P. (2022). Does it matter if students (dis)like school? Associations between school liking, teacher and school connectedness, and exclusionary discipline. *Frontiers in Psychology, 13,* 1–13. https://doi.org/10.3389/fpsyg.2022.825036

Gutzwiller-Helfenfinger, E., & Perren, S. (2022). The moral dimensions of bullying at school: A social-ecological process perspective. In M. Killen & J. G. Smetana (Eds.), *Handbook of moral development* (3rd ed.; pp. 437–453). Routledge.

Hall, E. T. (1976). *Beyond culture.* Anchor Press/Doubleday.

Harger, B. (2019). A culture of aggression: School culture and the normalization of aggression in two elementary schools. *British Journal of Sociology of Education, 40*(8), 1105–1120.

Hargreaves, D. H. (1995). School culture, school effectiveness and school improvement. *School Effectiveness and School Improvement, 6*(1), 23–46.

Heekes, S. L., Kruger, C. B., Lester, S. N., & Ward, C. L. (2022). A systematic review of corporal punishment in schools: Global prevalence and correlates. *Trauma, Violence, & Abuse, 23*(1), 52–72.

Hello, E., Scheepers, P., Vermulst, A., & Gerris, J. R. (2004). Association between educational attainment and ethnic distance in young adults: Socialization by schools or parents?. *Acta Sociologica, 47*(3), 253–275.

Henebery, B. (2019). Bullying against teachers: what can be done? *The Educator Australia.* https://www.theeducatoronline.com/k12/news/bullying-against-teachers-what-can-be-done/264550

Higgins-D'Alessandro, A., & Sadh, D. (1998). The dimensions and measurement of school culture: Understanding school culture as the basis for school reform. *International Journal of Educational Research, 27*(7), 553–569.

Hildebrandt, C. L. N., & Zan, B. (2014). Constructivist approaches to moral education in early childhood. In L. Nucci & D. Narvaez (Eds.), *Handbook of moral and character education* (2nd ed.; pp. 352–369). Routledge.

Hirschfield, P. J. (2008). Preparing for prison? The criminalization of school discipline in the USA. *Theoretical Criminology, 12*(1), 79–101.

Hussain, S., & Read, J. N. G. (2015). Islamic schools in the United States and England: Implications for integration and social cohesion. *Social Compass, 62*(4), 556–569.

Hwang, N., Penner, E. K., Davison, M., Sanabria, T., Hanselman, P., Domina, T., & Penner, A. M. (2022). Reining in punitive discipline: Recent trends in exclusionary school discipline disparities. *Socius, 8,* 1–8.

Hymel, S., & Bonanno, R. A. (2014). Moral disengagement processes in bullying. *Theory into Practice, 53*(4) 278–285.

Jackson, P. W., Boostrom, R. E., & Hansen, D. T. (1993). *The moral life of schools.* Jossey-Bass.

Johnson, N. B. (1982). Education as environmental socialization: Classroom spatial patterns and the transmission of sociocultural norms. *Anthropological Quarterly, 55*(1) 31–43.

Joseph, P. B. (2011). Conceptualizing curriculum. In P. B. Joseph (Ed.), *Cultures of curriculum* (pp. 3–22). Routledge.

Joseph, P. B., Green, N. S., Mikel, E. R., & Windschitl, M. A. (2011). Narrowing the curriculum. In P. B. Joseph (Ed.), *Cultures of curriculum* (pp. 52–70). Routledge.

Kaltenbach, E., Hermenau, K., Nkuba, M., Goessmann, K., & Hecker, T. (2018). Improving interaction competencies with children—A pilot feasibility study to reduce school corporal punishment. *Journal of Aggression, Maltreatment & Trauma, 27*(1), 35–53.

Kamii, C. (1984). Obedience is not enough. *Young Children, 39*(4), 11–14.

Kapferer, J. L. (1981). Socialization and the symbolic order of the school. *Anthropology & Education Quarterly, 12*(4), 258–274.

Kline, D. M. S. (2016). Can restorative practices help to reduce disparities in school discipline data? A review of the literature. *Multicultural Perspectives, 18*(2), 97–102.

Kohn, A. (1999). *Punished by rewards: The trouble with gold stars, incentive plans, A's, praise, and other bribes.* Houghton Mifflin.

Leman, P. J., & Björnberg, M. (2010). Conversation, development, and gender: A study of changes in children's concepts of punishment. *Child Development, 81*(3), 958–971.

Mannix-McNamara, P., Hickey, N., MacCurtain, S., & Blom, N. (2021). The dark side of school culture. *Societies, 11*(3), 1–19. https://doi.org/10.3390/soc11030087

Margolis, E., Soldatenko, M., Acker, S., & Gair, M. (2001). Peekaboo: Hiding and outing the curriculum. In E. Margolis (Ed.), *The hidden curriculum in higher education* (pp. 1–20). Routledge.

Migliaccio, T., & Raskauskas, J. (2015). *Bullying as a social experience: Social factors, prevention and intervention.* Routledge.

Moberly, D. A., Waddle, J. L., & Duff, R. E. (2005). The use of rewards and punishment in early childhood classrooms. *Journal of Early Childhood Teacher Education, 25*(4), 359–366.

Mowen, T. J., Brent, J. J., & Boman IV, J. H. (2020). The effect of school discipline on offending across time. *Justice Quarterly, 37*(4), 739–760.

Nese, R. N., Nese, J. F., McCroskey, C., Meng, P., Triplett, D., & Bastable, E. (2021). Moving away from disproportionate exclusionary discipline: Developing and utilizing a continuum of preventative and instructional supports. *Preventing School Failure: Alternative Education for Children and Youth, 65*(4), 301–311.

Nucci, L. (2006). Classroom management for moral and social development. In C. M. Evertson & C. S. Weinstein (Eds.), *Handbook of classroom management* (pp. 721–742). Lawrence Erlbaum.

Nucci, L. P. (2009). *Nice is not enough: Facilitating moral development.* Pearson.

O'Flaherty, J., & Mccormack, O. (2022). Values education: the understanding of values across Irish educational legislation, policies and curriculum. *Teachers and Teaching,* 1–23.

Orón Semper, J. V., & Blasco, M. (2018). Revealing the hidden curriculum in higher education. *Studies in Philosophy and Education, 37*(5), 481–498.

Osborn, M. (2006). Changing the context of teachers' work and professional development: A European perspective. *International Journal of Educational Research, 45*(4–5), 242–253.

Pallas, A. M. (2000). The effects of schooling on individual lives. In M. T. Hallinan (Ed.), *Handbook of the sociology of education* (pp. 499–525). Kluwer Academic/Plenum.

Peters, R. S. (1962). Moral education and the psychology of character, *Philosophy, 37*(139), 37–56.

Piaget, J. (1932/1965) *The moral judgement of the child.* Routledge and Kegan Paul.

Postholm, M. B. (2013). Classroom management: What does research tell us?. *European Educational Research Journal, 12*(3), 389–402.

Preiss, D. R., Arum, R., Edelman, L. B., Morrill, C., & Tyson, K. (2016). The more you talk, the worse it is: Student perceptions of law and authority in schools. *Social Currents, 3*(3), 234–255.

Prochner, L., & Hwang, Y. (2008). Cry and you cry alone': Timeout in early childhood settings. *Childhood, 15*(4), 517–534.

Prosser, J. (1999). The evolution of school culture research. *School culture,* In J. Prosser (Ed.), *School culture* (pp. 1–14). Paul Chapman.

Purpel, D. (1999). *Moral outrage in education.* Peter Lang.

Purpel, D., & Ryan, K. (1975). Moral education: Where sages fear to tread. *Phi Delta Kappan, 56*(10), 659–662.

Render, G. F., Padilla, J. N. M., & Krank, H. M. (1989). Assertive discipline: A critical review and analysis. *Teachers College Record, 90*(4), 607–630.

Robinson, G., & Maines, B. (1994). Assertive discipline: Jumping on a dated wagon. *Educational Psychology in Practice, 9*(4), 195–200.

Rodriguez, L. A., & Welsh, R. O. (2022). The dimensions of school discipline: Toward a comprehensive framework for measuring discipline patterns and outcomes in schools. *AERA Open, 8*(1), 1–23.

Saldana, J. (2013). Power and conformity in today's schools. *International Journal of Humanities and Social Science, 3*(1), 228–232.

Samson, M. G. (2018). Competition or cooperation? Jewish day schools, synagogues and the (re) construction of young people's Jewish identities in England. *Children's Geographies, 16*(3), 225–238.

Schoen, L. T., & Teddlie, C. (2008). A new model of school culture: A response to a call for conceptual clarity. *School Effectiveness and School Improvement, 19*(2), 129–153.

Smetana, J. G. (1999). The role of parents in moral development: A social domain analysis. *Journal of Moral Education, 28*(3), 311–321.

Stewart, J. S. (1974). The school as a values/moral agent. In *Essays on values development education.* Unpublished booklet, Michigan State University, College of Education, East Lansing, MI.

Stoll, L. (1998). School culture. *School Improvement Network's Bulletin, 9*(10), 9–14.

Straus, M. A. (1994). Beating the devil out of them: *Corporal punishment in American families.* Lexington Books.

Thornberg, R. (2008). Values education as the daily fostering of school rules. *Research in Education, 80*(1), 52–62.

Thornberg, R. (2009). The moral construction of the good pupil embedded in school rules. *Education, Citizenship and Social Justice, 4*(3), 245–261.

Thornberg, R. (2018). School bullying and fitting into the peer landscape: A grounded theory field study. *British Journal of Sociology of Education, 39*(1), 144–158.

Tuastad, S. (2016). What Is it like to be a student in a religious school?. *Religion & Education, 43*(1), 60–76.

Twemlow, S. W., & Sacco, F. C. (2013). Bullying is everywhere: Ten universal truths about bullying as a social process in schools & communities. *Psychoanalytic Inquiry, 33*(2), 73–89.

Veugelers, W. (2021). Teachers' ethos in moral learning: Strengthening teachers, supporting learners. In F. Oser, K. Heinrichs, J. Bauer, & T. Lovat (Eds.), *The international handbook of teacher ethos* (pp. 109–121). Springer.

Veugelers, W., & Vedder, P. (2003). Values in teaching. *Teachers and Teaching, 9*(4), 377–389.

Walker, V. S. E., & Snarey, J. R. (2004). *Race-ing moral formation: African American perspectives on care and justice.* Teachers College Press.

Watson, M. (2008). Developmental discipline and moral education. In L. P. Nucci, & D. Narvaez (Eds.), *Handbook of moral and character education* (pp. 175–203). Routledge.

Watson, M. S., Solomon, D., Battistich, V., Schaps, E., & Solomon, J. (1989). The Child Development Project: combining traditional and developmental approaches to values education. In L. Nucci (Ed.) *Moral development and character education: A dialogue* (pp. 51–92). McCutchan.

Welsh, R. O., & Little, S. (2018). The school discipline dilemma: A comprehensive review of disparities and alternative approaches. *Review of Educational Research, 88*(5), 752–794.

Wentzel, K. R. (2015). Socialization in school settings. In J. E. Grusec & P. D. Hastings (Eds.), *Handbook of socialization: Theory and research* (pp. 251–275). The Guilford Press.

Wiseman, A. W., Astiz, M. F., Fabrega, R., & Baker, D. P. (2011). Making citizens of the world: The political socialization of youth in formal mass education systems. *Compare: A Journal of Comparative and International Education, 41*(5), 561–577.

Woocher, J., & Woocher, M. (2014). Jewish education in a new century: An ecosystem in transition. In A. Dashefsky & I. Sheskin (Eds.), *American Jewish year book 2013* (pp. 3–57). Springer.

Woods, R. (2008). When rewards and sanctions fail: A case study of a primary school rule-breaker. *International Journal of Qualitative Studies in Education, 21*(2), 181–196.

Yang, C., Bear, G. G., Chen, F. F., Zhang, W., Blank, J. C., & Huang, X. (2013). Students' perceptions of school climate in the US and China. *School Psychology Quarterly, 28*(1), 7–24.

Zajda, J. (2014). Values education. In D.C. Phillips (Ed.), *Encyclopedia of educational theory and philosophy* (pp. 835–838). Sage.

Zhao, Z. (2014). The teacher–state relationship in China: An exploration of homeroom teachers' experiences. *International Studies in Sociology of Education, 24*(2), 148–164.

6

Moral Schools and Classrooms

A climate in which caring relations can flourish should be a goal for all teachers and educational policymakers. In such a climate, we can best meet individual needs, impart knowledge, and encourage the development of moral people.... A climate of care and trust is one in which most people will want to do the right thing, will want to be good.

—Nel Noddings, 2012, "The Caring Relationship in Teaching," p. 777

Critics of conventional schooling denounce the separation of school from students' vital moral interests by focusing on "conforming to school rules and routines," "failure to conceive and construct the school as a social institution" (Dewey, 1909, p. 15), and the view of "learners as passive recipients" dependent on "external motivation" (Postholm, 2013, p. 397), They also write about how the normalization of competition works against classrooms and schools as moral communities (Kohn, 1997) as the "competitive spirit undermines the richest aims of education" by thwarting teachers' work in helping children to live "full, moral, happy lives with generous concern for the welfare of others" (Noddings, 2012, p. 778). As well, there are critiques

Teaching for Moral Imagination, pages 115–139

about schools as “institutions of power” (Morrison & Vaandering, 2012, p. 140) with “punitive environments” in which “the goal of social control can overshadow the goal of education” (Perry & Morris, 2014, p. 1071). For these reasons, many scholars insist that classrooms and schools need to be transformed into moral communities where students learn and thrive in “a climate of care and trust” (Noddings, 2012, p. 777).

To achieve such transformation of schooling we might take to heart John Dewey’s (1909) observation that “every incident of school life is pregnant with moral possibility” (p. 58) so to imagine a multitude of opportunities for encouraging students’ moral emotions and reasoning. However, these efforts cannot be scattered or haphazard; rather, we have to engender intentional moral environments. As educational philosopher David Hansen (2002) cautions:

> For Dewey, a school or classroom environment that is left up to chance is as likely as not to be mideducative as educative. A chance environment is a random environment, a casual environment, and, in many respects, a thoughtless or mindless environment. Such an environment renders human outcomes a toss-up between the better and the worse, the helpful and the harmful, and the good and the bad. (p. 185)

Fortunately, we do not have to rely only on chance—nor on intuition and unexamined tradition. Instead, it is possible to draw from a rich body of conceptual and empirical research describing ways to create moral classrooms and schools.

Such scholarship highlights experiential moral learning that centers on both affective moral development (nurturing of caring and empathy) and cognitive moral development (fostering of moral reasoning, perspective taking, and appreciation of justice). Nevertheless, if students know caring and respect from their teachers and classmates but then encounter hostile school cultures, their experiences will be discordant and distressing. Consequently, educators also must cultivate school cultures as ethical and inclusive communities in which all members are committed to fairness and to bringing about the best in each other.

This chapter explores the moral possibilities of classroom and school life by exploring these questions:

- How can educators foster ethical school cultures?
- What educational practices nurture students’ empathy, respect, and appreciation of community?
- What educational practices encourage students’ understanding of others’ perspectives and reflection about self and others?

Ethical School Cultures

To understand how schools can become ethical communities, a starting place it to interrogate existing values and behaviors within school cultures, to begin by asking: Are there "overall goals and ideas which set the stage for every action"? Can all people within a school culture "define the values by which they live"? (Solomon, 1992, p. 3). And, is there a shared moral vision of commitment to caring and justice? Such inquiry allows perception of the existence or absence of an ethical environment.

Two interconnected constructs provide insight when considering such questions. First, *climate* "refers to the quality and character of school life" (Cohen et al., 2009, p. 182) and "involves impressions of school culture from students, parents, and educators of the social atmosphere of the learning environment" (Glover & Coleman, 2005, p. 254). Second, *ethos* represents shared "values and principles" that influence all aspects of school life and characterize the school's "philosophy or atmosphere" (Glover & Coleman, 2005, pp. 266, 258).

Climate

Although climate and culture often appear as interchangeable terms, scholars who define school climate especially highlight "patterns of people's experiences in schools" (Thapa et al., 2013, p. 358) and "impressions of the quality of relationships and way of living together" (Gutzwiller-Helfenfinger & Perren, 2022, p. 441). As such, they attend to "perceptions of school culture," e.g., examining how school culture "influences students' adjustment to school" and "interpersonal relationships between teachers and students" (Barr & Higgens-D'Alessandro, 2007, p. 234). However, "school climate is more than individual experience":

> It is a group phenomenon [referring] to spheres of school life (e.g., safety, relationships, teaching and learning, the environment) and larger organizational patterns (e.g., from fragmented to cohesive or "shared" vision, healthy or unhealthy, conscious or unrecognized). (Cohen et al., 2009, p. 182)

Various studies of school climate especially reveal configurations of students' impressions of the overall school environment and how people interact with each other.

Researchers synthesize school climate as patterns of experience: *survival-based, authoritarian,* and *authoritative.* "Survival-based" climates have few rules and poor teacher-student relationships; authoritarian or "power-based conflict resolution" climates rely on "directives" from teachers and administrators with expectations of "compliance" from students; and, "authoritative"—"care-based" and "respect-based conflict resolution" climates—accentuate communication, reciprocity, and collaboration among educators and students (Ferráns & Selman, 2014, p. 167). These categories provide a framework for investigating if and to what extent the school is an ethical environment.

A survival school climate is characterized by "student defiance and fighting as well as teacher ineffectiveness in maintaining order" (Bosworth & Judkins, 2014, p. 301); in such schools, students feel unprotected and unsafe because of heightened levels of "bullying, aggression, and victimization" (Espelage & Hong, 2019, p. 58) and are reluctant to report encounters with aggressive behaviors (p. 48). In schools where teachers and administrators do not assert moral authority or guidance, students can perceive that the school is "tolerant of harassment" (p. 49). As well, researchers document that negative school climates influence children's risk-taking behaviors, such as delinquency and misconduct (Ferráns & Selman, 2014, p. 167) and "elevate students' risk of bullying involvement and peer victimization" (Hong et al., 2018, p. 359).

Scholars also describe schools in which educators exercise a great deal of control, but in such environments, "teachers do not establish nurturing relationships and instead focus on maintaining strict order" (Ferráns & Selman, 2014, p. 167). This authoritarian school climate is replete with punitive disciplinary practices that are "highly structured and emphasize control and obedience without supporting students in correcting their behavior" (Bosworth & Judkins, 2014, p. 302). Without flexibility or helping students to understand rationales for discipline, educators can appear uncaring and unfair. The cumulative effect of such attitudes creates a school climate that provokes students' distrust and misconduct and "unfair or overly strict enforcement may undercut the school's legitimacy" (Preiss et al., 2016, p. 236).

In contrast, researchers refer to an authoritative school climate as comprising both "care-based" and "respect-based conflict resolution" environments. Its essential characteristics are "disciplinary structure and student support" (Cornell et al., 2015, p. 1187). Discipline in authoritative school cultures is "fair, reasonable, and unbiased" as fairness means that "students are treated fairly regardless of their race or ethnicity" (Cornell & Huang, 2016, p. 2254); subsequently, studies indicate that students' perception of "school discipline as fair is associated with significantly lower rates of disruptive behavior" (Arum & Way, 2005, p. 183). Such schools promote "shared decision-making" including students' participation in decisions about learning and discipline. Student support, "the other fundamental element of an authoritative school," involves students believing that "teachers care about all students and want them to do well" and "students feeling comfortable seeking help" from teachers (Cornell & Huang, 2016, p. 2254).

School climates that are "caring, participatory, and responsive" foster students' "attachment and bonding to school" (Bosworth & Judkins, 2014, p. 301; Ferráns & Selman, 2014, p. 167). Researchers emphasize that it is necessary to build communities "grounded in the premise that human beings are relational and thrive in contexts of social engagement over control" (Morrison & Vaandering, 2012, p. 139). These climates do not just happen but have to be "actively cultivated" (Schaps, 2003, p. 32).

Ethos

A powerful way of thinking of schools as moral communities is to comprehend the concept of ethos—a purposeful and unifying vision in which "all members of a group are aligned with a compelling ethic" (Goodman, 2007, p. 11) and "share attitudes, values, and beliefs that bond disparate individuals into a community" (Grant, 1988, p. 117). Educators devoted to a common ethical mission offer students congruent experiences that support moral growth and sustain teachers' efforts as moral educators. So too, as members of the school community, students would participate in creating ethos—in the development of "mission statements, codes of responsibility, and shared moral values" (Berreth & Berman, 1997, p. 25).

> A school with a strong positive ethos is one that affirms the ideals and imparts the intellectual and moral virtues proper to the functioning of an educational community in a democracy. It attempts to commit its members to those ideals and virtues in at least a provisional way through the espousal of goals, exemplary actions and practices, ritual celebrations and observance of norms. (Grant, 1988, p. 188)

Ethos would be reflected in school discipline (Goodman, 2006, p. 213), curricular content, activities, as well as decisions about resources (ASCD, 1988). Scholars who write about school ethos accentuate commitment to creating a moral world in which a strong sense of purpose leads all individuals in the community to have respect for each other and the school's values. As well, ethos means that all members of the school community take responsibility "to foster caring and respectful behavior by attending to moral and social development," "see it as part of their daily work to inspire students to be caring and respectful people," and "do so in ways that are ongoing and long-term" (Weissbourd et al., 2013, p. 2).

A necessary constituent of ethos is critical examination—comparing the ideal to real beliefs and interactions. A school's moral mission might represent "an ideal moral code about how things ought morally to be" (Boehm, 1977, p. 30) that may contrast with the reality of existing values represented by actual behaviors and policies. Critic and school reformer, John Holt (1970), emphatically conveyed this notion:

> The schools may well be saying all the time how much they like and respect children, how much they value their individual differences, how committed they are to democratic and human values, and so on. If I tell you that you are wise, but treat you like a fool; tell you that you are good, but treat you like a dangerous criminal, you will feel what I feel much more strongly than if I said it directly. (p. 56)

Articulation of ethos is crucial for creating guiding principles and cohesiveness, but schools are obligated to "put themselves under the microscope from time to time" (Glover & Coleman, 2005, p. 259) to scrutinize climate and ethos in light of values perceived by all those in the school community and to work towards making needed changes.

Moral Classroom and School Practices

To counter traditional schooling that emphasizes control, passivity, and individualism, there is an array of practices for creating moral experiences for children and young people: *caring community, democratic community, service learning, just community*, and *restorative justice*. Although they differ from one another in structures and lived experiences, in many ways these approaches are interrelated and share several aims. Altogether they embody significant components of moral imagination: heightening empathy, fostering perception and realistic understanding of others' needs, engaging in critical reflection about justice, and envisioning the goodness within ourselves and others (see Table 6.1).

Caring Community

Reflecting moral imagination's components of emotion (empathic feelings and connections with others) and perception (awareness of others' needs and interests), the caring community is a humanistic practice dedicated to holistic child development, the "relational ethic of care and connectedness" (Cefai & Cavioni, 2014, p. 81), and essential elements for human flourishing and moral development. This multidimensional approach that challenges conventional norms of schooling has numerous benefits for

TABLE 6.1 Moral Classroom and School Practices

Approach	Description
Caring Community	Emphasizes classrooms and schools adhering to the ethic of care—nurturing, closeness and attachment—focusing on the social and emotional health of all its community members.
Democratic Community	Provides opportunities for deliberation and participation in meaningful decisions and fosters respectful and sympathetic relationships.
Service Learning	Involves students in organized and sustained experiences to serve community needs and critical reflection to foster and strengthen academic skills, empathy, and agency.
Just Community	Features democratic deliberation about moral dilemmas, participation in cooperative decision making, and gaining perspectives on fairness and justice.
Restorative Justice	Focuses on interconnection of individuals in a community, viewing misconduct as a violation of relationships and involves a process of dialogue and consensus to acknowledge harm and commit to possible remedies.

students as well as for educators. The caring community requires a change from themes of competition and control to cooperation and trust, from "extrinsic rewards and consequences" to teachers guiding and supporting students within a "family atmosphere." It represents "a paradigmatic shift in classroom management and discipline" (Watson & Battistich, 2006, p. 275).

Caring communities emphasize nurturing, closeness, emotional attachment, and respectful, mutually supportive relationships—experienced by all in the community. While not indifferent to academic achievement, educators in a caring community especially value students' social and emotional wellbeing. So too, the caring community attends to the needs of teachers to cooperatively work together and to be mentored (p. 82). Proponents of caring communities recognize that among children's "basic psychological needs" are "emotional and physical safety" (Schaps, 2003, p. 31) and apprehend that emotional health is a requisite for moral development, enabling children to turn outward to others instead of concentrating primarily on satisfying their own needs. Akin to a nurturing family in which "caretakers are available and respond sensitively to children's needs," educators in the caring community need to build "warm, nurturing, and trusting relationships with students" as "children learn to become caring by being in caring relationships" (Watson, 2008, p. 180).

The primary moral relationship in a caring community is between the teacher and child. Philosopher Nel Noddings (2012) conceptualized the role of the teacher as a "carer" who is attentive and strives "to understand what the cared-for is experiencing" and "not simply the needs assumed by the school as an institution" (p. 772). She differentiated between teachers caring that students achieve and caring for students as human beings by engaging in "dialogue with students about what matters" to them (p. 774).

> A teacher-carer listening receptively to a student may hear that the student hates school and especially mathematics. How should the teacher respond? She is caught up in a real conflict. As one-caring, she must respond to the expressed need of the cared-for. She also has a clear responsibility to the school. Her job is to teach mathematics, and she must find a way to do this. She also has an intellectual responsibility to the field of her academic expertise, mathematics. Yet her most deeply felt moral responsibility is to the cared-for, her student. To respond as carer to him, she must put aside, temporarily, the demands of the institution. She needs time to build a relation of care and trust. (p. 774)

Similarly, scholars explain that students will not view their teachers as caring if attention primarily is paid to students' success in school and not to "awareness and understanding of the condition that students live under" (Antrop-González & De Jesús, 2006, p. 427). Also, in the caring community, students have opportunities to "engage in meaningful dialogic encounters based on caring relationships"; teachers need to "know each student personally" and really listen to them but also "share their own experiences and stories" (Cefai & Cavioni, 2014, p. 81). Through dialogue, teachers and students can "learn from each other" (Buzzelli & Johnston, 2014, p. 73) and engage in mutual, cooperative relationships (Watson, 2008, p. 181). This community features "an authentic form of caring emphasizing relations of reciprocity between teachers and students" (Valenzuela, 1999, p. 61).

Another constituent of the caring community is school belonging—"most consistently defined as the extent to which students feel personally accepted, respected, included, and supported by others in the school social environment" (Allen et al., 2018, p. 2). Teachers, administrators, parents, students, and students' caregivers feel that they are members of a community and all staff members demonstrate genuine concern for students; they communicate with each other and families about children's academic progress, social development, and emotional health. In the classroom and school, supportive peer relationships develop as students care for one another through informal and planned activities and family events. Inclusiveness is another theme in the caring community as students from diverse populations, including special education students, are valued members of the community (Antrop-González & De Jesús, 2006; Cefai & Cavioni, 2014; Schaps, 2003); in "an inclusive school community" all people, including teachers, feel "accepted, safe, respected, and celebrated, and know that their voice matters" (Creekmore & Creekmore, 2022, p. 42). In addition, this community provides "regular opportunities for service and cooperation" and students "experience the many satisfactions of contributing to the welfare of others" (Schaps, 2003, p. 32).

Elementary schools are more likely than secondary schools to develop caring communities because of their smaller enrollments and structures that facilitate knowing children and their families and for long-term relationships. But whereas "secondary schools tend to be large and impersonal places" (Ellerbrock, 2012, p. 34), some researchers do find caring environments on that level. The philosophy undergirding the middle-school movement highlights the social-emotional needs of young adolescents, the "need for caring adult relationships" and "sense of belonging" (Alder, 2002, p. 246). The "Caring Community Teaching Model" guides middle-school teachers to "create environments in which students feel connected, as demonstrated by meaningful participation in classroom activities, enjoyable relationships, and healthy social-emotional functioning" (Range et al., 2013, p. 48). Moreover, there are examples of high schools that have developed a transition year for entering students. In such programs, interdisciplinary teaming "helps teachers get to know their students well and aids in the promotion of positive relationships with students" (Ellerbrock, 2012, p. 49). Likewise, "teams provide a psychological home within the school that helps reduce the stress of isolation and anonymity" (Jackson & Davis, 2000, p. 125).

Researchers suggest that children educated in such communities perceive their classrooms as fair, safe, and caring places, and are more likely to act ethically and altruistically" (Schaps, 2003, p. 31). The caring community is especially important when students have experienced inadequate nurturing before coming to school as without "a view of relationships as cooperative and reciprocal, they will not have a basis for building a moral worldview" (Watson, 2008, p. 181). Likewise, for children "experiencing multiple adversity in their lives, a sense of belonging is a significant protective factor" (Roffey, 2013, p. 41) and "a sense of belonging is considered to play a fundamental role in adolescent development and identity formation" (Allen et al., 2016, p. 98). As well, inclusive school communities "know how to identify and respond quickly to racism and other forms of discrimination" (Creekmore & Creekmore, 2022, p. 46) and thereby ensuring caring for all and not for some.

Democratic Community

Advocates for caring communities believe that these settings likewise need to be democratic. They contend that children also thrive when classrooms and schools satisfy children's "psychological need for autonomy and competence" (Battistich et al., 1997, p. 137). Some scholars maintain that the democratic classroom community—comprising "joint problem-solving, listening as well as talking, grasping others' points of view, and using the common space to forge positions with others" (Mikel, 2011, p. 209)—is preparation for the "deliberative arts" of democracy" (Parker, 2003). Hence, conceptualizations of the democratic community express these themes: caring and respect, shared authority and agency, and deliberation and citizenship.

Scholars who associate caring communities with democratic classrooms posit that the democratic educational community is "interactive, interrelational, and interdependent" (Thayer-Bacon, 1996, p. 339), "includes caring as a value" (p. 344), and emphasizes "interpersonal concern and support" (Solomon et al., 1996, p. 723). Once more, several theorists specifically make connections between democracy and empathy (Gutmann, 1987), writing that it is necessary to "inculcate empathic dispositions" (Morrell, 2007, p. 385) as we "ought to want citizens predisposed to empathy" (p. 398). As follows, the democratic community also fosters "appreciation and respect for diversity" (Seigel & Rockwood, 1993, p. 65) because "democracy imposes on its adherents the public obligation to treat one another with the consideration, respect, and tolerance" (Gregory, 2000, p. 458). This outlook encourages us to "notice, inquire into, and articulate the needs and interests of others" (p. 456) and to be "mindful of the ways our conduct affects others" (p. 447).

Another portrayal of the democratic community is as a catalyst for students' empowerment. Agency develops when children have "ways to influence decisions that affect the community and opportunities to take responsibility for the community" (Watson, 2008, p. 182). Democratic communities ensure that children have "a say in establishing the agenda and climate for the classroom" and, for example, in such classrooms students believe that they "can get a rule changed if they think that it is unfair"; meaningful class meetings allow for children's participation in "setting goals and norms, planning activities, as well as identifying and solving problems" (Schaps, 2003, p. 32). Consequently, democratic environments "help students fight their feelings of powerlessness" (Berman, 1990, p. 75). Scholars depict such environments as a "shift from teacher control to shared control—from individual responsibility to shared responsibility" (Watson & Battistich, 2006, p. 275). When classrooms no longer are authoritarian, "teachers can be authorities and still enter into dialogue with their students; teachers' authority can inform their contribution to the dialogue, but does not dominate it" (Berman, 1990, p. 73).

A final theme in this literature is the belief that the democratic classroom as a deliberative community prepares for an engaged citizenship that "strengthens the democratic way of life" (Collins et al., 2019, p. 1). "Such a vision of democracy as deliberation, rather than democracy as procedures for majority rule, requires a rational, articulate and critical citizenry, who can participate productively in the public sphere" (Segal et al., 2017, p. 7). Key aspects of this community include "social interactions" and "the negotiation of everything from classroom processes to personal meanings" (Buzzelli & Johnson, 2014, p. 74). Scholars accentuate "reciprocal dialogue"—"active listening to one another as equal moral agents" (Alder, 2002, p. 263). In a democratic community, students are involved in "building a strong classroom community," participate in "critical dialogue," take responsibilities for decisions that are meaningful to their lives, have authentic roles as co-developers of curriculum (Collins et al., 2019, p. 1), and build a democratic curriculum based on their genuine questions and concerns (Beane, 2002).

Considering deliberation as "the hallmark of democratic life" forming "the nucleus of decision making," it serves as "the warp and woof of democratic society" (Mikel, 2011, p. 200). In this way, advocates for democratic classroom communities support John Dewey's concept of "democratic faith"—"an unshakable belief in democracy as the best mode of social life" (p. 199).

> To hold this faith is also to believe in the inherent capacity and goodwill of all members to make their experiment in democracy work in best way humanly possible. Faith in fellow members of a democratic community keeps alive the critical vision of mutual responsibility and shared authority. (Mikel, 2011, p. 199)

Or as Dewey (1939/1988) avowed, "democracy is a way of life controlled by a working faith in the possibilities of human nature" (p. 223), epitomizing moral imagination's envisioning of ideal versions of ourselves and society.

Service Learning

Referred to as "a pedagogy of engagement" (Stain, 2005, p. 71), scholars define service learning as "a form of experiential education where learning occurs through a cycle of action and reflection as students seek to achieve real objectives for the community and deeper understanding and skills for themselves" (Bandy, 2016). The two key goals of service learning are to provide opportunities for active learning "linking community service and academic study" (Ehrlich, 1996, p. xi) and for students to experience caring for others. Service learning actualizes components of the moral imagination: moral emotion as attentiveness to others' needs and critical reflection through examination of one's beliefs and actions. Scholars write that service learning "becomes a powerful approach to learning, because it not only connects theory with action, but also integrates cognitive learning with affective learning" (You & Rud, 2010, p. 38) and offers students opportunities to become moral agents.

> The desires to change the status quo of the community motivate these moral agents to collect and rearrange data, to balance reason and sense, and to imaginatively draw a blueprint with purpose in mind. Imagination interpenetrates the whole process of service, actively seeking meaning out of chaos and confusion and searching for new approaches in an effort to clarify and improve situations. (p. 39)

Service learning is widespread in secondary schools and higher education in the United States and numerous other countries; moreover, this "pedagogical approach for "fostering civic and social participation" (Spring et al., 2008, p. 8) has received partial support from governmental, corporate, and private grants (p. 29).

But before educators develop this practice in schools and communities, it is necessary to attend to this caveat: community service and service learning are not the same. "Community service becomes service-learning when there is a deliberate connection made between service and learning opportunities which are then accompanied by conscious and thoughtfully designed occasions for reflecting on the service experience" (Alliance for Service Learning in Education Reform, 1993, p. 71). In this way, service learning is distinguishable "from voluntarism, community service, and other forms of experiential education" (Weigert, 1998, p. 5). While community service by itself also engages students in projects to help others, this practice more often occurs in elementary schools but without the critical reflection requirement.

Advocates and scholars explain service learning as a reflective process: "looking back on the implications of actions taken, both good and bad, determining what has been gained, lost or achieved" (Alliance for Service Learning in Education Reform, 1993, pp. 71–72). For example, guided reflection assignments help students to ponder how they themselves have benefited from their experiences so "to avoid reinforcing a student-centered charity model" (Hammersley, 2012, p. 172). Through critical reflection, students are then able to interrogate the social and political implications to "consider problematic questions associated with power, history, and agency" (King, 2004, p. 125) and to recognize that their efforts are likely to have "marginal and tenuous effect on the deeply structured inequities of our society" (Purpel, 1998, p. 23). As such, "service learning is at its best when it is underpinned with a social justice ethos" (Asghar & Rowe, 2017, p. 119).

Furthermore, unlike other experiential models for promoting moral classrooms and schools, service learning is integrated with the academic curriculum and "must not be seen as an extracurricular volunteer activity" but instead as "a vehicle for enriching the curriculum" (Wade & Saxe, 1996, p. 333) with "clearly stated learning objectives" related to courses and skill development (Skinner & Chapman, 1999, p. 3). By "connecting young people to the community and placing them in challenging situations," students gain experiences and skills "that can strengthen traditional academic studies" and "make classroom study relevant" (Alliance for Service Learning in Education Reform, 1993, p. 71).

Service learning involves a complex process consisting of a number of components (Furco, 2016, p. 76; King, 2004, p. 124; Skinner & Chapman, 1999, p. 3; Weigert, 1998, p. 5):

- Co-equal planning with a community group or agency to learn about their actual needs and how students could make a contribution of mutual benefit;
- Coordinating with the community to design the service-learning experience and establish support and supervision for students;
- Developing goals and assignments connected to academic knowledge and skills;
- Developing forms of guided reflection for students to understand and theorize about their service-learning experience;
- Choosing and implementing means of assessment to evaluate students' attainment of skills and learning.

Consequently, educators need to appreciate that implementation "takes much time, coordination, and effort" (Furco, 2016, p. 78). Studies of service learning reveal difficulties stemming from limited resources, in particular, having enough time to prepare students for their assignments and the context of their activities. Also, as service learning often is a short-term assignment, community agencies experience frustration from a "lack of continuity"; moreover, some students can be resistant and resentful when this activity is a requirement and not a choice (Tyron et al, 2008, p. 18). Another concern is inadequate communication (Rosing et al, 2010, p. 471) between partners, including participating students.

Reciprocity as a crucial aspect of service learning. Scholars forewarn that when this practice is not understood as being mutually empowering, it "may actually reinforce prejudice and replicate power differentials between those conferring and those receiving the service" (King, 2004, p. 123) and the notion of service learning "as charity work" (Asghar & Rowe, 2017, p. 122).

> There is implicit in the concept of "service'" the notion that there are those who need help and there are those prepared to help, thus setting up a duality and hierarchy between the needy and the providers, the helpless and the helpful, there powerless and the powered, the takers and the givers. (Purpel, 1998, p. 23)

Relationships between schools and community agencies must be based on "respect, trust, genuine commitment, balancing power, sharing resources and clear communication" (Jacoby, 2015, p. p. 247) and service learning must be "mutually beneficial" (King, 2004, p. 124). Students, educators, and community members should become "colearners, coeducators, and cogenerators of knowledge"; as follows, service learning fosters "the capacity to engage with others as 'cobeings' and not as objects" (Felton & Clayton, 2011, p. 82).

Although studies are inconclusive about service learning advancing cognitive stages of moral development, a number of scholars declare that service learning has the potential for "transformative learning" (Felton & Clayton, 2011, p. 82) because it "enlivens moral imagination and sense of agency" (Stain, 2005, p. 71). For instance, programs integrating service and reflection stimulate moral growth as "students build relationships, struggle with social issues, and move toward self-authorship" (Scott, 2012, p. 30); students completing service-learning courses "perceive themselves to be more socially conscious, more effective in changing the world, and more compassionate" as compared with others who did not participate (Bernacki & Jaeger, 2008, p. 13). Therefore, as curriculum scholar and ethicist David Purpel (1998) concluded, service learning is a step toward "transcending our self-centeredness and mean-spiritedness and moving to a conscious caring, compassion, and love" (p. 26).

Just Community

The just community, a practice "integrating moral education with civic or citizenship education" (Althof, 2015, p. 73), has much in common with the democratic school community in that it provides opportunities for deliberation, student empowerment, and preparation for citizenship. However, this practice more intentionally emphasizes the attainment of justice and the fostering of students' moral reasoning as students engage in "ongoing reflections about fairness" as related to real-life situations (Oser et al., 2008, p. 396). The just community does not merely focus on abstract notions of fairness and rationality; it strives "to achieve a sense of community solidarity—to create a 'moral atmosphere'—through the practice of democratic governance" (Snarey & Samuelson, 2014, p. 78). It "repositions justice problems so that they [are] concurrently considered as issues of care and social cohesion" (McDonough, 2005, p. 208) as students and educators continually ask, "what would be best for the community?" (Fielding, 2013, p. 132). In addition, the just community "aims to promote moral development and moral responsibility through the organization, practices, and culture of the school itself" (Power & Higgins-D'Alessandro, 2008, p. 230).

Although many classrooms have democratic tendencies—allowing children to have a voice in some matters and, to some extent, encouraging deliberation—there are relatively few schools chronicled as having aims and structures of the just community. Albeit without the appellation of "just community," there are two significant historical examples. Referred to as the "forefather of the just community approach" (Oser, 2014, p. 201), Janusz Korczak was the director of a Jewish orphanage in Warsaw, Poland from 1911 to 1942 until he and his children perished in the Treblinka death camp during the Holocaust. Korczak believed that "democracy was intrinsically linked to moral education" (Efron, 2008, p. 50) and ran the orphanage as "the children's republic" with democratic self-government in which "the responsibility for operating the community affairs was shared between the adults and the students" and developed "jointly by the teachers and children in a democratic discourse" (pp. 48–48). In a very different context, A. S. Neill founded an English boarding school, Summerhill, in 1921. His purpose was to create a community that would foster children's happiness and counter authoritarian schooling (Darling, 1992, p. 47). Summerhill students primarily came from affluent families and many of these children manifested symptoms of neuroses that Neill believed were aggravated by their previously harsh schooling experiences. But, he also professed that "the aim of education is to teach people to be rational, reflective thinkers" (Thayer-Bacon, 1996, p. 342) through participating in a truly democratic environment. Thus, Summerhill is known for being a school that demonstrated that "the rights of the individual child were bound by the demands of the democratic, self-governing society" (Engel, 2013, p. 128).

The preeminent theorist and founder of just community schools was Lawrence Kohlberg. This cognitive-developmentalist psychologist admired Korczak's democratic model of the children's republic and was "inspired by the Anne Frank Haven school" in Israel, established in 1956 by kibbutz educators—with its democratic, deliberative governance shared by children and a community adult leader (Power & Higgins-D'Alessandro,

2008, p. 231). Eventually, Kohlberg realized that discussion of hypothetical moral dilemmas alone is not a sufficient moral education practice because "it does not take into account the moral atmosphere of the social context" (Snarey & Samuelson, 2014, p. 77); in doing so, Kohlberg "extended his theory from the moral reasoning of individuals to the moral cultures of communities" (p. 79). In 1974 Kohlberg took the lead in developing six just community high schools in the United States—primarily as alternative schools within public schools. Later, Kohlberg and colleagues involved in the just community movement met with European educators and, consequently, a number of just community schools or those using "the basic ideas but not the label" began in Germany and Switzerland for all grade levels (Oser et al., 2008, p. 397). In contemporary times, there are just community schools in several countries including Taiwan and Israel. Still, as this moral community practice truly challenges traditional school cultures, it was "always considered ambitious and never became widely adopted; nonetheless, the idea survived" (Althof, 2015, p. 51). There is still much interest in the just community concept and school as "an opportunity for moral and democratic learning" (Lind, 2019, p. 113)

From historical to recent manifestations, just community schools have similar features and structures. Korczak's orphanage had a children's council, parliament, and children's court of law to make the rules and consequences for violating them (Efron, 2008); Summerhill held "weekly town meetings to discuss issues and decide policy" and decide on "punishment for social offenses" (Thayer-Bacon, 1996, p. 340). Kohlberg's just community schools also held weekly community meetings in which students and staff met to "decide school policies and practices that dealt with issues of fairness and community" with adults and children having equal voices. Just community schools also maintain several committees, including advisory groups which discuss the agenda for the community meetings (Snarey & Samuelson, 2014, p. 78). Likewise, a contemporary just community school designates a "fairness committee to deal with violations of rules and norms" that is "chaired by a trained student leader and is made up of one teacher and six students" (Scarsdale High School, 2023).

Notwithstanding the many commonalities, there are divergent beliefs about the role of teachers in just community schools. Neil (1960) took pride in the fact that "my vote carries the same weight as that of a seven-year-old" (p. 45) whereas Kohlberg believed that adults in just community schools had to be more than facilitators but "to function as advocates for moral content" (Snarey & Samuelson, 2014, p. 78). Still, there is debate about "whether or not adults should take on an advocacy or an advisory role" (Fielding, 2013, p. 134). Because just communities began as "experiments in democratic education" (Oser et al., 2008, p. 395), they seem to be in dynamic formation as educators and their communities grapple with the practice of democracy in schools.

Restorative Justice

As an intentional response to aggression and punitive discipline, restorative justice is a strategy to create humane and cooperative classrooms and schools while addressing misconduct and hurtful behavior. This approach has been adopted in various countries by individual educators in classrooms as well as through whole-school programs (Darling-Hammond et al., 2020; Morrison, 2013). Restorative justice in schools evolved from programs for incarcerated juvenile and adults (McCluskey et al., 2008, p. 407). Its purpose is to create "nonadversarial dialogue among victims, offenders, and other affected individuals to address the harms caused by crime and to promote offender accountability" (Bergseth & Bouffard, 2013, p. 1055)—thus to provide insight to offenders and to "give voice to 'victims'" (McCluskey et al., 2008, p. 407). Subsequently, restorative justice in schools (sometimes known as restorative practices) "addresses a wide range of harmful behaviors" with the aim "to build the social and emotional intelligence and skills within the school community such that a normative capacity for safe and just schools can be realized" (Morrison, 2013, p. 326).

Restorative justice is a counterpart to the caring community with its affirmation of dialogue and interconnection. Whereas exclusionary discipline systems "are likely to reinforce the notion that the student cannot be part of the community" (Gomez et al., 2021, p. 461), restorative justice was introduced so to "keep the offender in the school community," to "repair relationships that were damaged" by the offender's actions, and as "a foundation for creating a culture of peace" (Carroll et al., 2022, p. 3).

> The central issue of restorative justice is how to move the individuals involved in an oppositional relationship in which they strive to dominate, exploit, and abuse each other to a promotive relationship in which they see themselves as members of the same moral community with responsibilities for each other's well-being. (Johnson & Johnson, 2012, p. 5)

Restorative justice "enables a process for the community to address harm through nurturing the human capacity for *restitution, resolution,* and *reconciliation,*" relying on relationships instead of institutional force to motivate behavior change and initiate reparation" (Morrison & Vaandering, 2012, p. 140). An essential premise of restorative justice is that misbehavior does not mean breaking school rules—a "violation of the institution"—but rather, "a violation against people and relationships in the school and wider community" (Cameron & Thorsborne, 2001, p. 183).

This practice emanates from "the belief that we are all connected through a web of relationships and when a wrongdoing has occurred, the web becomes torn" (Kline, 2016, p. 97); it centers on the premise that people "share a common humanity, learn from their mistakes and misfortunes, draw on their inner strengths, desire to live peaceably, and achieve healing by telling others their truths, [and] having those truths acknowledged" (Hansen & Umbreit, 2018, p. 101). Therefore, teachers facilitating restorative justice practices remind students—especially those who have been excluded from the community because of their misconduct—"about their own goodness and worth" (King, 2015, p. 18). This approach to cultivating a moral classroom resonates with the ultimate component of moral imagination—envisioning ideal versions of ourselves, others, and our communities.

Scholars discuss restorative justice practices as "occurring in two tiers": The first tier reflects cultural change in schools through "proactive practices . . . to foster relationships and prevent conflicts"—to "create an environment that is respectful, tolerant, accepting, and supportive" (Darling-Hammond, et al., 2020, p. 297) and to establish safe spaces through creation of smaller communities "to facilitate strong bonds between teachers and students" (Carroll et al., 2022, p. 14). The second tier focuses on "specific response to harm" (Reimer, 2020, p. 410) by "holding offenders accountable, repairing harm to the victims, and providing support and assistance to offenders to encourage their reintegration into community" (Suvall, 2009, p. 557).

Practices include restorative circles—"commonly referred to in schools as talking circles, community circles, conflict circles or peacemaking circles" (Reimer, 2020, p. 416) based on indigenous justice systems (Reimer, 2020). Such "collaborative problem-solving" (Anfara et al., 2013, p. 58) allows all individuals to communicate their feelings about the harm experienced with the goals of "resolving a dispute through dialogue and reaching a consensus agreement" (Kline, 2016, p. 100). Circles also can be organized to be "concentric," with the "the inner circle including those most affected by an incident, and the outer circle, the remaining classroom members" (Morrison, 2013, p. 326). These circles facilitate "connections, build and restore community, and allow healing for all parties involved" (Kline, 2016, p. 100). So, too, this practice may entail restorative conferencing and victim-offender mediation to "allow each participant to provide insight into the harm committed and to consider the possible solutions for repairing that harm" (Anfara et al., 2013, p. 58). Negotiated sanctions can be imposed following restorative practices such as "community service, restitution, apologies, or agreements to change specific behaviors, such as the offender agreeing to comply with certain conditions, sometimes in exchange for incentives" (Darling-Hammond et al., 2020, p. 296).

In educational settings, restorative justice involves the "whole school community, all school staff, pupils and sometimes parents" (McCluskey et al., 2008, p. 407). Implementation of restorative justice practices (restorative circles or mediation) requires teachers to make a commitment to participate in extensive training and administrators to make a "significant investment in staff development" (McCluskey et al., 2008, p. 415). Moreover, restorative justice calls into question traditional beliefs about discipline and compels schools to ""create a culture of peace"; such change necessitates "a philosophical shift in the way students, teachers, and administrators relate to each other" and calls for "a buy-in" from all individuals in the school community (Carroll et al., 2022, p. 19). Undoubtedly, such changes in school culture cannot happen quickly. Nonetheless, school-wide efforts are crucial as research suggests that restorative justice "is perceived to work best when it is integrated into the school's overall philosophy" (Darling-Hammond et al., 2020, p. 297).

References

Alder, N. (2002). Interpretations of the meaning of care: Creating caring relationships in urban middle school classrooms. *Urban Education, 37*(2), 241–266.

Allen, K. A., Vella-Brodrick, D., & Waters, L. (2016). Fostering school belonging in secondary schools using a socio-ecological framework. *The Educational and Developmental Psychologist, 33*(1), 97–121.

Allen, K., Kern, M. L., Vella-Brodrick, D., Hattie, J., & Waters, L. (2018). What schools need to know about fostering school belonging: A meta-analysis. *Educational Psychology Review, 30*(1), 1–34.

Alliance for Service Learning in Education Reform. (1993). Standards of quality for school-based service-learning. *Equity & Excellence in Education, 26*(2), 71–73.

Althof, W. (2015). Just community sources and transformations: A conceptual archeology of Kohlberg's approach to moral and democratic schooling. In B. Zizek, D. Garz, & E. Nowak (Eds.), *Kohlberg revisited* (pp. 51–89). Brill.

Anfara, Jr., V. A., Evans, K. R., & Lester, J. N. (2013). Restorative justice in education: What we know so far. *Middle School Journal, 44*(5), 57–63.

Antrop-González, R., & De Jesús, A. (2006). Toward a theory of critical care in urban small school reform: Examining structures and pedagogies of caring in two Latino community-based schools. *International Journal of Qualitative Studies in Education, 19*(4), 409–433.

Arum, R., & Way, S. (2005). School discipline and youth socialization. In R. Arum, *Judging school discipline: The crisis of moral authority* (pp. 159–187). Harvard University Press.

Asghar, M., & Rowe, N. (2017). Reciprocity and critical reflection as the key to social justice in service learning: A case study. *Innovations in Education and Teaching International, 54*(2), 117–125.

Association for Supervision and Curriculum Development. (1988). *Moral education in the life of the school. A report from the ASCD panel on moral education.* https://eric.ed.gov/?id=ED298651

Bandy, J. (2016). *What is service learning or community engagement.* Center for Teaching, Vanderbilt University. https://cft.Vanderbilt.edu/guides-subpages/teaching-through-community-engagement.

Barr, J. J., & Higgins-D'Alessandro, A. (2007). Adolescent empathy and prosocial behavior in the multidimensional context of school culture. *The Journal of Genetic Psychology, 168*(3), 231–250.

Battistich, V., Solomon, D., Watson, M., & Schaps, E. (1997). Caring school communities. *Educational Psychologist, 32*(3), 137–151.

Beane, J. (2002). Beyond self-interest: A democratic core curriculum. *Educational Leadership, 59*(7), 25–28.

Berman, S. (1990). Educating for social responsibility. *Educational Leadership, 48*(3), 75–80.

Bernacki, M. L., & Jaeger, E. A. (2008). The impact of service learning on moral development and moral orientation. *Michigan Journal of Community Service-Learning, 14*(2), 5–15.

Berreth, D., & Berman, S. (1997). The moral dimensions of schools. *Educational Leadership, 54*(8), 24–27.

Bergseth, K. J., & Bouffard, J. A. (2013). Examining the effectiveness of a restorative justice program for various types of juvenile offenders. *International Journal of Offender Therapy and Comparative Criminology, 57*(9), 1054–1075.

Boehm, C. (1977). The moral system. In L. J. Stiles & B. D. Johnson (Eds.), *Morality examined: Guidelines for teachers* (pp. 25–39). Princeton Book Company.

Bosworth, K., & Judkins, M. (2014). Tapping into the power of school climate to prevent bullying: One application of schoolwide positive behavior interventions and supports. *Theory Into Practice, 53*(4), 300–307.

Buzzelli, C., & Johnston, B. (2014). *The moral dimensions of teaching: Language, power, and culture in classroom interaction.* Routledge.

Cameron, L., and M. Thorsborne. 2001. Restorative justice and school discipline; mutually exclusive? In H. Strang & J. Braithwaite (Eds.), *Restorative justice and civil society* (pp. 180–195). Cambridge University Press.

Carroll, J. S., Kaugars, A., & Grych, J. (2022). Diverse approaches for implementing restorative practices in schools in the US. In G. Velez, & T. Gavrielides (Eds.), *Restorative justice: Promoting peace and wellbeing* (pp. 3–22). Springer.

Cefai, C., & Cavioni, V. (2014). *Social and emotional education in primary school: Integrating theory and research into practice.* Springer.

Cohen, J., McCabe, E. M., Michelli, N. M., & Pickeral, T. (2009). School climate: Research, policy, practice, and teacher education. *Teachers College Record, 111*(1), 180–213.

Collins, J., Hess, M. E., & Lowery, C. L. (2019). Democratic spaces: How teachers establish and sustain democracy and education in their classrooms. *Democracy and Education, 27*(1), Article 3.

Cornell, D., & Huang, F. (2016). Authoritative school climate and high school student risk behavior: A cross-sectional multi-level analysis of student self-reports. *Journal of Youth and Adolescence, 45*(11), 2246–2259.

Cornell, D., Shukla, K., & Konold, T. (2015). Peer victimization and authoritative school climate: A multilevel approach. *Journal of Educational Psychology, 107*(4), 1186.

Creekmore, N., & Creekmore, M. (2022). How to make your school psychologically safe. *Educational Leadership, 79*(9), 42–46.

Darling, J. (1992). A.S. Neill on democratic authority: A lesson from Summerhill?. *Oxford Review of Education, 18*(1), 45–57.

Darling-Hammond, S., Fronius, T. A., Sutherland, H., Guckenburg, S., Petrosino, A., & Hurley, N. (2020). Effectiveness of restorative justice in US K–12 schools: A review of quantitative research. *Contemporary School Psychology, 24*(3), 295–308.

Dewey, J. (1909). *Moral principles in education.* Houghton Mifflin.

Dewey, J. (1939/1988). Creative democracy—The task before us. In J. Boydston & J. Ratner (Eds.), *Later works of John Dewey* (pp. 224–230). Southern Illinois University Press.

Efron, E. S. (2008). Moral education between hope and hopelessness: The legacy of Janusz Korczak. *Curriculum Inquiry, 38*(1), 39–62.

Ellerbrock, C. R. (2012). Creating a family-like ninth-grade environment through interdisciplinary teaming. *Urban Education, 47*(1), 32–64.

Engel, L. H. (2013). The democratic school and the pedagogy of Janusz Korczak: A model of early twentieth century reform in modern Israel. *International Journal of Progressive Education, 9*(1), 119–132.

Espelage, D. L., & Hong, J. S. (2019). School climate, bullying, and school violence. In M. J. Mayer & S. R. Jimerson (Eds.), *School safety and violence prevention: Science, practice, policy* (pp. 45–69). American Psychological Association.

Felten, P., & Clayton, P. H. (2011). Service-learning. *New Directions for Teaching and Learning, 2011*(128), 75–84.

Ferráns, S. D., & Selman, R. (2014). How students' perceptions of the school climate influence their choice to upstand, bystand, or join perpetrators of bullying. *Harvard Educational Review, 84*(2), 162–187.

Fielding, M. (2013). Whole school meetings and the development of radical democratic community. *Studies in Philosophy and Education, 32*(2), 123–140

Furco, A. (2016). Institutionalising service-learning in higher education. In L. McIlrath & I. Mac Labhrainn (Eds.), *Higher education and civic engagement: International perspectives* (pp. 65–82). Routledge.

Glover, D., & Coleman, M. (2005). School culture, climate and ethos: interchangeable or distinctive concepts?. *Journal of In-service Education, 31*(2), 251–272.

Goodman, J. F. (2006). School discipline in moral disarray. *Journal of Moral Education, 35*(2), 213–230.

Goodman, J. F. (2007). School discipline, buy-in and belief. *Ethics and Education, 2*(1), 3–23.

Gomez, J. A., Rucinski, C. L., & Higgins-D'Alessandro, A. (2021). Promising pathways from school restorative practices to educational equity. *Journal of Moral Education, 50*(4), 452–470.

Grant, G. (1988). *The world we created at Hamilton High.* Harvard University Press.

Gregory, M. (2000). Care as a goal of democratic education. *Journal of Moral Education, 29*(4), 445–461.

Gutmann, A. (1987). *Democratic education.* Princeton University Press.

Gutzwiller-Helfenfinger, E., & Perren, S. (2022). The moral dimensions of bullying at school: A social-ecological process perspective. In M. Killen & J. G. Smetana (Eds.), *Handbook of moral development* (3rd ed.; pp. 437–453). Routledge.

Hammersley, L. (2012). Community-based service-learning: Partnerships of reciprocal exchange? *Asia-Pacific Journal of Cooperative Education, 14*(3), 171–184.

Hansen, D. T. (2002). The moral environment in an inner-city boys' high school. *Teaching and Teacher Education, 18*(2), 183–204.

Hansen, T., & Umbreit, M. (2018). State of knowledge: Four decades of victim–offender mediation research and practice: The evidence. *Conflict Resolution Quarterly, 36*(2), 99–113.

Holt, J. C. (1970). *What do I do Monday*? Dell Publishing.

Hong, J. S., Espelage, D. L., & Lee, J. M. (2018). School climate and bullying prevention programs. In H. Shapiro (Ed.), *The Wiley handbook on violence in education: Forms, factors, and preventions* (pp. 359–374). Wiley.

Jackson, A. W., & Davis, G. A. (2000). *Turning points 2000: Educating adolescents in the 21st century.* Teachers College Press.

Jacoby, B. (2015). *Service-learning essentials.* Jossey-Bass.

Johnson, D. W., & Johnson, R. T. (2012). Restorative justice in the classroom: Necessary roles of cooperative context, constructive conflict, and civic values. *Negotiation and Conflict Management Research, 5*(1), 4–28.

King, J. T. (2004). Service-learning as a site for critical pedagogy: A case of collaboration, caring, and defamiliarization across borders. *Journal of Experiential Education, 26*(3), 121–137.

King, L. (2015). Baby steps toward restorative justice. *Rethinking Schools, 29*(4), 16–19.

Kline, D. M. S. (2016). Can restorative practices help to reduce disparities in school discipline data? A review of the literature. *Multicultural Perspectives, 18*(2), 97–102.

Kohn, A. (1997). How not to teach values: A critical look at character education. *Phi Delta Kappan, 78,* 428–439.

Lind, G. (2019). *How to teach moral competence.* Logos Verlag.

McCluskey, G., Lloyd, G., Kane, J., Riddell, S., Stead, J., & Weedon, E. (2008). Can restorative practices in schools make a difference? *Educational Review, 60*(4), 405–417.

McDonough, G. P. (2005). Moral maturity and autonomy: Appreciating the significance of Lawrence Kolhberg's just community. *Journal of Moral Education, 34*(2), 199–213.

Mikel, E. R. (2011). Deliberating democracy. In P. B. Joseph (Ed.), *Cultures of curriculum* (pp. 196–218). Routledge.

Morrell, M. E. (2007). Empathy and democratic education. *Public Affairs Quarterly, 21*(4), 381–403.

Morrison, B. (2013). Schools and restorative justice. In G. Johnstone & D. Van Ness (Eds.), *Handbook of restorative justice* (pp. 347–372). Willan.

Morrison, B. E., & Vaandering, D. (2012). Restorative justice: Pedagogy, praxis, and discipline. *Journal of School Violence, 11*(2).

Noddings, N. (2012) The caring relation in teaching, *Oxford Review of Education, 38*(6), 771–781.

Neill, A. S. (1960). *Summerhill: A radical approach to child rearing.* Hart.

Oser, F. K. (2014). Toward a theory of the just community approach: Effects of collective moral, civic, and social education. In L. Nucci, D. Narvaez, & T. Krettenauer (Eds.), *Handbook of moral and character education* (pp. 198–222). Routledge.

Oser, F. K., Althof, W., & Higgins-D'Alessandro, A. (2008). The just community approach to moral education: System change or individual change?. *Journal of Moral Education, 37*(3), 395–415.

Parker, W. C. (2005). Teaching against idiocy. *Phi Delta Kappan, 86*(5), 344–351.

Perry, B. L., & Morris, E. W. (2014). Suspending progress: Collateral consequences of exclusionary punishment in public schools. *American Sociological Review, 79*(6), 1067–1087.

Postholm, M. B. (2013). Classroom management: What does research tell us?. *European Educational Research Journal, 12*(3), 389–402.

Power, F. C., & Higgins-D'Alessandro, A. (2008). The just community approach to moral education and the moral atmosphere of the school. In L. P. Nucci & D. Narvaez (Eds.), *Handbook of moral and character education* (pp. 246–263). Routledge.

Preiss, D. R., Arum, R., Edelman, L. B., Morrill, C., & Tyson, K. (2016). The more you talk, the worse it is: Student perceptions of law and authority in schools. *Social Currents, 3*(3), 234–255.

Purpel, D. E. (1998). Service learning: A critique and affirmation. *Encounter: Education for Meaning and Social Justice, 11*(2), 22–27.

Range, B., Carnes-Holt, K., & Bruce, M. A. (2013). Engaging middle-grade students to learn in a caring community. *The Clearing House: A Journal of Educational Strategies, Issues and Ideas, 86*(2), 48–52.

Reimer, K. E. (2020). "Here, it's like you don't have to leave the classroom to solve a problem": How restorative justice in schools contributes to students' individual and collective sense of coherence. *Social Justice Research, 33*(4), 406–427.

Roffey, S. (2013). Inclusive and exclusive belonging: The impact on individual and community wellbeing. *Educational and Child Psychology, 30*(1), 38–49.

Rosing, H., Reed, S., Ferrari, J. R., & Bothne, N. J. (2010). Understanding student complaints in the service learning pedagogy. *American Journal of Community Psychology, 46*(3–4), 472–481.

Scarsdale High School. (2023). *Structures of the S.A.S. just community.* https://www.scarsdaleschools.k12.ny.us/page/455

Schaps, E. (2003). Creating a school community. *Educational Leadership, 60*(6), 31–33.

Scott, J. H. (2012). The intersection of service-learning and moral growth. *New Directions for Student Services, 2012*(139), 27–38.

Segal, A., Pollak, I., & Lefstein, A. (2017). Democracy, voice and dialogic pedagogy: The struggle to be heard and heeded. *Language and Education, 31*(1), 6–25.

Seigel, S., & Rockwood, V. (1993). Democratic education, student empowerment, and community service: Theory and practice. *Equity & Excellence in Education, 26*(2), 65–70.

Skinner, R., & Chapman, C. (1999). *National Center for Education Statistics: Service-learning and community service in K–12 public schools.* Office of Research and Improvement.

Snarey, J., & Samuelson, P. L. (2014). Lawrence Kohlberg's revolutionary ideas: Moral education in the cognitive-developmental tradition. In L. Nucci, D. Narvaez, & T. Krettenauer (Eds.), *Handbook of moral and character education* (pp. 61–83). Routledge.

Solomon, D., Watson, M., Battistich, V., Schaps, E., & Delucchi, K. (1996). Creating classrooms that students experience as communities. *American Journal of Community Psychology, 24*(6), 719–748.

Spring, K., Grimm Jr, R., & Dietz, N. (2008). *Community service and service-learning in America's schools.* Corporation for National and Community Service.

Strain, C. R. (2005). Pedagogy and practice: Service-learning and students' moral development. *New Directions for Teaching and Learning, 2005*(103), 61–72.

Suvall, C. (2009). Restorative justice in schools: Learning from Jena High School. *Harvard Civil Rights–Civil Liberties Law Review, 44*, 547–569.

Thapa, A., Cohen, J., Guffey, S., & Higgins-D'Alessandro, A. (2013). A review of school climate research. *Review of Educational Research, 83*(3), 357–385.

Thayer-Bacon, B. J. (1996). Democratic classroom communities. *Studies in Philosophy and Education, 15*(4), 333–351.

Tryon, E., Stoecker, R., Martin, A., Seblonka, K., Hilgendorf, A., & Nellis, M. (2008). The challenge of short-term service-learning. *Michigan Journal of Community Service Learning, 14*(2), 16–26.

Valenzuela, A. (1999). *Subtractive schooling: U.S.—Mexican youth and the politics of caring*. State University of New York Press.

Wade, R. C., & Saxe, D. W. (1996). Community service-learning in the social studies: Historical roots, empirical evidence, critical issues. *Theory & Research in Social Education, 24*(4), 331–359.

Watson, M. (2008). Developmental discipline and moral education. In L. P. Nucci, & D. Narvaez (Eds.) *Handbook of moral and character education* (pp. 175–203). Routledge.

Watson, M., & Battistich, V. (2006). Building and sustaining caring communities. In C. M. Evertson & C. S. Weinstein (Eds.), *Handbook of classroom management* (pp. 263–280). Lawrence Erlbaum.

Weigert, K. M. (1998). Academic service learning: Its meaning and relevance. *New Directions for Teaching and Learning, 73*, 3–10.

Weissbourd, R., Bouffard, S. M., & Jones, S. M. (2013). *School climate and moral and social development: School climate practice brief*. National School Climate Center.

You, Z., & Rud, A. G. (2010). A model of Dewey's moral imagination for service learning: Theoretical explorations and implications for practice in higher education. *Education and Culture, 26*(2), 36–51.

7

Moral Education Curricula

From Tradition to Transformation

> *Defining mature moral functioning for today's world may require incorporating not only evolved propensities, ancient notions of moral virtue, and the effective moral practices of the majority of traditionalist societies around the world, but also skills required for global citizenship and humanity's sustainable flourishing.*
>
> —Darcia Narvaez, 2010, "Moral Complexity: The Fatal Attraction of Truthiness and the Importance of Mature Moral Functioning," p. 172

Moral education is broadly defined "as any activity explicitly aimed at or geared towards improving the moral beliefs, values or behaviors of children and adolescents" (Rehren & Sauer, 2022, p. 2). Among these activities are "curriculum-oriented approaches" (Schuitema et al., 2008, p. 70) that introduce students to moral education through curricular content—"subject matter as organized bodies of knowledge" (Schwab, 1973, p. 510). Although experiential learning is a crucial factor in moral development, moral education as curricular content allows for "deliberate teaching"

Teaching for Moral Imagination, pages 141–177

(Schuitema et al., 2008, p. 70), affording students opportunities to contemplate "the nature of morality" (Barrow, 2006, p. 6) and to "generate moral perspectives" (Nucci, 2016, p. 299). As such, moral education can become "a coherent endeavor created with purpose and deliberation" (Joseph & Efron, 2005, p. 525). Moreover, as curricular content, moral education can supplement or be integrated into a school's academic offerings.

In the literature on moral education curricula, major orientations reflect different positions about content and practices as well as morality itself. The first, *values transmission,* is the most traditional form of moral education and rests on the premise that young people must know and live by the moral values or virtues sanctioned by culture or religion in which "morality is a system of behaviors reflecting what societies regard as 'right' or 'wrong'" (Chazan, 2022, p. 25). A second orientation, *skills-based moral education,* refers to the "development of cognitive abilities to approach, think and reason about moral questions and problems" (Rehren & Sauer, 2022, p. 3) in real life and across the academic curriculum. A third orientation, *transformative moral education,* focuses on imagining "a more just and peaceful world" (Joseph & Mikel, 2014, p. 328) that "corrects existing social inequalities and inequities" (Nucci, 2016, p. 299). This chapter delineates moral education curricula and examines underlying beliefs as structured by these three orientations (see Table 7.1).

But no matter their chosen orientation to moral education, educators might consider these guiding questions to avoid creating superficial or haphazard curricula:

- In what ways can moral education help students to think deeply about moral values and the meaning of morality?
- How can moral education curricula stimulate ethical learning through academic subject areas?
- How can moral education curricula support the development of moral imagination?

Traditional Values and Virtues

Scholarship on moral education for transmitting traditional values and virtues evinces considerable complexity. Whereas moral education can embody historical values stemming from enduring religious traditions, some curricula reflect changing values in response to national circumstances or perceived needs for socialization of youth. Many nations specifically mandate moral education as a formal curriculum to be taught in schools whereas others allow decisions about content or about even about offering

TABLE 7.1 Moral Education Curricular Content

Curricula	Description
Traditional Values and Virtues	
Cultural Heritage	Transmission of values through sacred texts, oral traditions, and national curricula to inculcate in young people traditionally sanctioned beliefs, viewpoints, and behaviors.
Character Education	Virtues-based moral education characterized by direct instruction for traditional values, readings exemplifying virtues, and rewards for desirable behavior.
Moral Philosophy and Ethical Inquiry	
Moral Conversation	The underlying pedagogy of philosophical and ethical inquiry curriculum to foster respectful, egalitarian, and carefully facilitated discussions.
Philosophy with Children	Investigation of moral issues pertinent to individuals and society through a classroom community of philosophical inquiry, deliberation, and reflection.
Ethical Inquiry Across the Curriculum	Exploration of ethical issues and moral dilemmas germane to academic curricula by enhancing capacities for moral perception, ethical reasoning, and critical reflection.
Transformative Moral Education	
Critical Pedagogy	A process of investigations of social issues leading to critical awareness of injustice and to agency to effect change.
Human Rights Education	Study of human rights issues and codified documents guaranteeing rights as well as violations and the conditions that bring about them.
Ecojustice Education	A curriculum focused on real-life investigations of schools and communities as well as analysis of the destructive effects on the environment; interrogation of acceptance of human domination of nature.
Peace Studies	Curriculum and practices for learning about peace and nonviolence and how to be peaceful within classrooms, communities, and among nations.
Conflict Resolution Education	Teaching of skills for peaceful resolution of conflicts including perspective taking, negotiation, and collaborative problem-solving.
Global Education	Examination of international relationships and problems and emphasizes multicultural understanding, peaceful coexistence, and interdependency.
Environmental Education	Holistic curricular orientation emphasizing ecological consciousness, sustainability, and emotional or spiritual connection to nature.

moral education in any form left to local control. So too, in several countries schools embrace a form of moral education, character education, with its emphasis on cultivation of traits and values.

Cultural Heritage

The aim of moral education for the transmission of values is to inculcate in young people sanctioned beliefs, viewpoints, and behaviors. Such curricula emanate from sacred writings, oral traditions, and mandated national programs and textbooks. A way to comprehend moral education for values transmission is to become familiar with several predominant motifs:

- unity of religion and morality
- spirituality and relatedness
- community and social harmony
- national identity and patriotism
- diversity and citizenship

These themes capture a multiplicity of aims and cast light on the intricate social, political, and historical background gleaned from the international literature on moral education.

In the literature describing transmission of traditional cultural values, scholars consider the *unity of religion and morality* as a predominant theme of moral education endorsed by historical monotheistic religions of Judaism, Catholicism, and Islam. Despite profound differences in narratives, values, rules, and responsibilities, these traditions share an essential commonality: the assertion that "moral education is impossible" without a sense of the sacred (Green, 1999, p. 112). For example, "Jewish tradition sees religion and morality as intrinsically interrelated and integrated" (Efron, 1994, p. 52); "the aspiration of Catholic schooling is to educate the whole person in light of an all-embracing worldview based on divine revelation" (Cuypers, 2004, p. 426); and, "from an Islamic perspective, socially derived moral truths cannot replace the authority of divine revelation and inner experience as sources for moral understanding" (Hussain, 2007, p. 297). Once more, whether following the teachings of the Torah, Bible, or the Qur'an, these religious traditions turn to divine role models and moral exemplars for guidance about how to live ethically (Alexander, 2001; Nuzzi, 2004; Reetz, 2010). Finally, the scholarship on moral education from the Judaic, Catholic, and Islamic traditions illustrates that the concept of unity extends to a holistic understanding of moral education; all three religious traditions characterize the goal of moral education as an interface of religious faith, reason, and moral action (Chasan, 2022; Cuypers, 2004; Efron 1994; El-Moslimany, 2018; Memon & Alhashmi, 2018; Shapiro, 2005; Nuzzi, 2004).

Another theme—*spirituality and relatedness*—primarily comes from oral traditions transmitted by elders to young people (Armstrong, 2000;

Ikuenobe, 2018; Suina, 2000). Research about moral education within indigenous cultures reveals beliefs about "human interconnectedness with all other living things" and "nature relatedness" (Niigaaniin & MacNeill, 2022, p. 3): as spiritual connections "to each other as human beings, to the earth and to the whole cosmos" (Dei, 2002, p. 38). Scholars note that "most indigenous societies maintain a reciprocal relationship between the earth and humans" (Frisancho & Delgado, 2018, pp. 5–6), nature and the land have "spiritual dimensions" (Fonda, 2011, p. 4), and "other-than-human entities are treated typically as kin and as agentic subjects" (Narvaez, 2016, p. 230). This form of moral education also involves learning from cultural traditions and values, not through direct instruction but by deep understanding of and participation in a culture's arts and ceremonies. Scholarship about this motif especially highlights the nature of moral teachings from African and Native American cultures.

African traditional moral education emphasizes that "moral issues, even when they are issues between human beings, involve the relationship between spiritual and human beings" (Udeani, 2008, p. 67), the wisdom of elders and the spiritual guidance of ancestors (Ikuenobe, 2018, p. 32), the spiritual importance of "origin, ancestry, place, and history" (Dei, 2002, p. 44), and "the key moral relationships of kinship" (Metz & Gaie, 2010, p. 282). The concept of relatedness" is specifically taught as educators envision moral development not in "an individualistic way" as "the true self is inextricably bound up in relationships with other humans and non-human nature" (Le Grange, 2012, p. 338). Also, moral education involves storytelling to transmit moral values and cultural viewpoints (Tuwe, 2016); stories "convey important moral ideas or lessons to children since it is the duty of the storyteller to initiate children into the wisdom and custom of their society" (Ajayi & Iwuagwu, 2012, p. 2). In the United States, African-centered schools and enrichment programs draw from traditional African values and focus on developing students' spiritual identity and connection to ancestry.

Moral education in Native American traditions also centers on spirituality and relatedness in that "everything, including ourselves, is part of everything else... part of the land, community, family, and so on" (Armstrong, 2000, p. 40) as "Native people honor the integrity of the universe as a whole living being and inter-connected system" (Kawagley & Barnhardt, 1999, p. 8). A Native American scholar writes:

> We're all in this world to contribute to the well-being of all people. I think that these values of interconnectedness and responsibility need to be taught to our children. I think we can do that through our ceremonies and our

> dances. I also think that teaching these values in a natural settings, outdoors, is important. (Suina, 2000, p. 97)

In Native American belief systems, spirituality is "profoundly oriented to place" (McNally, 2017, p. 55) and "knowledge held by different tribal and indigenous groups cannot be understood as universal" (Yazzie-Mintz, 2011, p. 178). Therefore, "whereas all of nature is held in great respect, certain land forms or natural areas are experienced as the dwelling place of spirit beings whose presence gives special meaning and sacredness to the location" (Hendry, 2003, p. 5). Accordingly, Native American tribal and public schools have close relationships with community members and elders, integrate place-based knowledge and Native language into the curriculum, and attend to spirituality through oral traditions and cultural arts.

A third theme, *community and social harmony*, is both a historical and contemporary aim of moral education in various countries but most often in cultures influenced by the tradition of Confucianism (Shin & Koh, 2005, p. 1). These values influence both schools' moral socialization efforts and curricular content (Bamkin, 2020, p. 219) for the purpose of developing "students' knowledge, competence and practice to live better alongside others" (p. 221) and for "consideration of others" (p. 234). Scholars writing about moral education in China, Taiwan, Japan, Korea, and Singapore explore the continued influence of Confucianism as "a fundamental viewpoint in the conduct of life and society" (Yu, 2008, p. 122). A most essential Confucian moral value is filial piety—respect for and an obligation to care for parents—as there is "emphasis on strong families as the foundation of society" (Tan & Wong, 2010, p. 92). Thus, underlying the relationship of the individual to the community is "an intimate continuity between the family and the community" (Sim & Chow, 2019, pp. 467, 476). Unlike the Western philosophical orientation of individuality, in Confucianism "no comprehensive conception of 'self' can be reached without considering relational roles and responsibilities" (Sim & Chow, 2019, p. 466) and "the well-being of the community takes precedence over the interests of the individual" (Tan & Wong, 2010, p. 91). The Confucianist tradition endorses "an ideal of a meritocratic, harmonious social hierarchy in which people respect their social obligations" (O'Dwyer, 2003, p. 43). In this tradition, teachers desire to cultivate students' morality for taking their place in a "harmonious society" (Sim & Chow, 2019, p. 477).

A fourth motif of international moral education scholarship is the incorporation of *national identity and patriotism*. For example, a purpose for moral education in Japan is to impart "values necessary for becoming good citizens" (Anzai, 2015, p. 444); Singapore's integrated civics and moral education curriculum focuses on "nation building" and is "instrumental in holding Singapore's pluralistic society together and to instill "a collective national identity" (Sim & Chow, 2019 p. 469); moral education in Korea reflects esteem for traditional values as well as "developing students' sense of a democratic society" (Lee & Misco, 2014, p. 728). So too, Russia's mandated curriculum for "spiritual and moral development" revers "traditional national values" (Ozhiganova, 2019, p. 111). Researchers interpret the impetus for nationalistic curricula as a response to social, and political changes or historical upheavals (Han et al., 2018; Lee & Misco, 2014)—war, occupation, and regime change.

Moreover, several nations require the inclusion of patriotism as a civic value or a dominant creed (Bamkin, 2018; Wansheng & Wujie, 2004), however, the concept of patriotism varies profoundly. On one hand, in Russa "patriotic education as a part of moral education" is "militarized" and "continues the long-standing tradition to subdue and silence critical rationalization of patriotism in educational discourses in favor of a more traditional concept of State Patriotism" (Rapoport, 2009, p. 143). In the People's Republic of China (PRC) the government promotes a rigid and uncritical patriotism "as an ideology" (Lin & Jackson, 2022, pp. 1–2) with moral education textbooks dwelling on China's history of being "humiliated by foreign invaders" (Lee & Wang, 2023. p. 5). Alternately, the concept of patriotism seems somewhat benign in Japan with its focus on "love of community, country and culture" (Anzai, 2015, pp. 436) or characterized as "reflective patriotism" in Korea that "is not chauvinism or jingoism" and even "emphasizes the importance of civil disobedience" for violations of "universal human values" (Han et al., 2018, p. 74).

A final motif, *diversity and citizenship,* appears in studies of recent moral education efforts by nations wishing to respect their indigenous as well as their increasing immigrant populations. Such state-sponsored curricula acknowledge diversity and cultural plurality as moral values and essential elements of citizenship. Several nations in Asia promote these values. For example, "Korean moral textbooks encourage students to think that they live in a diverse community" and teach "respect for and consideration of others" (Lee & MIsco, 2014, p. 730). Scholars also comment on Taiwan's recognition of aboriginal peoples' cultures and languages (Lee, 2004, p. 577) and how this nation has been "moving from uniformity to diversity" (p. 578)—to "fostering pluralism and respect" (pp. 586). From the beginning of the 21st century, Taiwan's Ministry of Education replaced a singular course on moral education with "courses dealing with such general moral issues as humanism and self-understanding, respecting and appreciating others and their cultures, and taking care of oneself as well as the natural environment" (Wu, 2017, p. 74). Also, scholars write that "the social climate of Malaysia is pluralistic in nature" and that required moral education curriculum includes "having an enhanced understanding of cooperation by sustaining a peaceful and harmonious life in a democratic Malaysia" (Zulkifli & Hashim, 2019, p. 888).

Additionally, scholars document moral education curricula in Latin America reflecting recognition of diverse and democratic societies. An example is Colombia's efforts "towards building citizenship education that can foster the necessary ethical bond for social and political flourishing and which can be built from such diversity" (Jaramillo & Mesa, 2009, p. 469). Similarly, a moral education curriculum developed—but not mandated—by the Brazilian government "has four key themes: ethics, democratic coexistence, human rights, and social inclusion" (Araújo & Arantes, 2009, p. 490). Latin American countries have developed citizenship and moral education programs helped by resources from international initiatives "for the promotion of democratic culture" (Moreno-Gutiérrez & Frisancho, 2009, p. 391).

Character Education

While many nations refer to specific virtues in their curriculum guides and textbooks, character education is not dominant international moral education orientation. It is, however, the preponderant form of moral education in the United States and currently supported by the governments of the United Kingdom, Australia, and several Canadian provinces. Furthermore, there is a very large body of academic and popular literature about its aims and history as well as extensive critique of its ideology and practices.

In the United States from the 17th century to the present day, it has been a "taken-for-granted presupposition that schools should play a major role in transmitting 'good character' and fostering character development" (Boyles, 2005, p. 46). Moreover, from the beginning of the public-school movement in the early 19th century through the early 20th century, ubiquitous textbooks imparted moral and patriotic values; numerous generations of American children were schooled in traditional conceptions of morality and good citizenship.

> Textbooks taught "love of country, love of God, duty to parents, the necessity to develop habits of thrift, honesty, and hard work in order to accumulate property, the certainty of progress [and] the perfection of the United States." Famous spellers and readers, like those of Noah Webster and William Holmes McGuffey, warned ominously of the dangers of drunkenness,

> luxury, self-pride, and deception and promised handsome earthly rewards for courage, honesty, and respect for others. (McClellan, 1999, p. 25)

Into the 21st century, notwithstanding the availability of various other curricular approaches, character education with its explicit teaching of values remains popular in U.S. schools. In contemporary times, schools and school districts create their own character education programs—sometimes with input from parents and communities (Seider, 2012)—but often rely on commercial curriculum packages providing lists of virtues and teachers' guides. Christian fundamentalist schools also have endorsed character education and see it as compatible with their instruction as long as sanctioned values are attributed to religious tenets (Laats, 2010; Wilhelm & Firmin, 2008).

In contrast, character education is a relatively new development in the United Kingdom, regardless of its cultural congruence with the Victorian emphasis on character as a "personal disposition" (Taylor, 2018, pp. 404). Toward the beginning of the 21st century, character education in the UK was considered a "growing movement," but without "unity of understanding among members of this movement" (Arthur, 2005, p. 245). However, the UK government in 2011 endorsed programs for teaching of virtues in schools as a response to social unrest. As well, the Jubilee Centre for Character and Virtues launched in 2012 to conduct interdisciplinary research on how "virtues that make up good character can be learnt and taught" (Arthur et al., 2015, p. 3); the Centre has been influential in generating scholarship and professional development resources. Still, scholars suggest that "few in Britain would consider the school the most important location for character education" above other moral socialization influences, such as media, peers, and religion (Arthur, 2005, p. 246) and that character education "finds itself in a precarious position in the politico-educational landscape . . . coming under attack from both the political left and the political right" (Kristjánsson, 2021, p. 366). However, in the Commonwealth, the Australian government endorses implementation of a character education framework and resources for character-building education (Lovat & Dally, 2018) and several Canadian provincial governments support traditional character education initiatives to identify and teach common values (Pashby et al., 2014; Winton, 2008).

The literature on character education illustrates that this moral education approach has various meanings. "In the broad sense, character education refers to almost anything that schools might try to provide outside of academics, especially when the purpose is to help children grow into good people" (Kohn, 1997, p. 429). Most likely because moral education connotes religious education (Cassidy, 2022, p. 17), schools in various Western nations generally use the term character education to mean an umbrella of multiple moral education approaches. Indeed, research about "effective character-education" programs demonstrate "comprehensive, multifaceted approaches" including "social-skill training, caring communities, conflict resolution, parent involvement, opportunities for student reflection and grappling with moral issues, and adults modeling good character" (Berkowitz & Bier, 2004, p. 82).

Even so, scholars discuss how "moral education is broader than character education" (Obiagu, 2023, p. 238) and differentiate between character education "as the entire field" of moral education and the "more narrow approach of traditional character education" (Howard et al., 2004, p. 190). "In the narrow sense," character education "denotes a particular style of moral training" reflected in values as well as "assumptions about the nature of children and how they learn" (Kohn, 1997, p. 429). On the whole, authors identify the narrower or traditional concept of teaching specific values and traits when they discuss character education.

> In a phrase, character educators believe that the major purpose of education is to transmit "character, academics, and discipline"—the educational triad that incorporates the "traditional moral values" . . . Like Aristotle, character educators advocate the importance of exemplification, imitation, and habituation in the formation of moral character. (Nash, 1997, p. 21)

Three fundamental practices identify this form of character education: direct instruction for traditional values, readings that exemplify virtues and virtuous behavior, and rewards for desirable behavior.

Education for character is part of a long tradition of "virtue-based" moral education (Thoma & Walker, 2017) and "traces it roots to Aristotle" (Noddings, 2002, p. 61).

> Among the central tenets of an Aristotelian approach are the principles that: (a) there is an objective notion of human flourishing; (b) the virtues are a necessary condition for flourishing; and (c) these acquired attributes necessary for flourishing should be the ultimate ends of the education system. (Arthur et al., 2015, p. 9)

The "cornerstone of the neo-classical strategy is the Aristotelian argument that virtue is acquired in much the same way as other skills and abilities—through practice" (Hunter, 2002, p. 43). However, philosophers are not of one mind about education for virtues. Martha Nussbaum (1994) interprets Aristotle's virtue ethics to mean that good habits are not formed through "mindless behavioral conditioning, but patterns of increasingly intelligent choice guided by attachment and love" (p. 38). David Carr (2005), writes:

> [V]irtue ethics has something in common with modern character developmental approaches to moral education… [but] I believe that virtue ethics provides a rather more theoretically sophisticated view of the complexities of moral life than character education. Indeed, insofar as virtue ethical emotions require rational ordering, virtue ethics is undoubtedly an ethics of principled reflection (p. 140).

Nel Noddings (2002) feared that "character education concentrates on the development of virtues in contrast to views that emphasize reasoning, problem solving, and critical thinking (p. 61). Likewise, cognitive psychologist Lawrence Kohlberg (1975) concluded that if we are to conceptualize character as living by habitually examined principles, "an indoctrinative moral education" with its "imposition of the rules and values of the teacher and his culture on the child" (p. 673) is antithetical to education for moral development.

Critical examination of the rationale behind character education uncovers a motivation more disquieting than the desire for children's moral flourishing and "transmission of the community's best values and ethical ideals" (Wynne & Ryan, 1993 p. 58). Rather, advocates of character education expose their fear of young people's moral deficiencies, "a stunningly dark view of children" and belief that children "need fixing" (Kohn, 1997, p. 431) because they have lost the capacity "to control impulses and defer gratification" (Etzioni, 1993, p. 91). As well, some promoters hold a "pessimistic view of human nature" (Yu, 2004, p. 71) and fear that without a moral code "that has sustained Western society for centuries, adults become uncivilized" (Shannon, 1997, p. 152), resulting in "moral and social degeneration" (Spohrer, 2021, p. 4). Arguments for "moral literacy"—knowledge of core values as expressed in written heritage—indicate that virtues are no longer recognizable and "may have already been lost to the living memory of the culture" (Hunter, 2008, p. 222). Rationales for character education manifest a belief in "moral declinity" (Nash, 1997, p. 8) and that "character education in the public schools is the only way to reverse the erosion of moral standards" (p. 18).

Some scholars of character education conjecture that "the more people exhibit good character and virtues, the healthier our society" (Arthur et al., 2015, p. 3), deeming virtues as integral to moral functioning and the "core of selfhood" (p. 9). But whereas these authors view virtues as "stable and consistent states of character" (p. 9), they also believe that "the virtues that make up good character can be learnt and taught" (p. 3). Yet, it is not clear how children will understand virtues and internalize them when schools endorse trivial commonplace practices such as centering on a "value of the month" (Boyles, 2005; Smith, 2013). If moral educators teach a list of virtues in piecemeal fashion, young people cannot gain a deep understanding of morality. Philosopher John Dewey (1908/1996) envisioned that "unity is involved in the very idea of integrity of character" as well as the pitfalls resulting from "the notion that virtues may be kept apart, pigeon-hold in water-tight compartments" (p. 115). Similarly, sociologist James Davison Hunter (2002) explains the need for "a coherent moral philosophy rooted in social institutions and reflected in a communally shared narrative," otherwise moral codes can only deteriorate into arbitrary personal preferences" (p. 53).

Character education resources—texts, curricular packages, and academic writing—recommend a plentitude of virtues that should be taught to children. Some of these virtues unequivocally are of a moral nature and others, perhaps in a more convoluted way, might support moral functioning.

> It is helpful to divide the virtues into four main types: moral; intellectual; civic; and performance. Moral and civic virtues are essential to a good communal life; intellectual virtues are dispositions pertaining to inquiry, understanding, applying knowledge and respect for evidence; and performance virtues provide the strength of will to achieve goals, whatever they are. (Arthur et al., 2015, p. 9)

For example, two well-known character education books (intended also for parent audiences) are the *Book of Virtues* (Bennett, 1993) and *A Call to Character* (Greer & Kohl, 1995) that respectively showcase character traits admired by political conservatives and liberals. Nonetheless, despite their different perspectives, e.g., virtues of work and faith (on the conservative list) or creativity and idealism (revered by liberals), their editors hold five virtues in common: self-discipline, responsibility, honesty, loyalty, and courage. Moreover, a well-known character education organization names "The Six Pillars of Character": trustworthiness, respect, responsibility, fairness, caring, and citizenship (Character Counts, 2023). Nevertheless, notes a Christian educational scholar, "what one finds absent from Bennett, Greer, and Kohl's lists and almost every packaged character education program are [the] virtues [of] hope, forgiveness, gentleness, peace, patience, mercy" (Glanzer, 2000, p. 120). As well, a feature of character education is its attention to and glorification of individual virtues and efforts. A telling example in material from the UK's Jubilee Center is the treatment of US civil rights activist Rosa Parks focusing on "her image as an individual with particular character traits, acting on her own" but ignores her long involvement with civil rights organizations and movements (Suissa, 2015, p. 113).

Contemporary studies of school-wide character education efforts document wide-ranging values—compassion, cooperation, patriotism, and tolerance (Smith, 2013, p. 352)—along with recent initiatives that especially emphasize performance traits:

> Performance character initiatives focus on the skills and traits needed for students to attain excellence in school, the workplace, or any area of endeavor. This emphasis added a host of new virtues to character education, such as diligence, effort, perseverance, self-discipline, attention, motivation, self-confidence, and optimism. (pp. 352–353)

However, equating "performance virtues such as resilience and self-confidence" and ignoring "the compass provided by moral virtues" (Arthur et al., 2015) is problematic as these can have little to do with moral character. Also, in the tradition of "connecting upwards social mobility and employability with character" (Taylor, 2018, p. 408), scholars note that there is a "racist and classist discourse surrounding character education in schools" that connects academic failure "with character flaws" as a "disproportionate number of students with markers of academic failure are low-income or students of color" (Handsman, 2021, p. 273).

Once more, "the use of rewards for positive behavior is a mainstay of traditional approaches to character education" (Nucci, 2006, p. 720) as numerous character education programs recognize individual children for demonstrating virtuous traits. These programs employ "the 'catch them being good' concept" and rewards are "distributed whenever someone in authority catches a student doing something praiseworthy" (Watson, 2008, p. 187). These incentives might entail a treat from a fast-food restaurant (Boyles, 2005) or receiving "certificates, plaques, trophies, and other tokens of recognition" (Kohn 1997, p. 430) at "value award assemblies" (Lovat & Daily, 2018, p. 13). Critics of character education believe that at a result of this behavioristic emphasis, children learn "that the point of being good is to get rewards" (Kohn, 1997, p. 430).

> There is little dispute that rewards and positive feedback lead to an increase in rates of desirable behavior. What is in contention, however, is the impact of rewards on students' intrinsic motivation to do the right thing. There is now a considerable body of evidence indicating that an overreliance on rewards and positive feedback can undermine children's moral motivation. (Nucci, 2006, p. 720)

Since researchers confirm that rewards for good behavior decrease children's desire to act morally, the typical practice of character education calls into question if the narrow conceptualization of character education really can generate moral perspectives or sustain moral behaviors.

Ethical Reasoning

Moral education for enhancing students' ethical reasoning is grounded on the premise that deliberation promotes moral development by fostering understanding of others' viewpoints and critical self-reflection about moral decisions. Within respectful, egalitarian, and carefully facilitated discussions, students investigate ethical issues, explore moral dilemmas, imagine alternatives, and grapple with inherent complexities of decision-making.

Moral Conversation

The concept of moral conversation underpins curricula for ethical reasoning. Such conversations can be quite expansive, for instance, considering "how human beings should act," "life's meaning and the human place in the world," "the sources of evil and suffering," and "universal existential concerns and ways of knowing such as the meaning of friendship, love, and beauty" (Simon, 2001, pp. 37–38). Conversations also can center on specific moral dilemmas involving "a tension between two or more conflicting choices," often provoking further discussion rather than settling on "a concrete answer" (Wong, 2021, p. 369).

> A conversation is not an argument, although it can get heated. A conversation is at its best when the participants are not impatient to conclude their business, but wish instead to spend their time together in order to deepen and enrich their understanding of an idea, or… the ideas in a text (Nash, 1996, pp. 85–86)

In these conversations, participants must "consider alternatives and attempt to construct together a reasonable understanding of the world and ways in which human beings could be said to live well" (Sharp, 1984, p. 3).

So too, "conversing is an activity that recognizes the value of each of the participants"; everyone has something to say, everyone listens"—reinforcing a "sense of personal efficacy," "dignity, and "respect" (Grant, 1996, p, 480). Because "effective conversations must first be ethical conversations," conversation leaders need to ensure that a discussion group "agrees on an actual code of ethics: a set of mutual right and obligations to govern the conversational process" (Nash, 1996, p. 102). It should be the goal of educators to nurture such a "community of inquiry" (Sharp, 1984) in which participants "learn from one another's experience, share one another's understandings, and feel a sense of belonging to a larger community" (Lipman, 1995, p. 70).

Nonetheless, despite the respect and dignity afforded by moral conversations, participation in such discussions can be unsettling. Scholars write that the "experience of dialogue" can "undermine self-certainty" and compels participants "to recognize the complexity and ambiguity of the matter under discussion" (Grant, 1996, p. 474). Ultimately moral education "as critical inquiry" is "meant to cultivate independence of mind and to ensure that ethical precepts are adopted only after full examination—and not on the basis of authority" (p. 471). Moral conversation requires "that we scrupulously listen for the *truth* in other views, without rigid political preconceptions, and that we ruthlessly challenge the taken-for-granted truth we always assume in our own views" (Nash, 1996, p. 100). In this way, this form of discussion is integral to the cultivation of moral imagination by helping students to discern a moral situation and to examine beliefs and actions leading to critical self-reflection.

For instructors, it is crucial to become "fellow discussants" rather than "purveyors of wisdom" (Simon, 2001, p. 104) and "to step off the stage long enough for students to speak to one another" (p. 131). Teachers "can share puzzlement with their students, be open to unexpected but suggestive responses to the questions they and their students pose, and take pleasure in observing the exchanges students have with each other" (Pritchard, 2022). They "must not use their authority to impose their aims" but at the same time have insight about their students so that they can "tune onto their moral ideas and their pace of development" (Lind, 2006, p. 191). Educators have the responsibility of "allowing time for clarification of dilemmas" (p. 193) and to ensure that conversations have "a sharp intellectual focus"—to "promote stimulating, rather than aimless and overly personal discussions" (Nash, 1996, p. 101). This calls on educators to develop the craft of "asking good questions" that are essential for creating an "excellent moral conversation" (p. 103).

Philosophy With Children

Numerous scholars consider students' engagement with philosophy a valuable form of moral education for ethical reasoning. Characterized by the umbrella term, philosophy with children (Cassidy, 2012), this curricular orientation with its crucial component of investigation of moral issues began in the 1970s by philosopher and educator Mathew Lipman and has become an international movement "in every continent and region in the world" (Millett & Tapper, 2012, p. 547). Programs for engaging children and adolescents in philosophical inquiry include Philosophy for Children, Community of Philosophical Inquiry, Thinking Through Philosophy, and Ethical Understanding Curriculum. For teachers and schools interested in these curricula, numerous resources—books, articles, curricular content materials, and lesson plans for stimulating philosophical discussions—are available.

This approach is based on the discipline of philosophy that "focuses on thinking" and involves reflection—"thinking about thinking"—to allow students to gain "a rich understanding of issues and ideas that inform life and society" (Cam, 2014, pp. 1206–1207). It also builds expertise in "thinking together" as well as "rational questioning and intelligent agreement and disagreement" while students respectfully listen and respond to each other (Milett & Tapper, 2012, p. 547). The "classroom community of philosophical deliberation" is viewed as preparation for becoming "participating member of a democratic society" (Lipman, 1995, p. 70) as "extended dialogue into a philosophical question can contribute to the cultivation of a well-informed democratic citizenry" (Echeverria & Hannam, 2016, p. 4). Albeit, several contemporary scholars of this curriculum caution that discussion emphasizing "politeness and reasonableness" can "limit the range of emotional, experiential and intellectual responses to contentious issues, especially those who have been marginalized themselves" (Drane & Higham, 2023, p. 11) and does not attend to "underlying relationships of domination and their historical roots" (Chetty, 2018, p. 46).

Because of its emphasis on ethical inquiry, advocates for philosophy with children clearly link this curriculum with moral education. They insist that a reflective moral education grounded in ethical inquiry allows for self-reflection and for young people "to consider themselves in-relation to others and the world in which, and of which, they are a part" (Cassidy, 2022, p. 20). For instance, a researcher recounted philosophic inquiry in a fifth-grade classroom about the concept of retaliation with the teacher posing such questions as: "Can retaliating really 'get things even'?" "What alternatives to trying to 'get things even' might there be?" (Pritchard, 2022). Scholars point out the contrast between moral education as ethical inquiry and inculcation of values from moral socialization in the home and school; they criticize moral education as "teaching by telling" since it fails to cultivate "critical judgment" (Cam, 2016, p. 6) when children do not have "the opportunity to explore what they think about these values" (Cassidy, 2012, p. 247).

Lipman (1995) declared that "effective moral education requires that students actively engage in ethical inquiry, and ethical inquiry, in turn, requires that students cultivate all aspects of their thinking" (p. 61). Lipman's colleague and co-author, Ann Margaret Sharp (2007), advised that teachers guide students to contemplate "philosophical questions": "What kind of world (society, community) do you want to live in? What does it mean to be a person of the world? What values ought I to commit myself to? How should I attend to the other? (p. 251). As "an exercise of the moral imagination," philosophical inquiry "challenges the untried assumptions of each participant's cultural and traditional views, making it possible for participants to take on the perspectives of the others to view themselves" (Mizell, 2015, p. 323). Moral imagination thus "enables moral reasoning" but also is "essential for communal life" as it affords "understanding, and interacting with, those most different from us" (Bleazby, 2012, p. 101).

The founders of philosophy with children called for students to become "critical, creative and caring thinkers" (Lipman, 1995, p. 61). In particular, "caring thinking embodies three fundamental ethical tools: empathy, moral imagination and decentering" (Sharp, 2007, p. 250). They also argued that that stimulating moral imagination to rouse moral emotions is not adequate in itself.

> Children's moral imagination may be fired by tales of saints and heroes, but if we are going to expect them to engage in moral conduct in a reflective and responsible fashion they are going to have to have some degree of philosophical understanding as to what sainthood and heroism are about. (Lipman & Sharp, 1978, p. 90)

Accordingly, moral imagination stimulated by moral stories and dilemmas should be cultivated through disciplined philosophical inquiry.

Ethical Inquiry Across the Curriculum

By providing opportunities for teaching students "to interrogate and engage thoughtfully with the world they live in" (Bermudez, 2015, p. 116), ethical inquiry allows for the "infusion of critical and creative thinking into standard subject area instruction" (Swartz, 1992, p. 108). Moral education as ethical inquiry inspired by dilemmas and issues encountered through the academic curricula—literature and drama, social studies and history, media literacy and science—stimulates the moral imagination by rousing moral emotions and enhancing capacities for moral perception, ethical reasoning, and critical reflection. As well, through the process of ethical inquiry, "students ponder the effect of moral, immoral, and amoral actions upon themselves and others . . . and construct their understanding of what it means to be a moral human being" (Joseph & Efron, 2005, p. 531).

A primary springboard for ethical inquiry is literature—stories, novels, plays, and poetry. Whereas teaching literature as lessons about explicit moral values is a common educational practice, scholars instead urge that teachers choose readings and guide discussions for the purpose of imaginative engagement. They write that readings should not be chosen for blatant moral messages but to allow students to engage with uncertainties—"to offer space for students to discuss and provide a safe space for them to consider moral dilemmas by projecting their morality onto the story's characters" (Wong, 2021, p. 369). Educators should avoid stories with a "mostly didactic style . . . telling children what to do and not to do, but do not offer any opportunity to think further" (Koc & Buzzelli, 2004, p. 94) and instead to choose literature that "encourages them to think more deeply about moral issues" (p. 97).

Literature holds the potential for "affecting a person's perception of the world" (Heilbronn, 2021, p. 11) by enhancing the ability to think what it might be like to be in the shoes of someone different from oneself" (p. 7) and for "educating and refining the capacity for sympathy" (p. 8). But although scholars may emphasize the complexities of moral stories to enhance ethical reasoning, literature can have an emotional and imaginative impact; "literature offers that kind of experience, uniquely activating our metaphorical sensibilities to the might-be-could-be in our lives and worlds" (McGinley et al., 2017, p. 67). By experiencing literature, students "read and respond with both their hearts and minds" (p. 68) through emotional engagement with characteries in stories" (p. 77). "Literary texts . . . rarely tell us what to do"; instead, "they open up vistas of what it means to be human and to act humanely" (p. 75). For this reason, teachers should acknowledge young people's fascination with the forces of good and evil as portrayed in literature and film; they can build on such interest by encouraging students "to clarify, identify, and understand the details of the metaphysical tournament of narratives" (Glanzer, 2008, p. 528). By exploring powerful universal themes, moral imagination becomes "a source of moral seriousness that enables us to sympathize with others as engaged in our common humanity" (Heilbronn, 2021, pp. 3–4).

The field of social studies is another avenue for ethical inquiry. Often characterized as memorization of historical fact and stories (Byrd, 2012, p. 1073) and instilling values for socialization and patriotism (Sears & Parsons, 1991, p. 48), nonetheless, this discipline has a strong tradition of teaching critical thinking. Scholars consider this ability to be "essential to a democratic society" (p. 47) and see that an ethical responsibility is to prepare students to participate in democratic life (p. 65). They call for teachers to provoke questions about "how we ought to live together" (McAvoy & Hess, 2013, p. 16), "the relationships between the individual and the state" (p. 37), "our vision of the common good" (Milligan et al., 2018, p. 450), and the "immorality of denying basic human rights" (Byrd, 2012, p. 1073; p. 1074). Consequently, teachers need to "engage students in the pedagogical practice of deliberation" (McAvoy & Hess, 2013, p. 16) and to "give students concrete experiences wrestling with the value tensions" of political discourse (p. 37).

Scholars view the study of history as a way to "help students gain a critical understanding of the connections between past and present" and to "provide a reflective basis" for understanding contemporary values and contentious issues" (Bermudez, 2015, p. 105). Preparation for discussions or debates involves obtaining deep historical knowledge about "the perceived problems, values, and available intellectual frameworks of the time" and "understanding of the excruciating choices... experienced by historical actors"; teachers need to "introduce considerably more nuance in appreciating historical, ethical lives" so that students see beyond binary choices of "admiration or condemnation" (Milligan et al., 2018, p. 433).

An available history curriculum, used by numerous middle-school teachers in the United States and internationally, specifically attends to ethical inquiry. *Facing History and Ourselves*, implemented through lessons and units, provides resources about the history of 20th-century genocide, "on the Holocaust in particular, and presents the perspectives of perpetrators, bystanders, and victims" (Strom, et al., 1992, p. 131). This course of study especially relates to the moral concerns of young people by "using a historical case study to explore such questions as why some people conform to the norms of a group—even when those norms encourage wrongdoing—whereas others resist helps students explore these issues in depth" (Schen & Gilmore, 2009, p. 60). Although *Facing History* encourages "students to think about individual decision making" (Strom, et al., 1992, p. 131), another goal is to "participate in moral discourse with others" by "building a community of learners" (p. 137).

In addition, the subject of media literacy can be taught across various curricular areas but particularly in social studies and technology classes. Contemporary scholars view media literacy as a competency required for a participation in a democratic society. Deliberative democracy requires "distinguishing between factual truths, lies, and opinions" (Gordon, 2018, p. 64) and skills of "rational argumentation and critical assessment of arguments" as well as the ability to "treat others with compassion while maintaining a respect for truth and knowledge based on sound evidence"

(D'Olimpio, 2021, p. 94). This curricular area can "provide students with the requisite skills to navigate the contemporary information landscape" and cast light on "the sociocultural contexts in which media is produced" (Manfra & Holmes, 2020, pp. 127, 123). Media literacy education also enhances critical reflection by helping students to "understand their own positions on political and moral issues"; this capacity is crucial to rational and moral discourse (Gordon, 2018, p. 61).

So too, science is a subject area in the academic curriculum that opens the door for deep ethical inquiry. Among issues for discussion are researchers' ethical responsibilities (Garrecht, et al., 2022), "scientists' motives when they engage in scientific practices" (Mawasi et al., 2022, p. 355), and "intended and unintended consequences of scientific practices" (p. 363). Also, teachers can help students become aware of "the cultural factors that guide and generate knowledge" (Zeidler, et al., 2005, p. 372). For example, by bringing to light disparate viewpoints about "the relationship between humans and nature" (van der Leij, 2023, p. 3), students can better interrogate the values and beliefs systems undergirding scientific investigation. Contemporary scholars acknowledge the interdependence of science and society and call for socioscientific issues education (SSI) that raises moral dilemmas within science. This curriculum introduces "wicked problems" that are "controversial, open-ended... and can be addressed from multiple perspectives" (van der Leij, 2023, p. 2). As students grapple with such issues as climate change and genetic screening, they are prepared to "contribute to public debate" (Saunders & Rennie, 2013, p. 254)—not by falling back on unexamined beliefs or impressions from media—but equipped with knowledge of science and experience in ethical reasoning (Garrecht, et al., 2022).

Transformative Moral Education

Transformative moral education is a multidisciplinary study of human interactions and relationships with the natural world toward the goal of apprehending and embracing "core ethical obligations to strive for the protection of human fulfillment, freedom, and dignity and the welfare of nonhuman life and the Earth" (Joseph & Mikel, 2014, p. 318). This conception of moral education comprises affective and cognitive components of moral imagination—empathic feelings, awareness of others' needs, and critical reflection—but especially centers on visioning: confronting customary values and actions and conceiving of ideal versions of ourselves and society.

Moral Education for Transformation

Various scholars discern the inability of conventional moral education to teach for transformation of individuals and society. They write that "traditional moral education" cannot "help us to correct the existing social inequalities and inequities" because its goal is having "the new generation adopt and recapitulate existing socio-moral values and perspectives" (Nucci, 2016, p. 299). Similarly, "a school that rejects transformative education outright is one that ultimately allows the complex of formative cultural influences impacting on students to do their work unimpeded," perpetuating inequity, racism, and sexism (Yacek, 2020, p. 267). Along with concerns that moral education is too limited, individualistic, and nonvisionary, it also fails to educate people to have "commitment to nonviolence" (Toffolo & Harris, 2011, p. 369). Lastly, conventional moral education lacks "a moral mode of analysis for education" that is "grounded in a moral vision" (Purpel, 1991, p. 311).

For advocates of transformative moral education, a two-fold vision is central to curriculum and pedagogy: (a) critical consciousness of injustice and violence and (b) appreciation of interconnectedness and peace. In this way, transformative moral education involves analysis and contestation of immorality—of people's cruel and violent behaviors toward each other and toward non-human life form and the Earth. It also is based on a "holistic peace-based worldview acknowledging not only human bonds but that people are embedded within the environment and that reverence rather than ruthlessness is due to the natural world" (Joseph & Mikel, 2014, p. 328). "Transformative moral education . . . is more than simply teaching moral principles"; rather, it means that individuals internalize morality "for the purpose of effecting a change in society" and "believing wholeheartedly that such change is possible" (Laird, 2003, p. 47). This orientation educates for "a change in the human consciousness and in human society" corresponding to the "the transformative imperative" of teaching for peace leading to "a profound, global, cultural change that affects ways of thinking, world views, values, behaviors, relationships, and the structures that make up our public order" (Reardon 1988, p. x).

Transformative Curricula and Pedagogies

Transformative moral education draws from ethics-based pedagogies and curricular orientations that facilitate deepening of understanding and awakening to possibilities for moral agency: *critical pedagogy, human rights education, ecojustice education, peace studies, conflict resolution education, global education, and environmental education.* There are many opportunities to weave these pedagogies into academic subjects, especially social studies and science, but also through poetry, drama, and literature, and via interdisciplinary curriculum. One significant example of developing integrated practices for transformative moral education take place in schools guided by Maria Montessori's philosophy: "to understand the natural connection between education and peace" (Duckworth, 2006, p. 42), "the need to awaken and cultivate a universal consciousness in children" (Gynther & Ahlquist, 2022, p. 9), and to "make use of children's ability to imagine and visualize" (p. 10). Montessori schools embody transformative moral education across the curriculum by "fostering a keen sense of peace and social justice" (Sutton, 2009, p. 24) and "ecological sustainability principles" (p. 25).

Critical Knowledge of Injustice and Violence

To teach for critical knowledge of injustice and violence, scholars believe that we first need to perceive "a culture of violence" (Jenkins, 2016) or "an ecology of violence"—referring to "human interactions, discourse, and relationships with the natural world" (Joseph & Mikel, 2014, p. 317). This perception becomes a crucial step toward transformation of consciousness and eventual moral agency.

> Without attentiveness to aggression, discord, and habitual domination over other humans, nonhuman life, and the Earth, such beliefs and actions normalized by this worldview seem part of the natural order, moral sensibilities are numbed, and violence goes unquestioned and unchallenged. (Joseph & Mikel, 2014, p. 323)

The concept of an ecology of violence recognizes "persistence of murderous violence in the world" among peoples (Miller, 2003) along with "the devastating impact of human violence upon the Earth, its ecosystems, and the various species that inhabit it" (Harris & Mische, 2005, p. 171). Moreover, scholars argue for awareness about how individuals and societies are in the grip of the modern paradigm that is "individualistic, mechanistic, and ecologically hostile" and to understand "the hold that it has over human perceptions and actions, and its possible harm to cultures and the natural world" (Joseph & Mikel, 2014, p. 323). Likewise, they write that we need to "see the ecological crisis as at root a cultural crisis—direct outcome of the dominant western mechanistic worldview" based on "notions of separation and domination" (Selby, 2000, p. 88). To challenge dominant beliefs about competition, dominance over nature, and acceptance of violence, educators can draw from extensive scholarship on critical pedagogy, human rights education, and ecojustice education.

The literature on *critical pedagogy* describes a process of transformation as students name and investigate social issues and begin to "question their roles in society" (Kirylo et al., 2010, p. 332). This curriculum thus leads to both "critical awareness of existing social, political, and economic conditions and the belief in the possibility that society can be transformed to ensure that all people have the access to a free, fair, and humane life" (Windschitl & Joseph, 2011, p. 221). As follows, schools need to "help students see themselves as social, political beings with rights to access the legitimate systems of influence in schools, their workplaces and communities" (p. 223) and "should support students in transformation and action for personal empowerment and help engender more human and equal relationships" (Veugelers, 2017, p. 420). Influenced by Paulo Freire's (1985) ideas about pedagogy as liberation, scholars also refer to this curricular orientation as liberatory pedagogy because of its goal of new consciousness and transformation.

The ultimate goals for *human rights education* are to "promote universal respect for and observance of all human rights and fundamental freedoms," to "prevent human rights violations" (Tibbitts, 2017, p. 71), and to "press for governmental changes that protect human rights," especially for marginalized people (Brabeck & Rogers, 2000, p. 169). Through the study of "human rights documents, such as the Universal Declaration of Human Rights and the Convention on the Rights of the Child" (p. 168), students can move from holding a generalized sense of unfairness to having knowledge of their rights and those of others. Furthermore, this approach involves a potent emotional component as students empathize with people who endure war, cruelty, and suffering; eventually, young people develop "critical compassion" when they "begin to understand the conditions (structural inequalities, poverty, globalization, etc.) that give rise to human rights violations" (Zembylas, 2017, p. 63). This curriculum is "associated with transformative and emancipatory learning" (Tibbits, 2017, p. 74) because it cultivates students' knowledge and desire and take action to eliminate human rights violations.

Lastly, *ecojustice education* "analyzes the destructive effects of a worldview organized by a logic of domination" (Lowenstein et al., 2010, p. 101) and requires teachers and students to examine their local schools and communities "to consider which activities, beliefs, and practices... contribute to the support of living systems, and which do not" (p. 103). As delineated by environmental scholar and activist, C.A. Bowers (2001), this curricular orientation has four key themes: "understanding domination and oppression in ecological and cultural systems, alleviating environmental racism, revitalizing traditional ecological practices, and living sustainability with the natural world for future generations" (in Brantmeier, 2013, p. 251). For example, students need to learn about the "dumping of toxins in communities of economically and socially marginalized peoples" (Bowers 2006, p. 94) and to recognize that "the environmental commons include our relationships to the land, water, air and all the living creatures with whom we share the planet" (Lowenstein et al., 2010, p. 103). Through engagement with ecojustice, educators hope to "counter the pervasive forces of hopelessness and disempowerment" about environmental problems by developing students' "self-efficacy" as well as their "confidence, sense of agency, and hopefulness" (Bartlett et al., 2022, p. 3).

Appreciation of Interconnectedness and Peace

Whereas critical consciousness is an essential avenue of transformative moral education, critique is incomplete without understanding and deeply appreciating essential connections among all forms of life and adopting a peace-based worldview. Ultimately, individuals need to "imagine peaceful and equitable solutions rather than accepting the legitimacy of violence" (Joseph & Mikel, 2014, p. 328). To cultivate such realizations of interconnectedness and peace, there are abundant resources for curriculum and pedagogy from peace studies, conflict resolution education, global education, and environmental education.

Peace Studies is an area of peace education that "is oriented toward the transformation of a culture of violence" (Jenkins, 2016, p. 1) and focuses on learning about the meaning of peace and what it means to be peaceful. Through historical and contemporary studies, students learn how people have worked together to solve conflicts among nations, religions, and ethnic groups. Whereas the curriculum of peace studies involves "critical examination of militarism and the dangers and experiences of war," it also explores "the meaning of inner peace and peace in the world" and "aims to cultivate a deeply emotional understanding of peace and appreciation for the people and actions that build peace" (Joseph, 2011, p. 260). To help teachers and students have a deeper understanding of peace in their lives, a fundamental heuristic of this curriculum delineates three levels of approaching violence: peacekeeping, peacemaking and peacebuilding (Harris & Morrison's, 2003); this framework allows for discernment of peace as (a) merely prohibiting violence, (b) providing opportunities for conflict resolution, or (c) creating cultures of peace and stimulating the desire to be peaceful. Additionally, peace studies curriculum introduces Betty Reardon's (1988) conceptualization of negative and positive peace: the former is "defined as the absence of war, achieved by the prevention and/or the general reduction and eventual elimination of armed conflict" (Reardon,

1988, p. 6); the latter "includes but transcends negative peace" as it "entails not only the elimination of armed aggression but also the positive establishment of justice" (Snauwaert, 2012, p. 47). This learning of peace can be "viewed on a continuum: individuals first embrace nonviolence, commit to social justice, learn the skills of nonviolence, and, ultimately, imagine a world of peace" (Joseph, 2011, p. 247).

While *conflict resolution* education inherently is a part of peace studies, it often is taught independently in schools and is a distinctive field in educational literature. The scholarship makes clear that "individual children in conflict are in the process of developing and learning" and therefore when adults eliminate or resolve conflicts, that "would mean taking away an opportunity for them to grow and learn" (Hakvoort, 2010, p. 160). This learning and growth reflect the "core areas of conflict resolution education" that include perspective taking, compassion, negotiation, and collaborative problem-solving (p. 159). As well, "conflict resolution affords opportunities for students to recognize and describe their own feelings and others"—enhancing moral reasoning and empathy (Heydenberk et al., 2003, p. 29). Most importantly, conflict resolution educates individuals not to view another person as merely an "adversary" but to realize the humanity of the other—to "switch from I–It to I–Thou relations" and to "redirect energies engaged in fighting toward communication, empathy, creativity and resolution" (Cremin & Guilherme, 2016, p. 1131). Such skills and changed sensibilities allow individuals to live in peace but also to recognize that conflict does not have to be destructive.

On a wider scale than conflict resolution, *global education* focuses on dialogue and respect for differences (Hull & Hellmich, 2018, p. 6) but also "the interconnectedness of the world" (Barrow, 2017, p. 164). The aims of global education include "perspective consciousness," "knowledge of world conditions," "cross-cultural awareness of the world's diverse value systems and societal frameworks," understanding of "global system dynamics," and "knowledge of choices or alternatives to current management patterns" (Cook, 2008, p. 894). Based on the metaphor of a global village, it involves study of and participation in the world community, interdependency, and "improving the quality of life" for all humans and the Earth (Hendrix, 1998, p. 305). It also provides examination of international problems and relationships, emphasizing multicultural understanding and peaceful coexistence. Furthermore, global education facilitates students' "understanding of how cultural, national, regional, and global identifications are interrelated, complex, and evolving" (Banks, 2009, p. 108).

Lastly, *environmental education* shares several assumptions with ecojustice education—the necessity of ecological consciousness and a non-anthropocentric worldview—but environmental education is a broader and more holistic field of study encompassing both knowledge and emotion. A major theme of this orientation is environmental literacy: "knowledge, attitudes, dispositions, and competencies believed to equip people with what they need to effectively analyze and address important environmental problems" (Stern et al., 2014, p. 581). A second theme, environmental sustainability, focuses on developing awareness of "the need for reconciliation between economic development and environmental conservation" (Tilbury, 1995, p. 197) and on equipping students with skills of analysis to consider various alternatives (p. 207). A third theme, interconnectedness, expands on the concept of "viewing human beings as one part of the natural world" (Smith & Williams, 1999, p. 139) so to nurture a deep sense of inter-relatedness and a spiritual connection with nature. Researchers who study environmental education programs recognize that feelings of unity with nature are very important (Moroye & Ingman, 2013) and can be even more influential on behavior than environmental knowledge (Otto & Pensini, 2017, p. 89). From this viewpoint, love of the natural world inspires individuals' desire to learn about and protect the environment. Thus, it is essential that young people have sustained opportunities to "dwell in places and landscapes" so that they can "develop a sense of wonder in nature" (Bonnett, 2023, p. 8).

In conclusion, of all moral education approaches, transformative moral education is the most conceptually complex, not only because of its expansive curricular areas but because it requires simultaneously holding difficult and seemingly contradictory understandings and emotions. As students experience transformative moral education, sensibilities and feelings can be new or more intense. On one hand, they may feel frustration and outrage (Purpel, 1999; Zembylas, 2021) as they deepen their knowledge of harm and injustice; alternatively, through experiences in which students learn to actively engage in creating peaceful relationships and caring for the environment, they may experience "love and compassion, patience, and a sense of harmony" (Whang & Peralta Nash, 2005, p. 89) and peacefulness within the process of spiritual growth (McFarland, 2004).

References

Ajayi, A., & Iwuagwu, S. (2012). Reflection on moral education in Igbo folktale. *Journal of Qualitative Education, 8*(2), 1–6.

Alexander, H. A. (2001). God as teacher: Jewish reflections on a theology of pedagogy. *Journal of Beliefs and Values, 22*(1), 5–17.

Anzai, S. (2015). Re-examining patriotism in Japanese education: analysis of Japanese elementary school moral readers. *Educational Review, 67*(4), 436–458.

Araújo, U., & Arantes, V. (2009). The Ethics and Citizenship Program: A Brazilian experience in moral education. *Journal of Moral Education, 38*(4), 489–511.

Armstrong, J. (2000). A holistic education, teachings from the Dance House: We cannot afford to lose one Native child. In M. K. A. Nee-Benham & J. E. Cooper, J. E. (Eds.), *Indigenous educational models for contemporary practice: In our mother's voice* (pp. 35–44). Routledge.

Arthur, J. (2005). The re-emergence of character education in British education policy. *British Journal of Educational Studies, 53*(3), 239–254.

Arthur, J., Kristjánsson, K., Walker, D., Sanderse, W., & Jones, C. (2015). *Character education in UK schools.* The Jubilee Center for Character & Virtues. University of Birmingham UK.

Bamkin, S. (2018). Reforms to strengthen moral education in Japan: A preliminary analysis of implementation in schools. *Contemporary Japan, 30*(1), 78–96.

Bamkin, S. (2020). The taught curriculum of moral education at Japanese elementary school: the role of classtime in the broad curriculum. *Contemporary Japan, 32*(2), 218–239.

Banks, J. (2009). Human rights, diversity, and citizenship education. *Educational Forum, 73*(2), 100–110.

Barrow, E. (2017). No global citizenship? Re-envisioning global citizenship education in times of growing nationalism. *The High School Journal, 100*(3), 163–165.

Barrow, R. (2006). Moral education's modest agenda. *Ethics and Education, 1*(1), 3–13.

Bartlett, M. L., Larson, J., & Lee, S. (2022). Environmental justice pedagogies and self-efficacy for climate action. *Sustainability, 14*(22), 1–16.

Bennett, W. J. (Ed.) (1993). *Book of Virtues.* Simon and Schuster.

Berkowitz, M. W., & Bier, M. C. (2004). Research-based character education. *The Annals of the American Academy of Political and Social Science, 591*(1), 72–85.

Bermudez, A. (2015). Four tools for critical inquiry in history, social studies, and civic education. *Revista de Estudios Sociales, 52,* 102–118.

Bonnett, M. (2023). Environmental consciousness, nature, and the philosophy of education: Some key themes. *Environmental Education Research, 29*(6), 829–839.

Boyles, D. (2005). Would you like values with that? Chick-fil-A and character education. *Journal of Curriculum Theorizing, 21*(2), 45–62.

Brabeck, M. M., & Rogers, L. (2000). Human rights as a moral issue: Lessons for moral educators from human rights work. *Journal of Moral Education, 29*(2), 167–182.

Brantmeier, E. J. (2013). Toward a critical peace education for sustainability. *Journal of Peace Education, 10*(3), 242–258.

Byrd, D. (2012). Social studies education as a moral activity: Teaching towards a just society. *Educational Philosophy and Theory, 44*(10), 1073–1079.

Cam, P. (2014). Philosophy for children, values education and the inquiring society. *Educational Philosophy and Theory, 46*(11), 1203–1211.

Cam, P. (2016). A philosophical approach to moral education. *Journal of Philosophy in Schools, 3*(1), 5–15.

Carr, D. (2005). On the contribution of literature and the arts to the educational cultivation of moral virtue, feeling and emotion. *Journal of Moral Education, 34*(2), 137–151.

Cassidy, C. (2012). Philosophy with children: Learning to live well. *Childhood & Philosophy, 8*(16), 243–264.

Cassidy, C. (2022). Philosophy with children as and for moral education. In D. Mendonça & F. F. Figueiredo (Eds.), *Conceptions of childhood and moral education in philosophy for children* (pp. 13–28). Springer Berlin Heidelberg.

Character Counts. (2023). *The six pillars of character.* https://charactercounts.org/

Chazan, B. (2022). *Principles and pedagogies in Jewish education.* Springer Nature.

Chetty, D. (2018). Racism as 'reasonableness': Philosophy for children and the gated community of inquiry. *Ethics and Education, 13*(1), 39–54.

Cook, S. A. (2008). Give peace a chance: The diminution of peace in global education in the United States, United Kingdom, and Canada. *Canadian Journal of Education, 31*(4), 878–913.

Cremin, H., & Guilherme, A. (2016). Violence in schools: Perspectives (and hope) from Galtung and Buber. *Educational Philosophy and Theory, 48*(11), 1123–1137.

Cuypers, S. E. (2004). The ideal of a Catholic education in a secularized society. *Journal of Catholic Education, 7*(4), 426–445.

D'Olimpio, L. (2021). Critical perspectivism: Educating for a moral response to media. *Journal of Moral Education, 50*(1), 92–103.

Dei, G. J. S. (2002). Spirituality in African education: Issues, contentions and contestations from a Ghanaian case study. *International Journal of Children's spirituality, 7*(1), 37–56.

Dewey, J. (1908/1996). *Theory of the moral life.* Irvington.

Drane, R., & Higham, R. (2023). From polite agreement to passionate uncertainty: "Turning towards difference." In J. Biddulph, L. Rolls & J. Flutter (Eds.), *Philosophy for children (P4C) lessons. Unleashing children's voices in new democratic primary education* (pp. 160–175). Routledge.

Duckworth, C. (2006). Teaching peace: a dialogue on the Montessori method. *Journal of Peace Education, 3*(1), 39–53.

Echeverria, E., & Hannam, P. (2016). The community of philosophical inquiry (P4C): A pedagogical proposal for advancing democracy. In *The Routledge international handbook of philosophy for children* (pp. 3–10). Routledge.

Efron, S. E. (2008). Moral education between hope and hopelessness: The legacy of Janusz Korczak. *Curriculum Inquiry, 38*(1), 39–62.

Efron, S. G. (1994). Old wine, new bottles: Traditional moral education in the contemporary Jewish classroom. *Religious Education, 89*(1), 52–66.

El-Moslimany, A. (2018). *Teaching children: A moral, spiritual, and holistic approach to educational development.* International Institute of Islamic Thought (IIIT).

Etzioni, A. (1993). *The spirit of community: The reinvention of American society.* Touchstone.

Fonda, M. V. (2011). Are they like us, yet? Some thoughts on why religious freedom remains elusive for Aboriginals in North America. *The International Indigenous Policy Journal, 2*(4), 1–15.

Freire, P. (1985). *The politics of education. Culture, power and liberation.* Bergin & Garvey.

Frisancho, S., & Delgado, G. E. (2018). Moral education as intercultural moral education. *Intercultural Education, 29*(1), 18–39.

Garrecht, C., Czinczel, B., Kretschmann, M., & Reiss, M. J. (2022). "Should we be doing it, should we not be doing it, who could be harmed?" Addressing ethical issues in science education. *Science & Education,* 1–33. https://doi.org/10.1007/s11191-022-00342-2

Glanzer, P. L. (2000). Finding the gods in public school: A Christian deconstruction of character education. *Journal of Education and Christian Belief, 4*(2), 115–130.

Glanzer, P. L. (2008). Harry Potter's provocative moral world: Is there a place for good and evil in moral education?. *Phi Delta Kappan, 89*(7), 525–528.

Gordon, M. (2018). Lying in politics: Fake news, alternative facts, and the challenges for deliberative civics education. *Educational Theory, 68*(1), 49–64.

Grant, R. W. (1996). The ethics of talk: Classroom conversation and democratic politics. *Teachers College Record, 97*(3), 470–482.

Green, T. (1999). *Voices: The educational formation of conscience.* University of Notre Dame Press.

Greer, C., & Kohl, H. (Eds.) (1995). *A Call to character: A family treasury: of stories, poems, plays, proverbs, and fables to guide the development of values for you and your children.* HarperCollins.

Gynther, P., & Ahlquist, E. M. T. (2022). Education for sustainability and global citizenship for 6–12-year-olds in Montessori education. *Journal of Education for Sustainable Development, 16*(1–2), 5–18.

Hakvoort, I. (2010). The conflict pyramid: A holistic approach to structuring conflict resolution in schools. *Journal of Peace Education,* 7(2), 157–169.

Halstead, J. M. (2007). Islamic values: a distinctive framework for moral education?. *Journal of Moral Education, 36*(3), 283–296.

Han, H., Park, S. C., Kim, J., Jeong, C., Kunii, Y., & Kim, S. (2018). A quantitative analysis of moral exemplars presented in moral education textbooks in Korea and Japan. *Asia Pacific Journal of Education, 38*(1), 62–77.

Handsman, E. (2021). From virtue to grit: Changes in character education narratives in the US from 1985 to 2016. *Qualitative Sociology, 44*, 271–291.

Harris, I., & Mische, P. (2004). Environmental peacemaking, peacekeeping, and peacebuilding: Integrating education for ecological balance and a sustainable peace. In A. L. Wenden (Ed.), *Educating for a culture of social and ecological peace* (pp. 69–182). State University of New York Press.

Harris, I., & Morrison, M. L. (2003). *Peace education* (2nd ed.). McFarland and Company.

Heilbronn, R. (2021). Teaching literature in schools for democratic citizenship. In G. W. Noblit & J. R. Neikirk (Eds.). *Oxford research encyclopedia of education.* Oxford University Press. https://doi.org/10.1093/acrefore/9780190264093.013.1478

Hendrix, J. C. (1998). Globalizing the curriculum. *The Clearing House, 71*(5), 305–308.

Hendry, J. (2003). Mining the sacred mountain: The clash between the Western dualistic framework and Native American religions. *Multicultural Perspectives, 5*(1), 3–10.

Heydenberk, W. R., Heydenberk, R. A., & Bailey, S. P. (2003). Conflict resolution and moral reasoning. *Conflict Resolution Quarterly, 21*(1), 27–45.

Howard, R. W., Berkowitz, M. W., & Schaeffer, E. F. (2004). Politics of character education. *Educational Policy, 18*(1), 188–215.

Hull, G. A., & Hellmich, E. A. (2018). Locating the global: Schooling in an interconnected world. *Teachers College Record, 120*(3), 1–36.

Hunter, J. D. (2002). Virtue . . . on the cheap. *Society, 39*(3), 42–53.

Hunter, J. D. (2008). *The death of character: Moral education in an age without good or evil.* Basic Books.

Hussain, K. (2007). An Islamic consideration of western moral education: An exploration of the individual. *Journal of Moral Education, 36*(3), 297–308.

Ikuenobe, P. (2018). Oral tradition, epistemic dependence, and knowledge in African cultures. *Synthesis Philosophica, 33*(1), 23–40.

Jaramillo, R., & Mesa, J. A. (2009). Citizenship education as a response to Colombia's social and political context. *Journal of Moral Education, 38*(4), 467–487.

Jenkins, T. (2016). Transformative peace pedagogy: Fostering a reflective, critical, and inclusive praxis for peace studies. *Factis Pax, 10*(1), 1–7.

Joseph, P. B. (2011). Envisioning peace. In P. B. Joseph (Ed.), *Cultures of curriculum* (pp. 260–296). Routledge.

Joseph, P. B., & Efron, S. (2005). Seven worlds of moral education. *Phi Delta Kappan, 86*(7), 525–533.

Joseph, P. B., & Mikel, E. (2014). Transformative moral education: Challenging an ecology of violence. *Journal of Peace Education, 11*(3), 317–333.

Kawagley, A.O., & Barnhardt, R. (1999). Education indigenous to place: Western science meets native reality. In G. Smith and D. Williams (Eds.),

Ecological education in action: On weaving education, culture, and the environment (pp. 117–140). State University of New York Press.

Kirylo, J. D., Thirumurthy, V., Smith, M., & McLaren, P. (2010). Issues in education: Critical pedagogy: An overview. *Childhood Education, 86*(5), 332–334.

Koc, K., & Buzzelli, C. A. (2004). The moral of the story is . . . Using children's literature in moral education. *YC Young Children, 59*(1), 92–97.

Kohlberg, L. (1975). The cognitive-developmental approach to moral education. *Phi Delta Kappan, 56*(10), 670–677.

Kohn, A. (1997). How not to teach values: A critical look at character education. *Phi Delta Kappan, 78*(6), 428–439.

Kristjánsson, K. (2021). Recent attacks on character education in a UK context: a case of mistaken identities?. *Journal of Beliefs & Values, 42*(3), 363–377.

Laats, A. (2010). Forging a fundamentalist "One Best System": Struggles over curriculum and educational philosophy for Christian day schools, 1970–1989. *History of Education Quarterly, 50*(1), 55–83.

Laird, P. G. (2003). Bridging the divide: The role of perceived control in mediating reasoning and activism. *Journal of Moral Education, 32*(1), 35–49.

Le Grange, L. (2012). Ubuntu, ukama, environment and moral education. *Journal of Moral Education, 41*(3), 329–340.

Lee, C. M. (2004). Changes and challenges for moral education in Taiwan. *Journal of Moral Education, 33*(4), 575–595.

Lee, D. B., & Wang, Q. (2023). Portrayal of the national identity in Chinese language textbooks. *Journal of Curriculum Studies*, 1–16. https://doi.org/10.1080/00220272.2023.2181672

Lee, L., & Misco, T. (2014). All for one or one for all: An analysis of the concepts of patriotism and others in multicultural Korea through elementary moral education textbooks. *The Asia-Pacific Education Researcher, 23*, 727–734.

Lin, J. C., & Jackson, L. (2022). Patriotism in moral education: Toward a rational approach in China. *Journal of Moral Education*, 1–19.

Lind, G. (2006). Effective moral education: The Konstanz method of dilemma discussion. *Hellenic Journal of Psychology, 3*(3), 189–196.

Lipman, M. (1995). Moral education higher-order thinking and philosophy for children. *Early Child Development and Care, 107*(1), 61–70.

Lipman, M., & Sharp, A. M. (1978). Some educational presuppositions of philosophy for children. *Oxford Review of Education, 4*(1), 85–90.

Lovat, T., & Dally, K. (2018). Testing and measuring the impact of character education on the learning environment and its outcomes. *Journal of Character Education, 14*(2), 1–22.

Lowenstein, E., Martusewicz, R., & Voelker, L. (2010). Developing teachers' capacity for ecojustice education and community-based learning. *Teacher Education Quarterly, 37*(4), 99–118.

Manfra, M., & Holmes, C. (2020). Integrating media literacy in social studies teacher education. *Contemporary Issues in Technology and Teacher Education, 20*(1), 121–141.

Mawasi, A., Nagy, P., Finn, E., & Wylie, R. (2022). Using Frankenstein-themed science activities for science ethics education: An exploratory study. *Journal of Moral Education, 51*(3), 353–369.

McAvoy, P., & Hess, D. (2013). Classroom deliberation in an era of political polarization. *Curriculum Inquiry, 43*(1), 14–47.

McClellan, B. E. (1999). *Moral education in America: Schools and the shaping of character from colonial times to the present.* Teachers College Press.

McFarland, S. (2004). Educating for peace: A Montessori best practice. *Montessori Life, 16*(4), 24.

McGinley, W., Kamberelis, G., Welker, A., Kelly, M., & Swafford, J. (2017). Roles of affect and imagination in reading and responding to literature: Perspectives and possibilities for English classrooms. *Journal of Curriculum Theorizing, 32*(1), 67–85.

McKinnell, L. (2019). The ethics of enchantment: The role of folk tales and fairy tales in the ethical imagination. *Philosophy and Literature, 43*(1), 192–209.

McNally, M. D. (2017). Religion as peoplehood: Native American religious traditions and the discourse of indigenous rights. In G. Johnson & S. E. Kraft (Eds.), *Handbook of indigenous religion(s)* (pp. 52–79). Brill.

Memon, N. A., & Alhashmi, M. (2018). Islamic pedagogy: Potential and perspective. *Islamic schooling in the West: Pathways to renewal,* (pp. 169–194).

Metz, T., & Gaie, J. B. (2010). The African ethic of Ubuntu/Botho: Implications for research on morality. *Journal of Moral Education, 39*(3), 273–290.

Miller, R. (2003). Education for a culture of peace." *Encounter, 16*(2), 25–30.

Millett, S., & Tapper, A. (2012). Benefits of collaborative philosophical inquiry in schools. *Educational Philosophy and Theory, 44*(5), 546–567.

Milligan, A., Gibson, L., & Peck, C. L. (2018). Enriching ethical judgments in history education. *Theory & Research in Social Education, 46*(3), 449–479.

Mizell, K. (2015). Philosophy for children, community of inquiry, and human rights education. *Childhood & Philosophy, 11*(22), 319–328.

Moreno-Gutiérrez, M. C., & Frisancho, S. (2009). Transitions to democracy: the role of moral and citizenship education in Latin America. *Journal of Moral Education, 38*(4), 391–406.

Moroye, C. M., & Ingman, B. C. (2013). Ecological mindedness across the curriculum. *Curriculum Inquiry, 43*(5), 588–612.

Narvaez, D. (2010). Moral complexity: The fatal attraction of truthiness and the importance of mature moral functioning. *Perspectives on Psychological Science, 5*(2), 163–181.

Narvaez, D. (2016). Revitalizing human virtue by restoring organic morality. *Journal of Moral Education, 45*(3), 223–238.

Nash, R. J. (1996). Fostering moral conversations in the college classroom. *Journal on Excellence in College Teaching, 7*(1), 83–105.

Nash, R. J. (1997). *Answering the "virtuecrats": A moral conversation on character education.* Teachers College Press.

Niigaaniin, M., & MacNeill, T. (2022). Indigenous culture and nature relatedness: Results from a collaborative study. *Environmental Development, 44,* 1–15.

Noddings, N. (2002). *Educating moral people: A caring alternative to character education.* Teachers College Press.

Nucci, L. (2006). Classroom management for moral and social development. In C. M. Evertson & C. S. Weinstein (Eds.), *Handbook of classroom management* (pp. 721–742). Lawrence Erlbaum.

Nucci, L. (2016). Recovering the role of reasoning in moral education to address inequity and social justice. *Journal of Moral Education,* 1–17.

Nussbaum, M. C. (1994). Divided we stand. *New Republic, 210*(2–3), 38–42.

Nuzzi, R. J. (2004). Spirituality and religious education. In T. C. Hunt, E. A. Joseph, & R. J. Nuzzi (Eds.), *Handbook of research on Catholic education* (pp. 65–82). Greenwood.

O'Dwyer, S. (2003). Democracy and Confucian values. *Philosophy East and West, 53(1),* 39–63.

Obiagu, A. N. (2023). Toward a decolonized moral education for social justice in Africa. *Journal of Black Studies, 54*(3), 236–263.

Otto, S., & Pensini, P. (2017). Nature-based environmental education of children: Environmental knowledge and connectedness to nature, together, are related to ecological behaviour. *Global Environmental Change, 47,* 88–94.

Ozhiganova, A. (2019). "Spiritual and moral Education" in Russian public schools: Constructing a neo-traditionalist identity. *Forum for International Research in Education, 5*(1), 107–125.

Pashby, K., Ingram, L. A., & Joshee, R. (2014). Discovering, recovering, and covering-up Canada: Tracing historical citizenship discourses in K–12 and adult immigrant citizenship education. *Canadian Journal of Education, 37*(2), 1–26.

Pritchard, M. (2022). Philosophy for children. In E. N Zalta (Ed.), *The Stanford encyclopedia of philosophy.* https://plato.stanford.edu/archives/sum2022/entries/children

Purpel, D. E. (1991). Moral education: An idea whose time has gone. *The Clearing House, 64*(5), 309–312.

Purpel, D. E. (1999). *Moral outrage in education.* Peter Lang.

Rapoport, A. (2009). Patriotic education in Russia: Stylistic move or a sign of substantive counter-reform?. *The Educational Forum, 73*(2), 141–152.

Reardon, B. A. (1988). *Comprehensive peace education: Educating for global responsibility.* Teachers College Press.

Reetz, D. (2010). From madrasa to University—The Challenges and formats of Islamic Education. In A. S. Ahmed & T. Sonn (Eds.) *The Sage handbook of Islamic studies* (pp. 106–139). Sage Publishing.

Rehren, P., & Sauer, H. (2022). Another brick in the wall? Moral education, social learning, and moral progress. *Ethical Theory and Moral Practice,* 1–16.

Saunders, K. J., & Rennie, L. J. (2013). A pedagogical model for ethical inquiry into socioscientific issues in science. *Research in Science Education, 43,* 253–274.

Schen, M., & Gilmore, B. (2009). Lighting the moral imagination. *Educational Leadership, 66*(8), 59–63.

Schuitema, J., Dam, G. T., & Veugelers, W. (2008). Teaching strategies for moral education: A review. *Journal of Curriculum Studies, 40*(1), 69–89.

Schwab, J. J. (1973). The practical 3: Translation into curriculum. *The School Review, 81*(4), 501–522.

Sears, A., & Parsons, J. (1991). Towards critical thinking as an ethic. *Theory & Research in Social Education, 19*(1), 45–68.

Seider, S. (2012). *Character compass: How powerful school culture can point students toward success.* Harvard Education Press.

Selby, D. (2000). A darker shade of green: The importance of ecological thinking in global education and school reform. *Theory Into Practice, 39*(2), 88–89.

Shannon, P. (1997). Childhoods without children. *The Review of Education/Pedagogy/Cultural Studies, 19*(1), 151–166.

Shapiro, S. (2005). Elements of Jewish pedagogy. *Journal of Curriculum and Pedagogy, 2*(2), 24–29.

Sharp, A. M. (1984). Philosophical teaching as moral education. *Journal of Moral Education, 13*(1), 3–8.

Sharp, A. M. (2007). Education of the emotions in the classroom community of inquiry. *Gifted Education International, 22*(2–3), 248–257.

Shin, S., & Koh, M. S. (2005). Korean education in cultural context. *Essays in education, 14*(1), 1–10.

Sim, J. B. Y., & Chow, L. T. (2019). Confucian thinking in Singapore's citizenship education. *Journal of Moral Education, 48*(4), 465–482.

Simon, K. G. (2001). *Moral questions in the classroom: How to get kids to think deeply about real life and their schoolwork.* Yale University Press.

Smith, B. H. (2013). School-based character education in the United States. *Childhood Education, 89*(6), 350–355.

Smith, G., & Williams, D. (1999). Ecological education: Extending the definition of environmental education. *Australian Journal of Environmental Education, 15,* 139–146.

Snauwaert, D. T. (2012). Betty Reardon's conception of "peace" and its implications for a philosophy of peace education. *Peace Studies Journal, 5*(3), 45–52.

Spohrer, K. (2021). Resilience, self-discipline and good deeds—Examining enactments of character education in English secondary schools. *Pedagogy, Culture & Society*, 1–20. https://doi.org/10.1080/14681366.2021.2007986

Stern, M. J., Powell, R. B., & Hill, D. (2014). Environmental education program evaluation in the new millennium: What do we measure and what have we learned?. *Environmental Education Research, 20*(5), 581–611.

Strom, M. S., Sleeper, M., & Johnson, M. (1992). Facing History and Ourselves: A synthesis of history and ethics in effective history education. In A. Garrod (Ed.). *Learning for life: Moral education theory and practice* (pp. 131–153). Praeger.

Suina, S. (2000). Linking native people around the spirituality of all life:" The gifts of our grandmothers and grandfathers. In M. K. A. Nee-Benham & J. E. Cooper, J. E. (Eds.), *Indigenous educational models for contemporary practice: In our mother's voice* (pp. 93–100). Routledge.

Suissa, J. (2015). Character education and the disappearance of the political. *Ethics and Education, 10*(1), 105–117.

Sutton, A. (2009). Educating for ecological sustainability: Montessori education leads the way. *Montessori Life, 21*(4), 18–25.

Swartz, R. (1992). Teaching moral reasoning in the standard curriculum. In A. Garrod (Ed.), *Learning for life: Moral education theory and practice* (pp. 107–130). Praeger.

Tan, C., & Wong, Y. L. (2010). Moral education for young people in Singapore: Philosophy, policy and prospects. *Journal of Youth Studies, 13*(2), 89–102.

Taylor, N. (2018). The return of character: Parallels between late-Victorian and twenty-first century discourses. *Sociological Research Online, 23*(2), 399–415.

Thoma, S., & Walker, D. I. (2017). Moral and character education. In G. W. Noblit (Ed.), *The Oxford research encyclopedia of education.* Oxford University Press. https://doi.org/10.1093/acrefore/9780190264093.013.119

Tibbitts, F. (2017). Evolution of human rights education models. In M. Bajaj (Ed.), *Human rights education: Theory, research, praxis* (pp. 69–95). University of Pennsylvania Press.

Tilbury, D. (1995). Environmental education for sustainability: Defining the new focus of environmental education in the 1990s. *Environmental Education Research, 1*(2), 195–212.

Toffolo, C., & Harris, I. (2011). On the relationship of peace education to moral education. In J. L. DeVitis & T. Yu (Eds.). *Character and moral education: A reader* (pp. 369–381). Peter Lang.

Tuwe, K. (2016). The African oral tradition paradigm of storytelling as a methodological framework: Employment experiences for African communities in New Zealand. In *African studies association of Australasia and the Pacific (AFSAAP) proceedings of the 38th AFSAAP conference: 21st century tensions and transformation in Africa.* Deakin University.

Udeani, C. C. (2008). Traditional African spirituality and ethics—A panacea to leadership crisis and corruption in Africa?. *Phronimon, 9*(2), 65–72.

van der Leij, T., Goedhart, M., Avraamidou, L., & Wals, A. (2023). High school biology students' use of values in their moral argumentation and decision-making. *Journal of Moral Education*, 1–24.

Veugelers, W. (2017). The moral in Paulo Freire's educational work: What moral education can learn from Paulo Freire. *Journal of Moral Education, 46*(4), 412–421.

Wansheng, Z., & Wujie, N. (2004). The moral education curriculum for junior high schools in 21st century China. *Journal of Moral Education, 33*(4), 511–532.

Watson, M. (2008). Developmental discipline and moral education. In L. P. Nucci, & D. Narvaez (Eds.) *Handbook of moral and character education* (pp. 175–203). Routledge.

Whang, P. A., & Peralta Nash, C. (2005). Reclaiming compassion: Getting to the heart and soul of teacher education. *Journal of Peace Education, 2*(1), 79–92.

Wilhelm, G. M., & Firmin, M. W. (2008). Character education: Christian education perspectives. *Journal of Research on Christian Education*, 17(2), 182–198.

Windschitl, M. A., & Joseph, P. B. (2011). Confronting the dominant order. In P. B. Joseph (Ed.), *Cultures of curriculum* (pp. 235–259). Routledge.

Winton, S. (2008). Character education: Implications for critical democracy. *International Critical Childhood Policy Studies Journal, 1*(1), 42–63.

Wong, M. Y. (2021). Beyond asking "should" and "why" questions: Contextualised questioning techniques for moral discussions in moral education classes. *Journal of Moral Education, 50*(3), 368–383.

Wu, M. (2017). Moral education and the aboriginal peoples of Taiwan: From Sino-centrism to the ethic of multiculturalism. *Journal of Moral Education, 46*(1), 69–78.

Wynne, E., & Ryan, K. (1993). *Reclaiming our schools: A handbook on teaching character, academics, and discipline.* Macmillan.

Yacek, D. W. (2020). Should education be transformative?. *Journal of Moral Education, 49*(2), 257–274.

Yazzie-Mintz, T. (2011). Sustaining indigenous traditions. In P. B. Joseph (Ed.), *Cultures of curriculum* (pp. 190–211). Routledge.

Yu, T. (2004). *In the name of morality: Character education and political control.* Peter Lang.

Yu, T. (2008). The revival of Confucianism in Chinese schools: A historical-political review. *Asia Pacific Journal of Education, 28*(2), 113–129.

Zeidler, D. L., Sadler, T. D., Simmons, M. L., & Howes, E. V. (2005). Beyond STS: A research-based framework for socioscientific issues education. *Science Education, 89*(3), 357–377.

Zembylas, M. (2017). Emotions, critical pedagogy, and human rights education. In M. Bajaj (Ed.), *Human rights education: Theory, research, praxis* (pp. 47–68). University of Pennsylvania Press.

Zembylas, M. (2021). Encouraging moral outrage in education: A pedagogical goal for social justice or not?. *Ethics and Education*, 16(4), 424–439.

Zulkifli, H., & Hashim, R. (2019). Moral reasoning stages through Hikmah (Wisdom) pedagogy in moral education. *International Journal of Academic Research in Progressive Education and Development*, *8*(4), 886–899.

8

Ethical Teachers and the Moral Imagination

If teachers are not critically conscious, if they are not awake to their own values and commitments (and to the conditions working upon them), if they are not personally engaged with their subject matter and with the world around them, I do not see how they can initiate the young into critical questioning or the moral life.

—Maxine Greene, 1978, *Landscapes of Learning,* p. 48

Scholars view teaching as a moral profession (Hansen, 1998; Huebner, 1996), moral endeavor (Edling & Frelin, 2016; Klaassen et al., 2016), moral practice (Pring, 2001), and moral craft (Tom, 1980). They contend that teaching requires moral sensibility (Chubbuck et al., 2007), ethical knowledge (Campbell, 2006), and moral agency (Bergem, 1990; Campbell, 2014). Two essential characterizations of teaching as a moral profession correspond to this scholarship: first, the fields of educational history, sociology, and teacher education document community and professional requirements for teachers to maintain high moral standards; second, qualitative studies featuring interviews and reflective journals depict teachers'

Teaching for Moral Imagination, pages 179–206

perceptions of their motivations, moral nature of their work, and ethical dilemmas.

This chapter explores concepts and issues that cast light on the moral landscape of teachers' lives and work. It describes influences on teachers to be ethical professionals and attends to interpretations of moral imagination through teachers' perceptions of what inspired them to become teachers, their values and commitments, the moral nature of their work, and their desire to help students become moral people and to benefit society. The chapters' key questions are:

- What are expectations for teachers as ethical professionals?
- In what ways do teachers articulate their ethical identities, responsibilities, and aspirations?
- How does moral imagination inspire educators to discern forces and actions that limit the flourishing of their students and to envision teaching for a more ideal world?

Teaching as a Moral Profession

The teaching profession is intertwined with the notion of morality, especially reflected in the ethical standards required for individuals to become teachers and to retain their positions. Historically, there have been high societal expectations of moral fitness and strict prohibitions that separated teaching from most other occupations. As well, codes of ethics for the profession provide norms for teachers and licensure programs. More recently teacher educators and state agencies apply lists of dispositions to assess teaching candidates: some of these involve intellectual inclinations but others refer to virtues of character or morality.

Virtuous Teachers

A major purpose of schooling in the 19th and first half of 20th centuries in the United States was to inculcate children with a set of common values (Allison, 1995). Communities assumed that the teacher—"a paragon of moral virtue whose influence would be felt and imitated by the students in the common school" (Spring, 1990, p. 118)—should be the instrument for this moral socialization. Placed on moral pedestals, teachers were under scrutiny by their communities. Historians note the community pressures on teachers who "were expected to exhibit virtue both in and outside the classroom" and "had little privacy and virtually no latitude for mistakes in moral judgment" (McCellan, 1990, p. 24). A sociologist studying teachers as an occupational group in the first part of the 20th century concluded that the teacher is "psychologically isolated from the community because he must live within the teacher stereotype" (Waller, 1932, p. 49). In teacher education textbooks of that era, authors portray a "schoolteacher paragon" as a selfless altruist, dedicated soldier, patriot, saint, or redeemer" (Joseph, 2001, p. 136). Textbook authors insisted that teaching "is a way of life comparable with the way of the preacher and prophet" (Averill, 1939, p. 136) and emphasized the singularity of the teaching profession as "teachers are bound by a stricter moral code than other professional persons, ministers of the gospel alone excepted. (Jordan, 1930, p. 258)

International studies of the history of education also highlight teachers' roles in shaping their pupils' character (Bérard, 1984); teachers could not be hired unless they demonstrate respectability, good moral character (Coppock, 1997; Fischman, 2007; Stewart, 2006), and conform to "lists of normative expectations for teachers encompassing moral character and professional behavior" (Conway & Murphy, 2013, p. 12). Descriptions of communities' scrutiny of teachers' character and moral conduct as well as cultural norms of teachers as altruistic and self-sacrificing also appear in international studies in more modern times (Gao, 2008; Stewart, 2006).

Furthermore, historical studies confirm the gendered nature of expectations with "clear distinctions between what constitutes moral behavior for men and women" and "the expectation that part of a female teacher's role is to be caregiver, maternal and nurturing is deeply rooted in many societies" (Sperandio, 2014, p. 58). In the case of the United States that witnessed an expanding demand for public education in the mid-19th century, hiring morally virtuous female teachers became standard practice in response to "a pressing demand for a huge supply of relatively inexpensive teachers" (Blount, 2000, p. 85) and men did not stay in teaching because of many other occupational avenues (Melder, 1972, p. 21). Advocates for women to become teachers "popularized a vision of the ideal teacher" who exhibited "womanly purity, moral superiority, submissiveness, and nurturance" (Preston, 1993, p. 537). Well into the 20th century—especially in rural and small-town communities—teachers had to follow strict "paternalistic" rules of conduct in their professional and private lives including prohibitions against "marriage, drinking alcoholic beverages, smoking, wearing make-up, and riding in a carriage or automobile with any man except one's father or brother" (Allison, 1995, p. 52). However, such rules focused on social behavior that conformed to community standards and had little or nothing to do with teaching as an ethical endeavor.

Professional Codes of Ethics

Stringent behavioral requirements for being virtuous teachers placed teachers under repressive community control, disregarding the reality that teachers themselves wanted to codify standards for ethical teaching behavior. In the early 20th century, educators in the United States formed numerous professional associations in cities and states; a number of these developed their own code of ethics. Led by teacher associations and educational administrators, and influenced by the work of the National Education Association, by the 1930s most states established ethical codes (NEA, 1924, 1939). Internationally, a recent study of 30 nations (and five continents) reports that teachers' codes of ethics are omnipresent and that they "were developed collaboratively by educational leaders" as well as "government and teacher union representatives" (Shapira-Lishchinsky, 2020, p. 6).

Such codes deal with various standards of conduct relating to teachers' interactions with students, families, and the community. However, in early forms the first "general principle of character and conduct" was that "the teacher should be a person of high moral character"—defined by numerous personality traits such as kindness, cleanliness, honesty, and generosity (NEA, 1939, p. 4). In the United States, the NEA *Code of Ethics* evolved through the years and most recently its first principle is "commitment to the student"—a directive that includes fostering learning and refraining from discriminatory behavior (NEA, 2020). International codes of ethics for teachers represent "six primary categories: caring for students, teachers' professionalism, collegial relationships, parental involvement, community involvement and respecting the rules and regulations" (Shapira-Lishchinsky, 2020, p. 9). On the whole, recent international codes do not insist on teachers' overall moral character but on specific behaviors.

Scholars point out several limitations to ethical codes for teachers. In particular, there is not one unifying ethical code for the teaching profession nor one professional organization that has enforcement jurisdiction (Warnick & Silverman, 2011). Moreover, current codes promulgated by various organizations focus more on "a list of admonitions against improper behavior" and "they do not really address the problem of ethics" nor guide teachers in ethical decision-making (Barrett, et al., 2012, p. 891). As well, for future teachers, familiarity with ethical norms "is the bare minimum of an adequate ethics education" (Maxwell, 2017, p. 323).

Yet, notwithstanding limitations, authors see several purposes for developing teacher ethical codes, beginning with the belief that "no profession can really exist without a code of ethics to guide the conduct of its members" (Campbell, 2003, p. 108). Ethical codes can introduce new teachers to the ethical norms of the profession (O'Neill & Bourke, 2010, p. 164) and have the potential of "moving teachers into a state of awareness to apply a conscious ethical lens to their own view of daily practice" (Campbell, 2003, p. 108). Codes likewise can be catalysts for fostering teachers' consideration of professional ethics as "embedded in an enriched and ongoing examination of the ethical complexities of teaching" (Campbell, 2000, p. 204). Also, a list of ethical principles can be the starting point for developing case studies to examine real-life dilemmas faced by educators and to imaginatively consider alternatives and issues (Joseph, 1989).

Moral Dispositions

In the "standardized management paradigm" era (Henderson & Gornik, 2007) beginning in the late 20th century, efforts to systemize ethical attitudes and behaviors have led to the construct of teacher dispositors as "an integral aspect of teacher education" (von Hohenberg & Broderick, 2021, p. 221) and as constituents of accrediting and professional standards. As a result, teacher education programs in the United States "align dispositional assessments to existing teacher evaluations" (p. 224). In contrast, whereas "many countries understand teacher dispositions as key to promoting effective teaching, that general belief has not been operationalized in the same fashion or at the same rate" [as in the United States] (Fonseca-Chacana, 2019, p. 267). For instance, reports about teacher depositions in Europe state that "initial teacher education must provide teachers with dispositions and skills" (Romer, 2008, p. 21) but emphasize an "incremental perspective" in which "the whole set of competencies that teaching professionals require cannot be fully mastered by any individual, let alone at the very beginning of the career" (Caena, 2014, p. 2).

Dispositions refer to "the habits of professional action and moral commitments that underlie an educator's performance" (Bullough, 2023, p. 2) and serve the purpose "of identifying the required knowledge, skills, and dispositions of a well-qualified teacher" (Stooksberry et al., 2009, p. 719). Nonetheless, dispositions "can be difficult to define" because they refer to a multiplicity of attributes: "perceptions, expectations, qualities, behaviors, virtues, attitudes, temperaments, traits, characteristics, and philosophies" (von Hohenberg & Broderick, 2021, p. 223). As follows, dispositions contain a potpourri of virtues and behaviors for those becoming teachers—from "maintaining high standards of ethics within and outside school" to "planning and teaching well-structured lessons" (Department for Education UK Government, 2021), from "being truthful" to "maintaining professional dress and appropriate appearance" (Choi et al., 2016, p. 88).

Therefore, scholars "argue that the concept of disposition is often unclear in teacher education programs—sometimes referring to general personal values and beliefs and sometimes referring to professional commitments and actions" (Ruitenberg, 2011, p. 41).

Despite the fragmented characterization of dispositions, several scholars highlight their moral nature. They write that dispositions "reflect stances toward moral issues large and small, from 'caring' on an interpersonal level to 'social justice' on a broader societal scale" (Damon, 2007, p. 366). Responding to requirements for teachers to care about and educate all children, they see dispositions as providing a "moral framework" that "grows out of democracy's most fundamental commitment... to support human flourishing" (Bullough, 2023, p. 6).

In this literature, there are several frameworks for organizing dispositions thematically. One approach is to view dispositions as virtues of character, intellect, and care (Sockett, 2009); another distinguishes among intellectual, cultural, and moral dispositions (Stooksberry et al., 2009, p. 720). These tri-fold frameworks can become springboards for reflection. For example, rather than only representing dispositions as a superficial checklist, categories can be used "as a heuristic for... examining the ways candidates talk about their teaching" (p. 731). Similarly, we might consider dispositions as a platform for inquiry to be used by teacher candidates themselves by shaping their ongoing critical self-reflection on their beliefs and experiences.

Teachers and the Moral Imagination

Researchers studying the moral dimensions of teaching often conclude that educators lack a complex comprehension of ethics, moral agency and the moral nature of their work (Bergem, 1992; Sockett & LePage, 2002). Others view teachers as having moral purposes and desire to make moral contributions to their students and society (Sanger & Osguthorpe, 2013). The latter view indicates that teachers and teaching candidates have deep moral impulses and search for "moral meaning" in their lives (Brookfield, 1998). Such studies illustrate how teachers "reflect deeply upon their moral obligations and identities," "embrace ideas relating to moral sensitivity and capacity" (Joseph, 2016, p. 41), "integrate values and ethics" into their understanding of practice" (Afdal, 2019, p. 125), and "evaluate possibilities from a moral point of view" (Werhane, 1999, p. 5). Scholarship about teachers' cognizance of the moral nature of their identities and practice has various foci that parallel interconnected facets of moral imagination: emotions, perception, reasoning, reflection, and visioning (see Table 8.1).

TABLE 8.1 Teachers and the Moral Imagination

Dimensions	Description
Moral Emotions	
Caring	Love for children and adolescents, desire to help them, and aspiration to create caring environments.
Moral Calling	Feeling of being compelled to be of service and committed to caring for students.
Moral Perception	
Moral Presence	Attentiveness, receptivity, and engagement with students informed by moral sensibility and commitment.
Moral Identity	Ongoing development of self-concept as a moral person and ethical practitioner and awareness of self as role model.
Ethical Reasoning	
Ethical Knowledge	Understanding of ethical principles needed to guide teachers' decisions and actions.
Ethical Obligation	Responsibility for being ethical teachers and commitment to serve the best interests of students.
Critical Reflection	
Ethical Dilemmas	Conflicting choices for action between two or more competing ethical values.
Introspection	Inward process of examining personal ethics and ethical choices and their effects on others and upon oneself.
Visioning	
Moral Agency	Teacher's self-efficacy in acting for the well-being of their students and fostering their moral growth.
Transformative Pedagogy	Teaching students how to understand injustice, become global citizens, care for the planet, and appreciate nonviolence.
Activist Identity	Self-concept of teachers committed to challenging injustice and violence in schools, communities, and the wider world.

Once more, they offer examples of teachers—in their own voices—explaining their motivations, aims, and ideals.

Moral Emotions: Caring and Moral Calling

Studies of why individuals choose to become teachers reveal major themes: extrinsic, intrinsic, and altruistic motivations. Extrinsic factors mainly refer to job security, salary, working conditions, and compatibility with family demands. Intrinsic influences include job satisfaction, interest in subject areas, creativity, passion for teaching, and personal fulfillment. Altruistic motivations comprise love of children and the desire to help and empower them and aspirations to be of service to others and to make a social contribution (Campbell, 2013; Friedman, 2016; Heinz, 2015; Kohl, 1984; Lin et al., 2012; See et al., 2022; Watt et al., 2012).

These three rationales can be complex as well as overlapping. Scholars view teacher motivations within a socio-cultural context as local rewards and status influence people's choice and valuation of the teaching profession (Bergmark, et al., 2018; Klassen et al., 2011). For example, in societies that furnish few other career options or, in contrast, where teachers have high status and compensation, extrinsic motivation becomes more consequential than other inducements (Heinz, 2015; Lin et al., 2012; See et al., 2022). Yet, seldom do people choose teaching because of a singular motivation; the desire to be of service to others also can be intrinsically salient (Osguthorpe & Sanger, 2013).

Nonetheless, a preponderance of research in Western societies focuses on the altruistic nature of teachers' motivations emphasizing expressions of care and moral calling. Research about why people become teachers and what subsequently sustains them highlights the centrality of love for children and adolescents (Friedman, 2016; Osguthorpe & Sanger, 2013):

> [My students] need someone to recognize their uniqueness and specialness and respect it and nurture it. I need to be able to love them... I can imagine someone else coming into my classroom and being a sharper teacher, a better storyteller, more capable of choosing the right selections, and [with] a better sense of history and all that. But I feel like in terms of loving kids, that there I can do as good a job as anybody. (Hansen & Quek, 2022, p. 16)
>
> I get to see so many lovely things.... I work with a few children that have suffered quite a lot of neglect... there was one boy he wouldn't let anyone cuddle him... he was quite angry... I just remember at one point he really cuddled me. I was like, this is it, this is what it is all about. (Woolhouse, 2023, p. 10)

Once more, this literature illustrates teachers' devotion to caring for students and creating caring environments:

> I believe that teaching is a way of helping students. It is important to understand them and gain the knowledge needed for motivating them to do their best, not just academically but socially as well. You must be a good friend or counselor.... Good teaching is not just teaching, it is listening; it is hearing their voice, it is feeling and knowing their fears, and then putting yourself in a place to help them. (Mccray et al., 2002, p. 286)
>
> I am committed to fostering a sense of care within my classroom communities. As educational reform continues to center around accountability and standardization which tends to promote competition and individualism, it is important that I emphasize interdependence and caring for others so that

> my students and colleagues can extend this within their greater communities and ultimately, society. (Joseph, 2016, p. 39)

Teachers in these studies reveal that their rewards and joys come from working with and helping children, especially to overcome their difficulties:

> And there are all these small victories. And the small victories are important. Like say when a child is slow to talk, and one day they can say something. We see children develop, see them learn social skills and acquire new abilities. And we, the teachers, we watch this together and the joy unites us. (Harðarson & Magos, 2022, p. 1200)

> While I have sometimes felt unappreciated and lonely, I have also been able to feel deep satisfaction and joy in my work and moments of great inspiration.... I have felt my job to be an important position of trust despite the fact that society is now depriving teacherhood of its last traces of significance. (Estola et al., 2003, p. 245)

Scholars describe such moral purpose as moral calling—being compelled to become teachers to serve children and society, "suggesting just how central the moral work of teaching is to their view of themselves as educators" (Sanger & Osguthorpe, 2011, p. 572). The experiencing of moral feelings impels people to enter the teaching profession and provides intrinsic emotional incentives over time. The literature also offers examples of individuals who want to become teachers unlike those they endured in their youth; these individuals express "moral outrage" due to negative and even humiliating experiences with their own teachers (Campbell, 2013, p. 524). Irrespective of impetus, this sense of calling stems from "a moral passion" (Hansen, 2001, p. 734), coming from an inner drive within such individuals who "find teaching richly rewarding in ways that other vocations are not" (Buskist et al., 2005):

> ...I am not going to get a lot of money teaching school, but I am trying to help people in the community. I am doing my part in the community by trying to help the people's kids. (Mccray et al., 2002, p. 281)

> I can't think of any other profession that, for me, reaps as many benefits as being a teacher does. The sense of accomplishment one must feel at the end of the day, knowing you've done something truly valuable, has to be incredible. (Osguthorpe & Sanger, 2013, p. 184)

Moral calling obliges educators to "invest emotionally in both their work and their students" (Frelin & Fransson, 2017, p. 643), and "remain committed to the work of influencing students' lives for the better, even when one's journey as a teacher is fraught with uncertainties and disappointments" (Hansen & Quek, 2022, p. 12).

Moral Perception: Presence and Identity

Whereas moral perception allows individuals to "comprehend a moral situation encountered in experience" (Abowitz, 2007, p. 288) and "unique situations" (Simpson & Garrison, 1995, p. 252), it is this ability that also makes it possible for teachers to holistically understand the moral significance of their work and to be "attentive to the moral dimensions of existence" (Greene, 1978, p. 46). Such perception negates the concept of teaching solely as a technical practice and instead recognizes teachers' "engagement with students" (Beijaard et al., 2000, p. 751) and involvement in "moral relationships" (Chubbuck et al., 2007, p. 109). In that way, "moral sensibility underlies, prompts and permeates the entire practice" of teaching (p. 111). This component of moral imagination enables teachers to see the moral aspects of daily classroom interactions but also gives meaning to their expression of presence and moral identity.

Scholars writing about moral presence refer to teachers' attentiveness, receptivity, and engagement with students informed by moral sensibility and commitment (Edling & Frelin, 2016, p. 50). Teachers attuned to their presence apprehend the moral qualities inherent in their choices:

> I have realized that every decision I make as a teacher will have moral implications. This includes curriculum I choose, how I teach it, how I deal with discipline and classroom management, the choices I give students, and the list could go on and on. (Joseph, 2003, p. 13)
>
> Every action I make has "normative significance" within the classroom. My actions, what I choose to acknowledge or to ignore, contribute to the environment in the classroom and set the expectations of the classroom community. Those actions determine who is included in or excluded from the community and show my beliefs and attitudes toward different students. (Joseph, 2016, p. 39)

Teachers thus bring "their whole selves to full attention so as to perceive what is happening in the moment" (Rodgers & Raider-Roth, 2006, p. 267)—"to know and respond with intelligence and compassion" (p. 266). As such, presence involves "a sympathetic attitude towards students and their learning" (Hansen, 2000, p. 1) and reflects an "ethic of care over their careers through their classroom relationships and teaching, regardless of circumstance" (Day, 2019, p. 2).

By reacting to situations and engaging with students with a coherent moral presence, educators develop moral identities important to their self-concepts (Hardy & Carlo, 2011) with identity conceived as "the source of a moral imperative... an inner need to do the morally right thing" (Mustakova-Possardt, 2004, pp. 253–254). Studies of teachers' perceptions of their moral identities affirm that personal and professional identities entwine as "personal integrity intersects with the integrity of teaching" (Santoro, 2013, pp. 566–567):

> [*Question: Is your ongoing educational relationship with students part of your overall life as a person?*] You can't separate the one from the other. Because what we do is interact with human beings.... to say that one can be separate from the other is naïve at best, and maybe even detrimental to your practice at worst. (Hansen & Quek, 2022, p. 11)

Moral identity is a dynamic construct of teachers' knowledge and self-formation—"a long process" linked to "personal history and multiple affiliations... based upon relations with others" (Buxarrais, 2021, p. 132):

> As a new teacher, I expect that my values [as an educator] will continue to develop over time as I encounter new people and new situations. Despite this expected evolution, I do have a base with which to consider now the systems of ethics that influence my practice. (Joseph, 2016, p. 37)

> The moral philosophy that I bring to my teaching is obviously a complex product of my personal upbringing, the times in which I live, and the interpretation of life that I have developed through study and experience over the last twenty years. (Joseph, 2016, p. 37)

A way to understand how teachers construct their moral identities is to imagine this process as "identity work" (Clarke, 2009, p. 186) in which "our identities are thus partly given yet they are also something that has to be achieved" (p. 187).

Furthermore, scholars perceive a relationship between the development of moral identity and teachers' awareness of themselves as role models. In research about moral education, studies reveal that teachers typically portray themselves as role models who refrain from socially unacceptable behaviors, believing that they must be "paragons of virtue" (Bergem, 1990, p. 91). Still, some teachers realize that by being caring human beings "students will naturally look up to and identify with [them] because of their values and personal qualities" (p. 93):

> By a "model" I think of a person who shows by his own behaviour, for example, how he thinks the students in his class ought to treat each other. A

> teacher has to consider this . . . which standards he feels are important and what set of values he wants to base his own life upon. If he wants to convey this to the students, it'll be difficult to make any headway if he doesn't practise what he preaches. (Bergem, 1990, p. 93)

> I strive to be a role model for my students, not just as a person who loves math and has found a way to use it in everyday life, but as a thoughtful individual who makes careful decisions. I hope that my students see the care and concern that I put into everything I do, and use me as an example of the kind of person they want to grow to become. (Joseph, 2016, p. 39)

Such comments attest to role modeling as a "reflection of character and intentionality" on the part of teachers who "fulfill this responsibility and are motivated by it" (Campbell, 2013, p. 521). By manifesting caring moral identities, teachers serve "as an important means to nurture ethical caring in schools" (Sanderse, 2013, p. 29).

Ethical Reasoning: Ethical Knowledge and Obligations

Ethical reasoning as a component of teachers' moral imagination refers to recognition of issues and problems calling for ethical judgment and action. As an expanded conceptualization of moral perception, ethical reasoning introduces the elements of reflection and judgment informed by ethical understanding. Two major themes appear in this scholarship: ethical knowledge and ethical obligations. Scholars define the former as comprehension of principles needed to guide teachers' decisions and behaviors; they characterize the latter as teachers' responsibilities to serve the best interest of students.

To determine if they are meeting ethical obligations, teachers are obliged "to examine their own conduct and question their own intentions and actions" (Campbell, 2013, p. 529):

> I have to think about and examine the choices I make in everyday life, turning the seemingly mundane decisions I make daily into a study of ethical inquiry. . . . I reflect in order to ensure that the behavior I am modeling shows students how to treat others with respect and dignity. (Joseph, 2016, p. 37)

> I am obligated—I am morally obligated—to reflect on every moral choice I make in order to make myself as conscious as possible of where I stand. . . . Through this awareness of self, we are more likely to develop a system of values that is more consistent than chaotic. As educators and models of the value systems that we choose to live by, we are obligated to examine ourselves, our thoughts and our actions. (Joseph, 2016, p. 37)

But this scholarship also suggests that "teachers all too often mistake their personal values for ethics" (Malone, 2020, p. 87) and do not interrogate their self-justifications:

> I believe that integrity is something that I need to stick to, I don't think that any amount of faculty training is going to help me get there... I think that all morals are already in you and that you are not going to pick this up from a course. I don't think that a course is going to teach me how I should be treating people from a moral or ethical standpoint." (Campbell, 2013, p. 526)

> I cannot separate who I am from what I teach. At first, I wanted actual ideas and ways to teach morals. I have now come to realize that it is through myself, my decisions, and my own beliefs that I will come up with ways to teach morals. Some people might agree with my ways, and others may not. The important thing is that I am secure and positive in why I am doing things the way I am doing. If I can justify it to myself then I will be able to justify to anyone else. (Joseph, 2003, p. 14)

Moreover, ethical knowledge includes teachers' obligations "to be aware of the many norms and values involved in their interaction and relationship with students" (Damon, 1992, p. 751). Thus, because of their power held over students, it is crucial for teachers "to make ethical choices about the 'right' way to proceed in a myriad of situations" (Davies & Heyward, 2019, p. 372). Scholars appreciate that all of educators' actions have ethical repercussions: "examining these implications is our responsibility as members of society and especially as teachers and as teacher educators" (Burant et al., 2007, p. 405).

Ethical knowledge also compels teachers to see educational issues as "questions of right and wrong" and to engage in "ethical discourse... that commonly includes such words as ought and should, fair and unfair" (Strike, 1988, p. 156). Such knowledge "enables teachers to make conceptual and practical links between core moral and ethical values such as honesty, compassion, fairness, and respect for others and their own daily choices and actions" (Campbell, 2006, p. 33):

> Ethics and professionalism should go hand-in-hand in order to promote effective welcoming learning environments, but they basically set a minimum standard for me and only begin to address the multitude of other values which I and other teachers strive to live by... to name a few: empathy, trust, sincerity, compassion and even sympathy once you are faced with a classroom full of children in varying cognitive and emotional states. (Joseph, 2016, p. 37)

Cognizance of "the ethical dimensions of their practice" allows teachers to be aware of "which issues of right and wrong conduct are at stake" and that complex decisions about appropriate responses must be made (Campbell, 2000, p. 215).

Critical Reflection: Ethical Dilemmas and Introspection

Critical reflection involves an inward process of examining personal ethics and ethical choices (made and not made) and their effects on others and upon oneself. This component of moral imagination reveals that awareness of ethical issues and obligations does not always involve easy decisions for teachers and that "ethical dilemmas will exist... wherever different principles lead to different resolutions—where there is no evident right answer and we must make a tough choice between two or more conflicting answers" (Shapira-Lishchinsky, 2016, pp. 246–247). Ethical dilemmas—with compelling accounts of how teachers experience them—is a significant topic in the literature on the moral dimensions of teaching.

Some authors insist that to educate teachers to face ethical quandaries, novices must understand "the ethical standards of their profession" (Tirri, 2010, p. 154) and to be introduced to "key ethical principles explicit in the formation of morally responsible practitioners" (Maxwell & Schwimmer, 2016, p. 359). Others, however, believe that teacher education cannot fully prepare teachers to deal with ethical dilemmas nor can these quandaries be easily resolved as "teachers can seldom rely on commonly held and acknowledged ethical principles" and even with such knowledge, teachers "have to make the transfer from the abstract principle to the demands of concrete 'real life' situations" (Kelchtermans, 1996, p. 317).

Researchers document how both new and experienced educators deal with ethical dilemmas in their practice (Campbell, 2000; Koc & Buzzelli, 2016, p. 34), noting that "ethical conflicts are constantly present" (Conerud, 2015, p. 347). Teachers "who believe they should be moral agents may recurrently experience ethical dilemmas about how to serve the best interests of children and when they encounter barriers to living according to their moral obligations" (Joseph, 2016, p. 39). Educators face dilemmas centering on their concerns about fairness as well as equitable resources for students and schools (Shapira-Lishchinsky, 2011, pp. 648–649). They also feel torn between maintaining their students' trust and following school rules "which obligate them to report confided information to administration and parents" (p. 649). Another predicament is whether or not to confront a colleague when they believe a student is being mistreated (p. 649). Scholars also point out that ethical dilemmas surface when there is conflict between teachers and parents about what is best for students (p. 649) and when teachers' "beliefs and values clash with those of administrators, colleagues, and the greater society" (Koc & Buzzelli, 2016, p. 30):

> When you have a pupil with a parent whom I personally think often behaves inappropriately towards their child, it can be hard to strike a balance between maintaining a decent relationship with the parent and making the child as happy as possible. The child's well-being is my primary concern, of course, but where is the boundary? Maintaining a good relationship with the parents is also important. I sometimes feel frustrated in this type of situation. (Colnerud, 2015, p. 355)

A way of characterizing several of these dilemmas is to recognize the tensions generated by "two ethical dimensions of school climate": "the caring climate promotes attention to individual and social needs while the formal climate focuses on adhering to organizational rules" (Shapira-Lishchinsky, 2011, p. 648). Such studies illustrate "value differences between teachers and students, administrators, or communities" and "portray the vulnerability of teachers" who feel "apprehension about offending people or fear of doing what is forbidden" (Joseph & Efron, 1993, p. 218):

> If [teachers are] "awake" and utilizing their moral agency and considering the moral dimensions of decisions, since they are an example for the students, this will have a positive impact. On the other hand, if teachers just do their job and play their role without weighing moral dimensions of their choices, that would have a detrimental effect on their students' process of moral learning.... That is the disconnect I felt while student teaching. I was just playing the role of a passive teacher in the system (appropriate for the situation of student teaching), and I was not showing the students an example of what it means to be "moral" or "awake." (Joseph, 2016, p. 40)

A related topic in this scholarship is moral stress (Colnerud, 2015). This emotional reaction occurs because teachers do not experience ethical dilemmas on just a cognitive level; the decision-making process and aftermath can create considerable emotional discomfort. Moral stress, expressed throughout the literature about perceptions of ethical dilemmas, stems from teachers' feelings of regret and powerlessness:

> A student came to me; she was crying. She was upset because her mother was living with someone. This person was mistreating her mother.... the girl came to me and asked me to intervene, but I had to tell her that I can't. It was very hard for me to do. I did the right thing in the eyes of the board of education. I didn't do the right thing in my eyes. I saw what it was doing to

> the child. Do you do the right thing for the students or for yourself? (Joseph & Efron, 1993, pp. 214–215)

> Iris deserved to be sent abroad as part of a school delegation. However, I was put under a lot of outside pressure to exclude her because the municipality was only willing to pay for residents, and Iris was a dorming pupil. Iris's family was too poor to pay for the trip. I believed in her, but instead of helping her I caved in. Iris lost her trust in me and in adults in general. I am very angry at myself. I folded. There were other ways to fund her trip. I should have listened to my own truth, my values. Sometimes, by avoiding conflicts we cause even bigger and more acute problems. (Shapira-Lishchinsky, 2011, p. 653)

This distress often results because "teachers often act in ways that conflict with their own conscience" (Colnerud, 2015, p. 347) and "this moral dimension in teaching contributes a great deal to teachers' vulnerability" (Kelchtermans, 1996, p. 318).

Yet, there are scholars who believe that ethical dilemmas that foster introspection can be catalysts for teachers' learning and growth as "they provide an opportunity for reflective processes by questioning the way things in school operate" (Shapira-Lishchinsky, 2016, p. 246). Experiencing ethical dilemmas can stimulate reflection leading to moral learning and growth (Brookfield, 1998) when teachers identify their conundrums and realize the myriad of moral choices and issues involved in their decisions:

> The moral and ethical beliefs of my practice have continually revealed themselves through "dilemmas" I experienced during my student teaching experience both in the classroom and working with various staff. A majority of the dilemmas I faced involved providing equitable resources for my special needs population and my English language learners. Each moment I stopped and paused about what I was teaching or planning and how it would affect each of these populations, I realized I was defining my system of ethics as a professional. (Joseph, 2016, p. 40)

Accordingly, "dilemmatic situations do not automatically lead to negative affective states" as these quandaries might eventually inspire attainable solutions and teachers might even "experience positive moral emotions" (Ittner & Hascher, 2021, p. 224) when they discover the benefits of their struggle and learning, including self-knowledge.

Visioning: Moral Agency, Transformative Pedagogy, and Activist Identity

Lastly, the component of visioning means that teachers envision their moral agency in their ethical relationships with students and their roles as professionals in schools—even when that means countering customary values and behaviors. Educators also expand their professional identities by teaching transformative pedagogy—educating their students to understand the meaning and necessity of social justice, nonviolence and restoration of the natural world. This component of moral imagination involves educators' consciousness transformation stimulated by profoundly different ways of thinking about not only about teaching but about the world. As they contemplate ideal versions of society and conceive of more ethical and dynamic roles, they take on identities as activists in schools, communities, and broader spheres.

Teachers as moral agents foster students' moral values and development (Aloni, 2008; Bergem, 1990; Campbell, 2003; Ezer et al., 2010) and strive to create a moral universe in the classroom and school; "by conducting education morally, the teacher hopes to induce an enhanced moral sense in the student" (Noddings, 1984, p. 179):

> Teachers should not be in a classroom unless they truly care about the students they deal with and have a desire to make some kind of positive impact in these children's lives.... We must as teachers help our students to feel the brotherhood of humanity, regardless of race, religion, and gender. No one should be excluded from the worldwide moral community.... Above all, we must help our students to feel, to take the risk of being hurt, to share the triumph of spirit. (Joseph, 2003, p. 11)

> [We as] educators have the responsibility to make school a safe place by helping students understand the consequences of the choices they make.... This can take the form of stepping in when I see bullying occurring, or making a stand against racism and prejudice. (Joseph, 2016, p. 39)

For some scholars, "the very essence of teaching lies in moral agency" (Johnston et al., 1998, p. 163). Educators who are conscious of "their moral agent state of being" (Campbell, 2008, p. 603) have "deep awareness of the significance of their choices and how those choices influence the development and well-being of others" (Buzzelli & Johnston, 2002, p. 120). As is the case of other components of moral imagination, visioning necessitates attentiveness and reflection.

Visioning also encompasses teachers' moral action on behalf of their students and society, to "revise and transform social and cultural practices" and not to "passively submit to them" (Sugarman, 2005, p. 808). Scholars explore how teachers as moral agents "work collaboratively for the common good" (Diez, 2007, p. 395) and act "in the broader rather than narrower interests of the student" (Day, 2019, p. 3):

> I see teaching as a political act. This is about justice. This is about giving our children what they deserve. I [want to] be part of it standing up to righting some wrongs. (Santoro, 2013, p. 569)

> One of the most important qualities of respect is a commitment to equity. This idea goes beyond the simple idea of fairness and instead addresses students' true needs for learning and ultimately allows me as a teacher to respect those needs .... It is my responsibility as an educator to treat these students with respect and provide for them what they need to be successful. (Joseph, 2016, p. 38)

In this light, moral agency is what motivates teachers to challenge dominant paradigms of schooling and society that impede students' flourishing—"to actively apply their moral responsibilities to make a difference" in students' academic, social, and personal learning experiences (Day, 2019, p. 3). These educators contemplate how schooling and their own practices "contribute or fail to contribute to a just and humane society" (Adler, 1991, p. 142).

Teachers also express moral agency through transformative pedagogy with its goals of recognizing the dignity of all human beings (Merry & de Ruyter, 2011), creating a more just society (Morrison, 2016), and confronting the environmental crisis and valuing environmental justice (Lowenstein et al., 2010, p. 105). This practice of transformative moral education reflects educators' societal and ecological concerns as well as their hopes for possibilities for change. Teachers involved with forms of transformative pedagogy have a moral commitment to "prepare students to develop their own vision of justice and the skills to enact the vision themselves" (Picower, 2012, p. 566) and "are applying a philosophy in the classroom that includes a clear investment in their students' developing identities" (Harrell-Levy & Kerpelman, 2010, p. 77):

> I love taking myself and children's minds out beyond what they are comfortable with. And to be just really aware of what's happening in the world. And relate it back to their lives. To be helpful in a global way.... I'm hoping that I'll be able to plant some seeds to help them create a better world at some point in the future. (Rosenberg, 2018, p. 122)

> It means teaching... [students] about the world as it is and how they can be part of changing the world to be more the way... they would want the world to be. [Teaching students] to think about their situation in the world and their experiences and their family's experiences and what's right about that and what's wrong about that and how those things can be changed. (Picower, 2012, p. 566)

Teachers of transformative pedagogy acknowledge the need to cultivate their students' agency. A justice-centered pedagogy becomes "a catalyst for social transformation by positioning students as transformative intellectuals who exhibit complexity, commitment, and credibility" (Morales-Doyle, 2017, p. 1055). Teaching about social justice involves fostering students' ability to recognize and challenge injustice by "developing their own understandings of inequality and skills to take action" (Picower, 2012, p. 564):

> We used our community to show the kids how they could make change in the world, essentially. We did that by having a large meeting where each class sent representatives where we could discuss topics that the kids brought up that were important to them, urgent things that were on their minds.... (Santoro, 2011, p. 14)
>
> I'm trying to teach [my students] to be responsible global citizens. I try to weave through everything I do, not only with the curriculum but also with the students and how my classroom is set up [for] compassion and respect and human rights.... (Joseph & Duss, 2009, p. 199)

So too, teaching about environmental justice requires teachers to "help students form a critical relationship with the cultural roots of current crises" and to be involved in cultural changes to sustain a healthy environment (Lowenstein et al., 2010, p. 105) as well as "embracing greening of classrooms and schools for environmental sustainability" (Mueller 2009, p. 1050).

As educators imagine a more just and peaceful world, they contemplate their curricular content, classroom milieu, and goals for their students; they look for ways to actualize their ethical commitments through their teaching. In particular, their teaching realizes their mission to "remove the hold of violence upon individuals, cultures, and the Earth" (Joseph & Mikel, 2014, p. 328) and to strive for "a reorientation of a world view" with "peace as a moral and ethical pursuit" (Jenkins, 2016, p. 3):

> I think what actually motivates me the most in teaching languages is that, in the end, the aim of learning languages is that there would be no wars, no hatred, because language helps you to come closer to other human beings who do not share your culture. (Rissanen et al., 2018, p. 69)
>
> *We pledge to be peacemakers, to treat others with respect and live by the golden rule.* I [often ask] especially at the beginning of the year after the pledge, how did you treat someone with respect today?... how have you been a peacemaker, how have you been kind, who have you helped? How have you lived by the golden rule and I constantly refer to what the golden rule is. (Joseph & Duss, 2009, p. 200)

Yet, these teachers do not aim to "simply replace violent ideologies with more peaceful ones" as "such an approach is indoctrination"; toward this end, they demonstrate the importance of nonviolence and peace awareness through "an ethical, elicitive and learner-centered approach" (Jenkins, 2016, p. 3). Educators accordingly need to afford students a knowledge base and opportunities to critically understand violence and to gain an experiential appreciation of peace.

Concurrently, doing the work of transformative pedagogy coheres teachers' identities as activists working for social justice in schools, communities, and beyond. Scholars suggest that these individuals experience "a personal transformative process" and "develop a dialectical consciousness—of violence and peace, of ecological devastation and harmony" (Joseph & Mikel, 2014, p. 327). Activist teachers "hold a vision of a socially just world and work to reconcile this vision with the realities of inequality that they see in the world around them" (Picower, 2012, p. 564). They "take risks and face resistance and likelihood of overt conflict" but "live with such hope and commitment" (Mikel & Hiserman, 2000, pp. 130). Activist identity includes visions of agency and self-efficacy for changing schooling and for challenging the ways that "schooling reproduces existing inequalities and maintains the status quo" (Picower, 2012, p. 564):

> As soon as I got into teaching, I recognized the way that education policy and the larger forces of capitalism affect what goes on in the classrooms. It became clear to me that I couldn't just teach and expect the world to get better, I had to be involved in changing the way that education works in society. (Picower, 2012, p. 570)

> I wake up in the morning and I believe that the world can be better and that's why I do the work that I do. [Teacher activism] is founded in the belief that the systems and structures and the ways in which people relate to each other doesn't have to be the only way. (Picower, 2012, p. 565)

For some teachers, their activism also focuses on societal transformation; they "consider teaching peace and nonviolence as extensions of their personalities as activists" (Joseph & Duss, 2009, p. 204):

> ...If you're a progressive teacher and your emphasis is on social justice, to me there's probably nothing less just than war or violence, whether that violence is physical or poverty or whatever. So, as far as I'm concerned, advocating for peace is advocating for way of transforming society without violence....I am a proponent of peace because it's a proponent of change. (Joseph & Duss, 2009, p. 195)

Moreover, activist teachers learn that collaboration is crucial "for both immediate and systemic educational change" (Boylan, 2016, p. 65):

> I don't think that individual teachers can just struggle alone in their own classroom and be like, "Oh well, that's the system I'm living in so I'll just make the best of it." I think unless we're struggling with the larger issues that make it so our classroom is not as productive of an environment for students as it could be, then well, I don't see the point in teaching... I feel like I have to be involved in the struggle for change... by being connected to movements that are going on, that need more people working in them. (Picower, 2012, p. 570)

Working "in coalition with others" provides support for activist teachers and encouragement "to keep going in the face of adversity" (Picower, 2012, p. 570). For instance, researchers report that teachers of peace pedagogy have "backgrounds of activism in anti-war, nonviolence, peace and social justice activities" and are remain involved with organizations working for similar goals (Joseph & Duss, 2009, p. 204).

Finally, transformative work inside of classrooms and schools is only part of what activist educators recognize as their ethical obligations. For these educators, "consciousness transformation culminates in agency" with their own "ongoing efforts to end brutality, dominance, and oppression in private and public spheres and the natural world" (Joseph & Mikel, 2014, p. 328). Teaching for transformation "inside of the classroom without fighting injustice outside inadequately reconciles their vision of the world they wish to see" (Picower, 2012, p. 564); activist teachers "are not content to depend on their students alone to change the world" (p. 569). Therefore, teachers who hold visions of justice and nonviolence make a commitment to personally take moral responsibility in a difficult world.

References

Abowitz, K. K. (2007). Moral perception through aesthetics engaging imaginations in educational ethics. *Journal of Teacher Education, 58* (4), 287–298.

Adler, S. (1991). The reflective practitioner and the curriculum of teacher education. *Journal of Education for Teaching, 17,* 139–150.

Afdal, G. (2019). Ethical logics in teacher education. *Teaching and Teacher Education, 84,* 118–127.

Allison, C. B. (1995). Women teachers and the struggle for occupational justice: Is feminism an answer?. *Counterpoints, 6,* 47–69.

Aloni, N. (2008). The fundamental commitments of educators. *Ethics and Education, 3,* 149–159.

Averill, L. A . (1939). *Mental hygiene for the classroom teacher.* Pitman.

Barrett, D. E., Casey, J. E., Visser, R. D., & Headley, K. N. (2012). How do teachers make judgments about ethical and unethical behaviors? Toward the development of a code of conduct for teachers. *Teaching and Teacher Education, 28*(6), 890–898.

Beijaard, D., Verloop, N., & Vermunt, J. D. (2000). Teachers' perceptions of professional identity: An exploratory study from a personal knowledge perspective. *Teaching and Teacher Education, 16*(7), 749–764.

Bérard, R. N. (1984). Moral education in Nova Scotia, 1880–1920. *Acadiensis, 14*(1), 49–63.

Bergem, T. (1990). The teacher as moral agent: A Scandinavian perspective. *Journal of Moral Education, 19*, 88–100.

Bergem, T. (1992). Teaching the art of living: Lessons learned from a study of teacher education. In F. K. Oser, A. Dick, & J. L. Patry (Eds.), *Effective and responsible teaching: The new synthesis* (pp. 349–364). Jossey Bass.

Bergmark, U., Lundström, S., Manderstedt, L., & Palo, A. (2018). Why become a teacher? Student teachers' perceptions of the teaching profession and motives for career choice. *European Journal of Teacher Education, 41*(3), 266–281.

Blount, J. M. (2000). Spinsters, bachelors, and other gender transgressors in school employment, 1850–1990. *Review of Educational Research, 70*(1), 83–101.

Boylan, M. (2016). Deepening system leadership: Teachers leading from below. *Educational Management Administration & Leadership, 44*(1), 57–72.

Brookfield, S. (1998). Understanding and facilitating moral learning in adults. *Journal of Moral Education, 27*, 283–300.

Bullough Jr, R. V. (2023). Rethinking dispositions in teaching and teacher education: Virtue and the manners of democracy as a way of life. *Journal of Teacher Education*, 1–12. https://doi.org/10.1177/002248712311549

Burant, T. J., Chubbuck, S. M., & Whipp, J. L. (2007). Reclaiming the moral in the dispositions debate. *Journal of Teacher Education, 58*(5), 397–411.

Buskist, W., Benson, T., & Sikorski, J. F. (2005). The call to teach. *Journal of Social and Clinical Psychology, 24*(1), 111–122.

Buxarrais, M. R. (2021). Teacher's ethos and moral and professional identity. In F. Oser, K. Heinrichs, J. Bauer, & T. Lovat (Eds.), *The international handbook of teacher ethos: Strengthening teachers, supporting learners* (pp. 125–143). Springer International.

Buzzelli, C. A., & Johnston, B. (2002). *The moral dimensions of teaching: Language, power, and culture in classroom interactio*n. Routledge/Falmer.

Caena, F. (2014). *Initial teacher education in Europe: An overview of policy issues.* European Commission. ET2020 Working Group of Schools Policy. http://ec.europa.eu/education/policy/strategic--framework/expert--groups/documents/initial--teacher--education_en.pdf

Campbell, E. (2000). Professional ethics in teaching: Towards the development of a code of practice. *Cambridge Journal of Education, 30*(2), 203–221.

Campbell, E. (2003). *The ethical teacher.* Open University Press.

Campbell, E. (2006). Ethical knowledge in teaching: A moral imperative of professionalism. *Education Canada-Toronto, 46*(4), 32–35.

Campbell, E. (2008). The ethics of teaching as a moral profession. *Curriculum Inquiry, 38*(4), 357–385.

Campbell, E. (2013). Ethical intentions and the moral motivation of teachers. In K. Heinrichs, F. Oser, & T. Lovat (Eds.), *Handbook of moral motivation* (pp. 517–532). Brill.

Campbell, E. (2014). Teaching ethically as a moral condition of professionalism. In *Handbook of moral and character education* (pp. 117–134). Routledge.

Choi, H. S., Benson, N. F., & Shudak, N. J. (2016). Assessment of teacher candidate dispositions: Evidence of reliability and validity. *Teacher Education Quarterly, 43*(3), 71–89.

Chubbuck, S. M., Burant, T. J., & Whipp, J. L. (2007). The presence and possibility of moral sensibility in beginning pre-service teachers. *Ethics and Education, 2*(2), 109–130.

Clarke, M. (2009). The ethico-politics of teacher identity. *Educational Philosophy and Theory, 41*(2), 185–200.

Colnerud, G. (2015). Moral stress in teaching practice. *Teachers and Teaching, 21*(3), 346–360.

Conway, P. F., & Murphy, R. (2013). A rising tide meets a perfect storm: New accountabilities in teaching and teacher education in Ireland. *Irish Educational Studies, 32*(1), 11–36.

Coppock, D. A. (1997). Respectability as a prerequisite of moral character: the social and occupational mobility of pupil teachers in the late nineteenth and early twentieth centuries. *History of Education, 26*(2), 165–186.

Damon, W. (1992). Teaching as a moral craft and developmental expedition. In F. K. Oser, A. Dick, & J. L. Patry (Eds.), *Effective and responsible teaching: The new synthesis* (pp. 139–153). Jossey-Bass.

Damon, W. (2007). Dispositions and teacher assessment: The need for a more rigorous definition. *Journal of Teacher Education, 58*(5), 365–369.

Davies, M., & Heyward, P. (2019). Between a hard place and a hard place: A study of ethical dilemmas experienced by student teachers while on practicum. *British Educational Research Journal, 45*(2), 372–387.

Day, C. (2019). Teachers' moral purposes: A necessary but insufficient condition for successful teaching and learning. In M. Peters (Ed.), *Encyclopedia of teacher education.* Springer. https://doi.org/10.1007/978-981-13-1179-6_191-1

Department for Education, UK Government. (2021). *Teachers' standards.* https://www.gov.uk/government/publications/teachers-standards

Diez, M. E. (2007). Looking back and moving forward: Three tensions in the teacher dispositions discourse. *Journal of Teacher Education, 58*(5), 388–396.

Edling, S., & Frelin, A. (2016). Sensing as an ethical dimension of teacher professionality. *Journal of Moral Education, 45*(1), 46–58.

Estola, E., Erkkila, R., & Syrjala, L. (2003). A moral voice of vocation in teachers' narratives. *Teachers and Teaching, 9*(3), 239–256.

Ezer, H., Gilat, I., & Sagee, R. (2010). Perception of teacher education and professional identity among novice teachers. *European Journal of Teacher Education, 33*(4), 391–404.

Fischman, G. E. (2007). Persistence and ruptures: The feminization of teaching and teacher education in Argentina. *Gender and education, 19*(3), 353–368.

Fonseca-Chacana, J. (2019). Making teacher dispositions explicit: A participatory approach. *Teaching and Teacher Education, 77*, 266–276.

Frelin, A., & Fransson, G. (2017). Four components that sustain teachers' commitment to students—A relational and temporal model. *Reflective Practice, 18*(5), 641–654.

Friedman, I. A. (2016). Being a teacher: Altruistic and narcissistic expectations of pre-service teachers. *Teachers and Teaching, 22*(5), 625–648.

Gao, X. (2008). Teachers' professional vulnerability and cultural tradition: A Chinese paradox. *Teaching and Teacher Education, 24*(1), 154–165.

Greene, M. (1978). *Landscapes of learning.* Teachers College Press.

Hansen, D. T. (1998). The moral is in the practice. *Teaching and Teacher Education, 14*(6), 643–655.

Hansen, D. T. (2000). *Cultivating an intellectual and moral sensibility as teacher.* Paper presented at the Annual Meeting of the American Educational Research Association (New Orleans, LA, April 24–28, 2000).

Hansen, D. T. (2001). Reflections on the manner in teaching project. *Journal of Curriculum Studies, 33*(6), 729–735.

Hansen, D.T., & Quek, Y. (2023). The call to teach and the ethics of care: A dynamic educational crossroads. *Journal of Curriculum Studies, 55*(1), 8–20.

Harðarson, A., & Magos, K. (2022). Emotional demands and moral rewards: A story told by fifteen teachers. *Scandinavian Journal of Educational Research, 66*(7), 1194–1203.

Harrell-Levy, M. K., & Kerpelman, J. L. (2010). Identity process and transformative pedagogy: Teachers as agents of identity formation. *Identity: An International Journal of Theory and Research, 10*(2), 76–91.

Heinz, M. (2015). Why choose teaching? An international review of empirical studies exploring student teachers' career motivations and levels of commitment to teaching. *Educational Research and Evaluation, 21*(3), 258–297.

Henderson, J. G., & Gornik, R. (2007). *Transformative curriculum leadership* (3rd ed.). Merrill/Prentice Hall.

Huebner, D. (1996). Teaching as moral activity. *Journal of Curriculum and Supervision, 11*(3), 267–275.

Ittner, D., & Hascher, T. (2021). Towards a model of teachers' moral health: Professional satisfaction, moral emotions and teacher ethos. In F. Oser, K. Heinrichs, J. Bauer, & T. Lovat (Eds.), *The international handbook of teacher ethos: Strengthening teachers, supporting learners* (pp. 211–234). Springer International.

Jenkins, T. (2016). Transformative peace pedagogy: Fostering a reflective, critical, and inclusive praxis for peace studies. *Factis Pax, 10*(1), 1–7.

Johnston, B., Juhasz, A., Marken, J., & Ruiz, B. R. (1998). The ESL teacher as moral agent. *Research in the Teaching of English*, 161–181.

Jordan, R. H. (1930). *Education as a life work: An introduction into education.* Century.

Joseph, P. B. (1989). Ethical choices for social studies professionals. *Social Education, 59*(1), 55–57.

Joseph, P. B. (2001). "The Ideal Teacher": Images in early 20th-century teacher education textbooks. In P. B. Joseph & G. E. Burnaford (Eds.) *Images of schoolteachers in America* (pp. 147–170). Routledge.

Joseph, P. B. (2003). Teaching about the moral classroom: Infusing the moral imagination into teacher education. *Asia-Pacific Journal of Teacher Education, 31*(1), 7–20.

Joseph, P. B. (2016). Ethical reflections on becoming teachers. *Journal of Moral Education, 45*(1), 31–45.

Joseph, P. B., & Duss, L. S. (2009). Teaching a pedagogy of peace: A study of peace educators in United States schools in the aftermath of September 11. *Journal of Peace Education, 6*(2), 189–207.

Joseph, P. B., & Efron, S. (1993). Moral choices/moral conflicts: Teachers' self-perceptions. *Journal of Moral Education, 22*(3), 201–220.

Joseph, P. B., & Mikel, E. (2014). Transformative moral education: Challenging an ecology of violence. *Journal of Peace Education, 11*(3), 317–333.

Kelchtermans, G. (1996). Teacher vulnerability: Understanding its moral and political roots. *Cambridge Journal of Education, 26*(3), 307–323.

Klassen, R. M., Al-Dhafri, S., Hannok, W., & Betts, S. M. (2011). Investigating pre-service teacher motivation across cultures using the Teachers' Ten Statements Test. *Teaching and Teacher Education, 27*(3), 579–588.

Koc, K., & Buzzelli, C. A. (2016). Turkish teachers' accounts of moral dilemmas in early childhood settings. *Journal of Early Childhood Research, 14*(1), 28–42.

Kohl, H. (1984). *Growing minds: On becoming a teacher.* Harper & Row.

Lin, E., Shi, Q., Wang, J., Zhang, S., & Hui, L. (2012). Initial motivations for teaching: Comparison between preservice teachers in the United States and China. *Asia-Pacific Journal of Teacher Education, 40*(3), 227–248.

Lindqvist, H., Thornberg, R., & Colnerud, G. (2021). Ethical dilemmas at work placements in teacher education. *Teaching Education, 32*(4), 403–419.

Malone, D. M. (2020). Ethics education in teacher preparation: a case for stakeholder responsibility. *Ethics and Education, 15*(1), 77–97.

Maxwell, B. (2017). Codes of professional conduct and ethics education for future teachers. *Philosophical Inquiry in Education, 24*(4), 323–347.

Maxwell, B., & Schwimmer, M. (2016). Professional ethics education for future teachers: A narrative review of the scholarly writings. *Journal of Moral Education, 45*(3), 354–371.

McClellan, B. E. (1999). *Moral education in America: Schools and the shaping of character from colonial times to the present.* Teachers College Press.

Mccray, A. D., Sindelar, P. T., Kilgore, K. K., & Neal, L. I. (2002). African-American women's decisions to become teachers: Sociocultural perspectives. *International Journal of Qualitative Studies in Education, 15*(3), 269–290.

Melder, K. E. (1972). Woman's high calling: The teaching profession in America, 1830–1860. *American Studies, 13*(2), 19–32.

Merry, M. S., & de Ruyter, D. J. (2011). The relevance of cosmopolitanism for moral education. *Journal of Moral Education, 40*(1), 1–18.

Mikel, E. R., & Hiserman, S. (2000). Beyond the classroom: Progressive activist teachers and images of experience, meaning, purpose, and identity. In P. B. Joseph & G. E. Burnaford (Eds.), *Images of schoolteachers in America* (pp. 115–131). Routledge.

Morales-Doyle, D. (2017). Justice-centered science pedagogy: A catalyst for academic achievement and social transformation. *Science Education, 101*(6), 1034–1060.

Morrison, P. (2016). School home interactive curriculum development: Teachers and families in partnership. In *Handbook of research on effective communication in culturally diverse classrooms* (pp. 129–152). IGI Global.

Mueller, M. P. (2009). Educational reflections on the "ecological crisis": Ecojustice, environmentalism, and sustainability. *Science & Education, 18*(8), 1031–1056.

Mustakova-Possardt, E. (2004). Education for critical moral consciousness. *Journal of Moral Education, 33*(3), 245–269.

National Education Association. (1939). *Ethics in the teaching profession: Codes of state and national educational associations.* Washington DC: Research Division. https://babel.hathitrust.org/cgi/pt?id=nnc1.cu17217334&view=1up&seq=2

National Education Association. (1975/2010/2020). *Code of ethics.* http://www.nea.org/home/30442.htm

National Education Association. (1924). Professional ethics for educators. *Journal of the National Education Association, 13*(2), 64–67. https://babel.hathitrust.org/cgi/pt?id=pur1.32754076535305&view=1up&seq=85&q1=ethics

Noddings, N, (1984). *Caring: A feminine approach to ethics and moral education.* University of California Press.

O'Neill, J., & Bourke, R. (2010). Educating teachers about a code of ethical conduct. *Ethics and Education, 5*(2), 159–172.

Osguthorpe, R., & Sanger, M. (2013). The moral nature of teacher candidate beliefs about the purposes of schooling and their reasons for choosing teaching as a career. *Peabody Journal of Education, 88*(2), 180–197.

Picower, B. (2012). Teacher activism: Enacting a vision for social justice. *Equity & Excellence in Education, 45*(4), 561–574.

Preston, J. A. (1993). Domestic ideology, school reformers, and female teachers: Schoolteaching becomes women's work in nineteenth-century New England. *The New England Quarterly, 66*(4), 531–551.

Pring, T. (2001). Education as moral practice. *Journal of Moral Education, 30*(2), 101–112.

Rissanen, I., Kuusisto, E., Hanhimäki, E., & Tirri, K. (2018). The implications of teachers' implicit theories for moral education: A case study from Finland. *Journal of Moral Education, 47*(1), 63–77.

Rodgers, C. R., & Raider-Roth, M. B. (2006). Presence in teaching. *Teachers and Teaching: Theory and Practice, 12*(3), 265–287.

Romer, M. (2008). *Teacher education in Europe: An ETUCE policy paper.* https://www.csee-etuce.org/images/attachments/ETUCE_PolicyPaper_en.pdf

Rosenberg, G. R. (2018). Moral agency as teaching morally and teaching morality: A practical approach to moral education. In T. Harrison & D. I. Walker (Eds.), *The theory and practice of virtue education* (pp. 112–125). Routledge.

Ruitenberg, C. W. (2011). The trouble with dispositions: A critical examination of personal beliefs, professional commitments and actual conduct in teacher education. *Ethics and Education, 6*(1), 41–52.

Sanderse, W. (2013). The meaning of role modelling in moral and character education. *Journal of Moral education, 42*(1), 28–42.

Sanger, M., & Osguthorpe, R. (2013). The moral vacuum in teacher education research and practice. In H. Sockett & R. Boostrom (Eds.), *NSSE yearbook: A moral critique of contemporary education, 112* (pp. 41–60). Teachers College, Columbia University.

Sanger, M. N., & Osguthorpe, R. D. (2011). Teacher education, preservice teacher beliefs, and the moral work of teaching. *Teaching and Teacher Education, 27*(3), 569–578.

Santoro, D. A. (2013). "I was becoming increasingly uneasy about the profession and what was being asked of me": Preserving integrity in teaching. *Curriculum Inquiry, 43*(5), 563–587.

See, B. H., Munthe, E., Ross, S. A., Hitt, L., & El Soufi, N. (2022). Who becomes a teacher and why?. *Review of Education, 10*(3), e3377.

Shapira-Lishchinsky, O. (2011). Teachers' critical incidents: Ethical dilemmas in teaching practice. *Teaching and Teacher Education, 27*(3), 648–656.

Shapira-Lishchinsky, O. (2016). From ethical reasoning to teacher education for social justice. *Teaching and Teacher Education, 60*, 245–255.

Shapira-Lishchinsky, O. (2020). A multinational study of teachers' codes of ethics: Attitudes of educational leaders. *NASSP Bulletin, 104*(1), 5–19.

Simpson, P. J., & Garrison, J. (1995). Teaching and moral perception. *Teachers College Record, 97*(2), 252–278.

Sockett, H. (2009). Dispositions as virtues: The complexity of the construct. *Journal of Teacher Education, 60*(3), 291–303.

Sockett, H., & LePage, P. (2002). The missing language of the classroom. *Teaching and Teacher Education, 18*, 159–171.

Sperandio, J. (2014). A question of role and respect: The status of female teachers in societies in change. In *Inequalities in the teaching profession* (pp. 50–66). Palgrave Macmillan.

Spring, J. (1990). *The American school: 1642–1990.* Longman.

Stewart, D. J. (2006). Teachers as exemplars: An Australian perspective. *Education and Urban Society, 38*(3), 345–358.

Stooksberry, L. M., Schussler, D. L., & Bercaw, L. A. (2009). Conceptualizing dispositions: Intellectual, cultural, and moral domains of teaching. *Teachers and Teaching: Theory and practice, 15*(6), 719–736.

Strike, K. A. (1988). The ethics of teaching. *Phi Delta Kappan, 70*(2), 156–158.

Sugarman, J. (2005). Persons and moral agency. *Theory & Psychology, 15*(6), 793–811.

Tirri, K. (2010). Teacher values underlying professional ethics. In T. Lovat, R. Toomey, & N. Clement (Eds.) *International research handbook on values education and student wellbeing* (pp. 153–161). Springer.

Tom, A. R. (1980). Teacher as a moral craft: A metaphor for teaching and teacher education. *Curriculum Inquiry, 10*(3), 317–323.

von Hohenberg, S. C., & Broderick, M. (2021). The role of teacher dispositions in a global teaching context. In *Interdisciplinary approaches toward enhancing teacher education* (pp. 221–240). IGI Global.

Waller, W. (1932). *The sociology of teaching.* Wiley.

Warnick, B. R., & Silverman, S. K. (2011). A framework for professional ethics courses in teacher education. *Journal of Teacher Education, 62*(3), 273–285.

Watt, H. M., Richardson, P. W., Klusmann, U., Kunter, M., Beyer, B., Trautwein, U., & Baumert, J. (2012). Motivations for choosing teaching as a career: An international comparison using the FIT-Choice scale. *Teaching and Teacher Education, 28*(6), 791–805.

Werhane, P. H. (1999). *Moral imagination and management decision making.* Oxford University Press.

Woolhouse, C. (2023). Technologies of the self and narrating an ethical teacher identity, or how to tell stories of a life well lived. *International Journal of Qualitative Studies in Education.* 1–17. https://doi.org/10.1080/09518398.2023.2181453

About the Author

Pamela Bolotin Joseph, PhD is principal lecturer emerita in the School of Education Studies, University of Washington Bothell. She received a Bachelor of Arts degree with an interdisciplinary major, History of American Thought and Culture, from Lawrence University and a Master of Arts in Teaching in education and history and a Doctor of Philosophy degree in social studies education from Northwestern University; her doctoral studies culminated in an interdisciplinary conceptual dissertation centered on emotion and culture in moral development and implications for schooling and moral education.

She has been a been a history and language arts teacher in high school and middle school and university faculty within graduate studies for experienced educators and teacher preparation programs at National-Louis University, Antioch University Seattle, and University of Washington Bothell. Her teaching areas include the moral dimensions of education, curriculum studies, curriculum development, reflective practice, history of education in the United States, education and popular culture, educational research, and organizational change and school reform.

She is editor and author of chapters in *Cultures of Curriculum* and coeditor and author of chapters in *Images of Schoolteachers in America.* Her articles on teachers' ethical reflections, moral education orientations, moral dimensions of teacher education, professional ethics, and transformative moral education have been published in the *Journal of Moral Education, Phi*

Teaching for Moral Imagination, pages 207–208

Delta Kappan, *Asia-Pacific Journal of Teacher Education*, *Theory and Research in Social Education*, *Social Education*, and *Journal of Peace* Education. Additionally, she has published articles about the teaching profession and curriculum inquiry in the *Journal of Teacher Education*, *Journal of Curriculum Studies*, and *Journal of Curriculum & Pedagogy*. She also has contributed to the *Encyclopedia of Teacher Education*, *Oxford Encyclopedia of Curriculum Studies*, *Encyclopedia of Curriculum Studies*, *Encyclopedia of Teacher Education*, and *Encyclopedia of the Social and Cultural Foundations of Education*.

Index

A

abuse, 24, 31, 37, 80, 84, 130
achievement, 33–34, 71, 92–94, 121
A Call to Character, 152
adolescence, 75, 77–78, 82
administrators, 92, 107, 118, 122, 133, 182, 193
affect (affective development, domain, realm), xvii, 12, 29, 46–48, 60–61, 70–71, 73, 93, 116, 126, 160, 194
African moral traditions, 6, 145
aggression, xvii, 28, 31, 38–40, 47, 70–71, 77, 80–81, 83–84, 101, 106, 118, 131, 162, 165
altruism, 26, 35–36, 181, 185, 186
anger, 26, 31, 39, 81
Anne Frank Haven School, 129
Aristotle, 150
attachment (attachment theory), 29–33, 46, 51, 119, 121, 151
authority, 4, 53–54, 56, 59, 80, 82, 96, 102, 105–106, 124–125, 153, 155
 moral, 101 102 118
autonomy, 35, 46, 54–56, 58–59, 72, 98, 102, 124

B

Baier, K., 7
Bandura, A., 76
behavior (conduct), 4, 8–10, 31, 37, 49, 50, 58, 69, 71, 74, 75– 77, 79–83, 91–92, 94–107, 117–120, 131, 133, 141–144, 150, 153–154, 161, 166
 amoral, 37, 157
 immoral (immorality), 13, 29, 38, 47, 58, 81, 157, 159, 161
 antisocial, 83, 101
 moral, 5, 11, 30, 47, 52, 75, 91,104, 157, 181

Teaching for Moral Imagination, pages 209–219

prosocial, 34, 47, 78–79, 83, 98
socially acceptable, xv, 8
standards (norms), 3, 5, 182–183
behaviorism in schooling, 97–101, 150
behavioral conditioning, 150
behavioral requirements, 182
belonging (belongingness), 30, 33–35, 40, 82–83, 106, 122, 123, 155
Bettelheim, B., 97
Bloom, P., 28
Boehm, C., 3, 26, 27
bonding (bonds), 26, 29–32, 77, 93, 119, 132, 148, 161
Book of Virtues, The, 152
Bowers, C. A., 164
Bregman, R., 50
bullying (bullies), 24, 32, 34, 47, 81–84, 106, 107, 118, 195
cyberbullying 84
bystanders, 82, 106, 159

C

caring, x, 6, 26, 29, 32, 46–47, 49–52, 78–79, 93, 116–117, 119, 121–124, 126, 128, 152, 157, 162, 184, 186, 189–190
caregiving (caregivers), xviii, 25 29–32, 34, 38, 70, 75, 77, 80–81, 97, 122, 181
caring community, xviii, 120–124, 131
environment, 185–186
Carr, D., 151
change, 15, 37, 50, 58–59, 104, 107, 121, 126, 131, 133, 143, 147, 161, 196–199
climate 28, 160
cultural 132, 161
character, xvi, xvii, 8–10, 46, 57, 94
childhood, 26, 31, 33, 38, 50–51, 56, 73, 75, 77, 93
childrearing (childrearing practices), xi, 73, 77, 79, 81, 99
citizenship (citizenry, citizens), 2, 92–94, 96, 124–125, 128, 141, 144, 146–148, 152, 156, 185, 197
citizenship education, 128, 148
codes of conduct (ethical codes), 11, 92 154, 180, 182
coercion (coercive power), 53, 58, 79–81, 101
cognition (cognitive realm, domain), xvii, 9–10, 12, 14–15, 28, 45–46, 52–53, 59–61, 76, 82, 126, 142, 160, 191, 193
cognitive moral development (cognitive developmental theory), 46, 52–53, 55–58, 60, 70
cognitive stages (cognitive stage theory), 55–58, 60, 128
collaboration, 36, 104, 118, 132, 143, 165, 182, 195, 198
communities, xix, 6–7, 11, 25, 29, 32, 47, 50, 59, 71–72, 75, 94, 98 ,103, 116 ,119, 121, 124–128, 132, 144–147, 155, 157, 166, 179–182, 187
classroom, 124–125, 143, 156, 159, 186, 188
inclusive, 116, 122, 123
moral, x, 27, 92, 107, 115–117, 119, 130, 131, 195
school, 119–120, 131, 133
community service, 120, 125–126, 132
compassion, xii, 8, 23, 25, 29, 31, 46, 47, 49–50, 76, 78–79, 128, 153, 159, 162–163, 165, 188, 191, 197
competence (competencies), 98, 124, 146, 166, 183
moral, 25, 61, 79
competition, xii, xvii, 39, 93, 115, 121, 163, 186,
complexity, xvi, 2–3, 11, 24, 45–46, 57, 70, 74, 77, 142, 155, 197

conflict, ix, 27, 53, 57, 72, 81, 122, 132, 143, 154, 164–165, 185, 192–194, 198
conflict resolution, 79, 118, 150, 165
conformity, xii, 4, 5 38, 54, 95, 159, 181
connection, 6–8, 13, 29–30, 51, 120–121, 124, 131–132, 143, 145, 159, 162, 164, 166
conscience, 4, 46, 50, 194
consciousness, 5, 11–12, 57, 74, 126, 128, 161–162, 166, 190, 195
  critical, 17, 161, 164, 179, 183
control, 38, 79, 95–96, 98, 102, 105, 107, 116, 118–121, 124, 151
  community, 182
  local, 143
conversation, 79, 84, 154–155
  ethical 154
  moral xvii, 143, 154–155
conventions, 9, 15, 55, 59, 73, 94
cooperation, xvii, 26–27, 29–30, 39, 54, 55, 78–80, 82, 93–94, 97, 121–123, 131, 148, 153
crisis, 163, 196
  ecological 163
culture, ix–x, xi, xviii, 3–4, 12, 56, 70–74, 77, 91–92, 94, 96, 100, 102–103, 107, 142, 147, 149, 151,197
  classroom, xii
  dominant, 96
  levels of, 73–74
  organizational, 16
  school (*See* school cultures)
  subcultures, 70, 103
  of violence, 162, 164
curricula (content, study), xvi, 93, 102–105, 125, 127, 141–143, 146–149, 152, 157, 159, 162, 188, 197
  academic, x, xi, xviii, 125 127 142–143, 157, 160, 162
  drama, 157, 162
  history, 126, 145, 147, 157, 159
  interdisciplinary, 123, 162
  literature, 157–158
  media literacy, 157, 159–160, 162
  poetry, 158, 162
  science, 157, 160, 162
  social studies, 157–159, 162
  technology, 159
curriculum studies, xv, xvi, 92

D

decisions (decision–making), 1, 7, 15–16, 52, 71–72, 102, 105, 118–119, 121, 124–125, 142, 154 ,159, 185, 188, 190–194
  moral (ethical), ix, 1, 3 5, 11, 52–53, 58–61, 70, 154, 182
deliberation, xi, xviii, 9, 14, 59, 121, 124–125, 128–129, 142–143, 154, 156, 159
delinquency (delinquents), 31, 37, 118
democracy (democratic society, values), 54–55, 80, 119–120, 124–125, 129, 131, 147–148, 158–159, 184
democratic community, xviii, 16, 120–121, 123–125, 128–130, 156
dependency, 29, 33
deprivation, 34, 36–39, 80, 98, 100
Dewey, J., 4, 7, 10, 58, 61, 116, 125, 152
dialogue, 12, 27, 121, 122, 124–125, 131–132, 155–156, 165
dignity, 34, 58–59, 154–155, 160, 190, 196
dilemmas, x, 55, 97, 155, 183, 194
  moral (ethical), ix, xvi, xix, 1, 11, 51–52, 56, 121, 130, 143, 154, 157, 158, 160, 180, 185, 192–194
discipline, xviii 80, 92, 95–97, 99, 101, 104–105, 118–119, 121, 133, 150, 188

assertive, 99
coercive, 79–81
developmental, 102
disproportional, 106
exclusionary, 99–100, 105–106, 131
punitive, 80, 99, 101, 131
zero tolerance policy, 100, 105
discourse, x, xvii, 2, 8, 16, 48, 71, 129, 153, 159–160, 162, 191
discrimination, 96, 107, 123, 182
discussions, 11, 130,143, 154–156, 158–160
disequilibrium, 2, 53
dispositions, 124, 149, 152, 166, 180, 183–184
distress, x, 30, 46–49, 60, 79, 194
diversity, 72, 122, 124, 144, 147–148, 165
divinity, 72, 144
domination (dominance), 16, 37–38, 106, 143, 156, 162–164, 199
Dreikurs, R., 80
dysfunction, xvii, 24, 37, 39–40

E

ecojustice, 16
ecological consciousness (concerns), 143, 166, 196
ecology of violence x, 2, 162
ecological systems, 7, 162, 165
efficacy, ix, 101, 154, 164, 185, 198
egocentrism, 54
egotism, 27, 97
emotions (feelings), xvii, ix, xix, 28, 45, 47–51, 55, 60–61, 74, 120, 166
moral, xi, 13, 32, 34, 37, 46–49, 60, 73, 126
empathy (empathic feelings), xv, xvii, xviii, 2, 7, 13–14, 24–25, 29, 31–32, 36, 46–50, 56, 70, 78–79, 81–82, 84, 93, 102, 116, 120–121, 124, 157, 160, 165, 191
empowerment, 124, 128, 163, 185
environments, 15–16, 25, 38, 53, 58, 76, 78, 83
classroom, xvi, 92, 188, 199
democratic, 124, 129
ethical, xviii, 117–118, 191
school, x, xvi, xviii, 93–94, 105, 107, 116–118, 122–123, 132
Erikson, E., 34
esteem (esteem needs), 33–35, 37–40, 49, 101, 147
ethic of care, 6, 46, 50–52, 60, 120–121, 188
ethic of justice, 57, 60
ethics, 2, 6, 10–12, 37, 72, 76, 148, 150–151, 154, 162, 182–185, 189, 191–192, 194
ethnicity, 52, 71, 118
ethnocentrism, 27
ethos, 72, 117, 119–120, 127
evil, 24, 27, 154

F

Facing History and Ourselves, 159
fairness, 9, 25, 53–55, 72, 78, 82, 116, 118, 121, 128–130, 152, 191–192, 196
faith, 16, 24, 36, 40, 59, 125, 152
families, x, xviii, 4, 6, 25, 31–32, 34 ,50, 52, 69–70, 73, 77–78, 80–83, 91, 93–95, 121–123, 129, 145, 146, 182
flourishing, 34–35, 115, 120, 141, 148, 150–151, 180, 184, 196
Fromm, E., 38–40
frustration, 81, 127, 161

G

gender, 51–52, 82–83, 195
generosity, 26, 115, 182
Gilligan, C., 51
good and evil, 3, 10, 158
Greene, J., 26
Greene, M., 61
groups, 10, 26–30, 33, 38–40, 72–73, 77, 103, 119, 159
  marginalized, 106
  peer, 34, 82, 83
  social, 75, 82, 83
growth, 33, 34, 165, 194
  moral, xv, xvi, xviii, 53, 80, 92, 119, 128, 185, 194
  spiritual, 162
guidance, 101, 118
  cultural, 56
  moral, 73, 78, 144
  spiritual, 145
guilt, xvii, 46–47, 49–50, 61, 81

H

habits, 4, 9, 16, 56, 74, 97, 148, 150, 183
Haidt, J., 26, 56
Hall, E. T., 73–75
Hansen, D. T., 116
harm, 5, 7, 24, 56–57, 79–81, 96, 98–99, 101–102, 121, 131–132, 161, 163
harmony, 162, 198
  social, 92, 144, 146
heteronomy, 54–55
hierarchies, 33, 35, 37, 80, 128, 146
Holocaust, 129, 159
Holt, J., 120
human evolution, theory of, 7, 25–29
human nature, xvii, 24, 26–28, 33, 125, 145, 151
human needs, x, xvii, 24, 33–35
human rights, 36, 58, 143, 148, 159, 163–164, 197
Hunter, J. D., 152

I

identification, 27, 31, 35, 46, 48, 71, 189
identity, 34, 36, 39–40, 82–83, 123, 189
  activist, 185, 198
  cultural, 70
  development, 82
  moral, xvii, 9–10, 34, 36, 185, 188–189
  national, 92, 144, 146–147
  religious, 94
  spiritual, 145
ideology, 2 147–148
imagination, 13, 16–17, 23, 35, 126
imitation, 37, 76, 81, 150, 180
individualism, xii, 2, 39, 92, 120 ,186
incentives, 97–98, 133, 153, 187
Indigenous cultures (groups, traditions), 132, 145–147
indoctrination, 101, 151, 197
inducements, 29, 79–80, 186
induction, 79, 102
inequality (inequity), 15, 54, 127, 142, 161, 163, 197–198
injustice, xvii, 8, 13, 16–17, 79, 143, 161–162, 185, 197, 199
inquiry, 117, 152, 184
  analytical, 27
  critical, 15, 155
  curriculum, xv, xvi, 2
  ethical, 143, 156–160, 190
  philosophical, 143, 156–157
instincts, 24–25, 29, 57
integrity, 8, 12, 152,189, 191
intelligence, 95, 188
  emotional, 131
  moral, 53

interconnectedness, 7, 145, 161, 164–166
interdependence, 6–7, 124, 143, 160, 186
internalization, 53, 70, 75, 77, 79, 101, 152 ,161
introspection, 185, 194
irrationality, 28–29, 56
isolation, 38, 56, 83, 95, 99–100, 123, 181

J

Johnson, M., 37, 38
Jubilee Center, the, 149, 152
judgments, 3, 9, 12–13, 28, 55, 58, 71–72, 91, 104, 190
  critical, 156
  moral (ethical), 13–14, 52, 54, 56–57, 60, 181, 190
  principled, 52
  rational, 57
  value, 76
justice, x, 25, 40, 46, 51, 58–60, 82, 116–117, 120–121, 128–129, 165, 196, 199
  environmental 196–197
  social, 127, 162, 165, 184, 195, 197–199
just community, 121, 128–130

K

kibbutz, kibbutzim, 30, 129
knowledge, x, xi, xvii, 2, 6, 13, 15, 27, 31, 58, 61, 69, 71, 74, 76–77, 84, 92, 95, 103, 115, 127–128, 141, 146, 152, 160–161, 164–166, 183
  critical, 162–163, 198
  cultural, 71, 74, 95
  empirical, 9
  environmental, 166
  historical, 159
  moral (ethical), 10, 12, 94, 151, 179, 185, 190–191
  place-based, 146
  of self, 13, 15, 58, 194
  teacher, 183, 186, 189, 192
Kohlberg, L., 52, 55–58, 60, 129, 130, 151
Korczak, J., 129, 130

L

language, 71, 73, 103, 146–147,197
leaders, 38, 50, 129, 130, 154
  educational, xii, 182
  school, 106–107
learning, 2, 54, 70, 76–77, 94–95, 97, 101, 105, 117, 119, 127, 165, 182, 188, 194, 196–197
  autonomous, 102
  constructivist, 101
  cultural, 56, 70, 73–74, 130, 145
  democratic, 130
  emancipatory, 164
  experiential (active), 116, 125, 141
  moral (ethical), 54, 77, 80–81, 97, 102, 130, 142, 145, 193, 194
  social, 76–77
  transformative (emancipatory), 164
Lipman, M., 157
love, 7, 29–34, 37–38, 40, 50–51, 78, 128, 147–148, 151, 154, 162, 166, 185–186

M

manipulation, 98–99, 101
marginalization (marginalized groups), 52, 106, 156, 163–164
Maslow, A., 33–35, 37–38
media, xviii, 70, 75, 83–84, 91, 149, 160
  social media, 83

militarism, 23, 147, 164
misbehavior, misconduct, xviii, 47, 70, 80, 96, 99–102, 106, 118, 121, 131–132
modeling (models), xviii, 25, 70, 73–76, 78–80, 83–84,150
  role models, xv, 78, 104, 144, 185, 189, 190
monitoring, 78, 84
Montessori, M., 162
  Montessori schools, 162
moral action, xvii, 10, 13, 15, 23, 27, 46, 57, 60–61, 72, 98, 144, 157, 195
moral agency, x, 12–13, 24, 36, 40, 162, 179, 184–185, 193–196
moral agents, xi, xv, xvi, 9, 36, 71, 125–126, 192, 195
moral beliefs, ix, 3, 5, 11–12, 24, 59, 91, 94, 141
moral calling, 8, 185–187
moral codes, 3, 4,10, 97, 119, 120, 151, 181
moral concern, xvii, 6, 36, 159
moral development, ix–x, xvi–xviii, 2, 24–25, 29–30, 37, 45–46, 50–58, 60–61, 69–70, 73, 76, 78, 81, 92, 95, 97–98, 100–102, 107, 116, 120–121, 128–129, 141, 145, 147, 151, 154
moral dimensions, ix–xii, xv–xvi, 1–2, 14, 70, 184, 188, 192–193
moral disengagement, 47, 81, 83–84, 106
moral dysfunction, xvii, 24, 37, 39
moral education curricula, xviii–xix, 142–143, 148
  cultural heritage, 144–148
  character education, xix, 143, 148–154
  ethical inquiry across the curriculum, 157–160
  moral conversation, 154–155
  philosophy with children, 155–157
  transformative moral education, 160–166
moral education orientations, xvi, 142
moral educators, x–xi, xv–xvi, 2, 23, 119, 152
moral exemplars, 36, 144
moral functioning, xvii, 3, 9, 24, 26, 34, 36, 47, 50, 60, 71, 97, 141, 151–152
moral imagination, 2, 12–17, 24, 45, 61, 76, 92, 120, 125–126, 128, 132, 142, 155, 157–158, 160, 180, 184–185, 188, 190, 192, 195
moral (ethical) responsibility, xvii, 6–8, 34, 54, 76, 122, 129, 158, 199
morality, xi, xv–xvi, 1–12, 23–24, 26–29, 34–35, 37–38, 46–47, 49, 53–54, 56, 59–61, 69 72–73, 76, 78, 91, 94, 96–97, 102, 104 ,142, 144, 146, 148, 152, 158, 161, 180
Moral Judgment of the Child, The, 53
Moral Life of Schools, The, 104
moral messages, xviii, 70–71, 92, 158
moral outrage, 74, 101, 187
moral perception, 13, 14, 15, 16, 143, 157, 185, 188, 190
moral sense, 25–26, 29, 195
moral sensitivity, 46, 57, 184
moral socialization, xviii, 53, 75–107, 146, 149, 156, 180
motivations, 10, 33, 35, 57, 80, 96–98, 115, 151, 153, 186
motivations to become teachers, 185–187

N

narcissism (narcissists), xvii, 38–39, 40, 49
Narvaez, D., 25
National Education Association, 182

natural world (environment, nature), 2, 7, 15–16, 143, 145–146, 160–164, 166, 195, 197, 199
neglect, 32, 37, 186
negotiation, 125, 143, 165
Neill, A. S., 129
nest, 29, 32
Noddings, N., 51, 52, 121, 151
nonviolence, xvii, 16, 143, 161, 165, 185, 195, 197–199
norms, 5, 11, 16, 53, 55, 70, 72–77, 92–93, 96, 103–105, 119–120, 124, 130, 159, 180–182, 191
nurturing, xv, 29–32, 46, 49, 51, 107, 116, 118, 121, 123, 181, 186, 190

O

obedience, 7, 59, 101, 105, 118 124 146 191
obligations, x, 6–8, 51, 105, 154
  moral (ethical), xi, 6–8, 57, 96, 160, 184–185, 190, 192, 199
  social, 146
offenders, 131–133
organizational cultures, 16, 103, 117, 193

P

parenting (parents), 31, 32, 39, 50, 52–54, 73, 77– 82, 84, 94, 99, 101, 107, 117, 122, 133, 146, 148, 149, 192, 193
Parks, R., 152
passivity, 73, 82–83, 95, 115, 120, 193
patriotism, 40, 144, 146–147, 153, 158
peace (peacefulness), xix, 16 17 71 131 133 142–143, 148, 152 161–162, 164–166, 197–198
pedagogy, 95, 125, 143, 161, 164
  folk, 95
  peace, 199
  transformative, 185, 195–196, 198
peer group (peers), x, xviii, 24–25, 31, 34, 53, 70, 75, 77, 81–83, 91, 95, 106, 149
perspective taking, xviii, 46, 53, 79, 82, 116, 143, 165
Peters, R. S., 9, 61, 97
philosophy, xv, 3, 6, 10–11, 117, 123, 133, 155–156, 162, 196
  moral, x, xvii, 4, 11, 46, 50, 70, 143, 152, 189
  with children, xix, 155–157
Piaget, J., 52–56, 60, 99, 101
Pinker, S., 28, 59
pity, 31, 47–48
poverty, 106, 163, 198
power, xviii, 37, 54, 70, 79–81, 83, 96, 105–107, 116, 118, 126, 128, 191
powerlessness, 15, 38, 124, 128, 194
praise, 79, 98
predispositions, 26–27, 29
prejudice, xii, 27–28, 95, 105–106, 128, 195
presence, 1, 146, 188
  moral, xvii, 101, 185, 188–189
principles, 1, 3–7, 9–11, 24, 36, 47, 52, 55–58, 60, 76, 98, 102, 117, 120, 150–151, 161–162, 182–183, 185, 190, 192
problem solving, 132, 143, 151, 165
prohibitions, 29, 47, 75, 97, 180–181
psychoanalytic theory, 46, 50
punishment, xv, 55– 56, 70, 73, 76, 79–80, 97–100, 104–106, 130
  corporal punishment, 81, 100–101, 106
  expiatory, 99
  reciprocal, 99
Purpel, D., 128

Q

questioning, 5, 12, 59, 156, 179, 194

R

race, 28, 82, 106, 118, 195
racism, 24, 84, 96, 123, 161, 164, 195
rationality (rational thinking), ix, xvii, 5, 9, 27–29, 46, 51, 56–59, 61, 95, 101, 125, 129, 151, 156, 159–160
rational morality, 46, 55, 57–60, 72
reality, 4, 13, 15, 27–28, 58, 71, 120, 182, 198
reasoning, xvii–xix, 2, 12, 14, 34, 36, 45–46, 52–53, 55–61, 71, 79, 116, 151, 184
  moral (ethical), xii, xv, 13–15, 24, 35, 51–53, 55–57, 59–60, 71–71, 78–79, 84, 102, 116, 128, 130, 143, 154–155, 157–158, 160, 165, 185, 190
reciprocity, 58, 99, 118, 122, 127
  reciprocal dialogue, 125
  reciprocal relationships, 30, 51, 53, 70, 77, 82, 123
  reciprocal understanding, 54, 80
reflection, xvii–xix, 5, 9, 11–12, 15, 26, 46, 58–59, 61, 70, 76, 116, 125, 128, 143, 150–151, 156, 184, 190, 194–195
  critical, xv, 13, 15, 120–121, 126, 143, 157, 160
  guided, 126–127
  moral (ethical), 23–24, 55
  self (critical self), 49, 154–156, 184–185, 192
regulation, 30, 49, 101, 104, 182
  internal (self), 37, 74, 81–82
reinforcement, 76, 80, 98–99
relatedness, 144–145, 166
relationships, 6–7, 30–33, 38, 47, 50–51, 53–54, 70, 77–78, 80, 82, 92–93, 99, 102–103, 117–118, 121–123, 128, 131–132, 143, 145–146, 161–163, 166, 182, 188, 194
religion (faith traditions), 5–6, 40, 94, 100, 104, 142, 144, 149, 164, 195
  religious beliefs (doctrine, traditions, values), 5, 24, 49, 74, 104, 142, 144, 149
  religious education, 149
  religious schools, 94
  religious socialization, 94
remorse, 31, 47, 50, 61, 81, 99
resilience, 31, 35, 83–84, 153
respect, 7, 34–35, 54–55, 58–59, 78, 82, 97, 116, 118–120, 124, 128, 146–147, 149, 152, 154–155, 160, 163, 165, 186, 190–191, 196–197
responsibility, 49, 51, 78, 81, 101–102, 119, 122, 124–125, 129, 145, 152, 155, 185, 190–191, 195–196
restorative justice, xviii 99, 120–121, 131–133
retaliation (retribution), 99, 102, 156
rewards, xv, 25, 55, 70, 76, 79–80, 94, 96–99, 104, 121, 143, 149–150, 153–154, 186–187
routines, 37, 71, 96, 115
rules, 4, 5, 7, 9, 11, 14, 53–57, 59–60, 73–75, 82, 92–93, 96–98, 101–102, 104–105, 115, 117, 124, 130–131, 144, 151, 181–182, 192–193, 197

S

safety, 24, 33–34, 37–38, 100, 117, 121
sanctions, 11, 56, 81, 96, 99, 132
school climate, 105, 115–119 193
school culture, xviii, 91–92, 103–104, 107, 117, 133
schooling, xvi, xviii, 91–96, 99, 102, 104–105, 107, 115–116, 120, 129, 180, 196, 198

school reform, 104
security, 24, 27, 30–31, 33–35, 37–38, 185
self-actualization, 33–36
self-concept, 10, 36, 185
self control, 46, 61, 70, 79, 81, 100
self-interest, 7–8, 15, 35–37, 97
selfishness, 35
selflessness, 26, 181
service learning, 120–121, 125–128
Sharp, A., 157
shame, xvii, 31, 46–47, 49–50, 81
Singer, P., 8
Skinner, B. F., 76
skills, 33, 74, 79, 82, 84, 92–93, 95, 125, 127, 131
  academic, 121
  social, 96, 187
socialization, xviii, 70, 73, 75–79, 82–84, 92–95, 142, 158
  moral, xviii, 53, 77–80, 82, 91–97, 101–104, 107, 146, 149, 156, 180
socialization theoies, 76, 95
  behaviorism, 76
  social domain theory, 77
  social learning theory, 70, 77
special education, 97, 122
spirituality, 72, 144–146
  spiritual beliefs, 74
  spiritual connection, 143, 145, 166
  spiritual development, 147
standards, 3–4, 9, 11, 70, 75, 92, 182, 190
  community, 181
  moral (ethical), xviii–xix, 11, 47, 69, 81, 91, 151, 179–180
  professional, 182–183, 192
status, 39, 80, 83, 186
stories, 122, 145, 157, 158
  storytelling 145, 186
stress, 30, 31, 32, 37, 105, 123
  moral, 193
submission, 37, 101
Summerhill School, 129–130
survival, 29, 3
  needs, 33–39
  school climate, 117–118
  systems, 37
sustainability, 143, 162, 164, 166, 197
sympathy, 2, 6, 13–14, 28, 34, 47, 48, 60–61, 78–79, 98, 121, 158, 188, 191

T

teacher activism, 195, 198
teacher education, xix 179, 181, 183–184, 192
teaching profession, 11, 105, 180–183, 186–187
textbooks, 144, 147–148, 181
traditions, 2, 5–6, 49, 55, 94, 103, 116 142, 144–147, 150, 153, 158
traits, xv–xvi, 8–10, 24, 31, 38, 91, 143, 150, 152–153, 182– 183
transformation, 15, 69, 116, 161–164, 195, 197–199
transformative moral education curricula, xi 142–143, 161–162
  conflict resolution education, 143, 162, 164–165
  critical pedagogy (justice-centered, liberatory), xix, 143, 162–163, 196
  ecojustice education, 143, 162–164, 166
  environmental education, 143, 162, 164, 166
  global education, 143, 162, 164–166
  human rights education, 143, 162–163
  peace education (studies), 143, 162, 164–165, 198–199
transcendence, 61
  self-transcendence, 33–35

transgressions, 49, 56, 75, 77, 96
trust, 34, 106, 115–116, 121–122, 128, 187, 191–193
truth, 9, 59, 155, 160, 193
Tufts, J. H., 9, 61

V

values, ix–x, xv–xvi, xviii, 3–5, 10–16, 25, 28, 37, 39, 46, 50–51, 59, 70–79, 92–95, 102–104, 117, 119–120, 142–151, 153, 156–161, 179–180, 184, 189–191, 193, 195
  cultural values, xviii, 46, 53,71, 73, 75, 144–146, 151
  moral (ethical), xviii, 3–4, 12–13, 25, 36, 47, 53, 58, 69–71, 73, 75, 91, 93, 119, 142, 145, 147, 150, 158, 161, 185, 191, 195
values transmission, xviii, 75, 77, 91, 93–94, 103, 142–145, 148, 150, 156
victimization (victims), 31, 48, 77, 83–84, 106–107, 118, 131–132, 159
violence, xii, xvi, xvii, xviii, 8, 16, 17, 24 32 71 81 84 101 117 161 162 163 164 165 185 197 198
virtues, xvii, 6, 9, 59, 119, 141–143, 148–153, 180, 183–184, 189
  virtue ethics 150–151
vision (visioning), 13, 15–16, 103, 117, 119, 125, 159–161, 181, 184–185, 194–196, 198–199

W

wellbeing, 6, 30, 121
withdrawal, 31, 32, 49, 100
worldview, 123, 144, 161–164, 166

Printed in the USA
CPSIA information can be obtained
at www.ICGtesting.com
LVHW020635080424
776700LV00001B/65